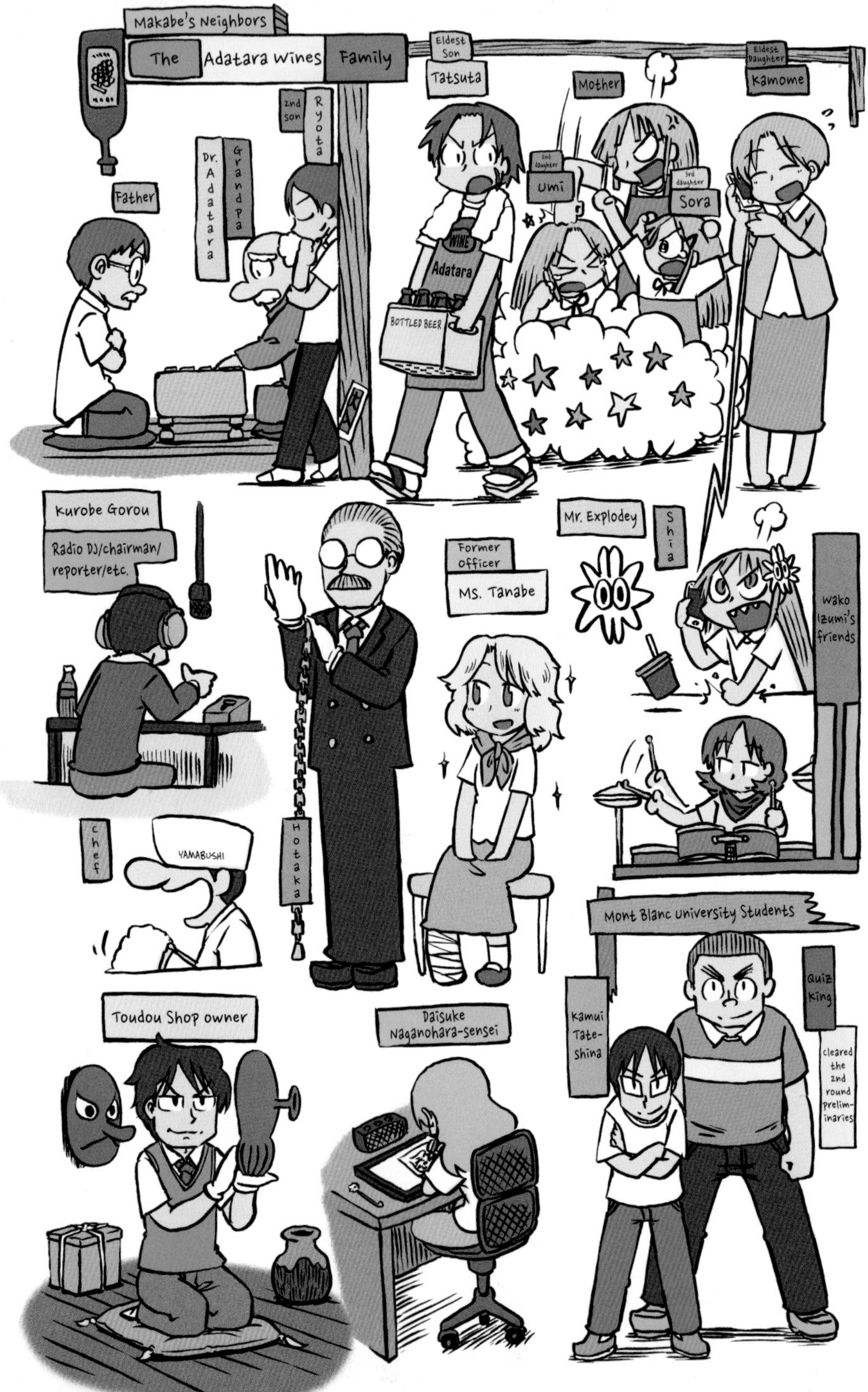

Makabe's Neighbors
The Adatara Wines Family
Eldest Daughter
Kamome
Mother
3rd daughter
Sora
2nd daughter
Umi
Eldest Son
Tatsuta
WINE
Adatara
BOTTLED BEER
2nd son
Ryota
Grandpa
Dr. Adatara
Father
Wako Izumi's friends
Shia
Mr. Explodey
Former officer
Ms. Tanabe
Hotaka
Kurobe Gorou
Radio DJ/chairman/reporter/etc.
Chef
YAMABUSHI
Mont Blanc University Students
Quiz King
cleared the 2nd round prelim-inaries
Kamui Tate-shina
Daisuke Naganohara-sensei
Toudou Shop owner

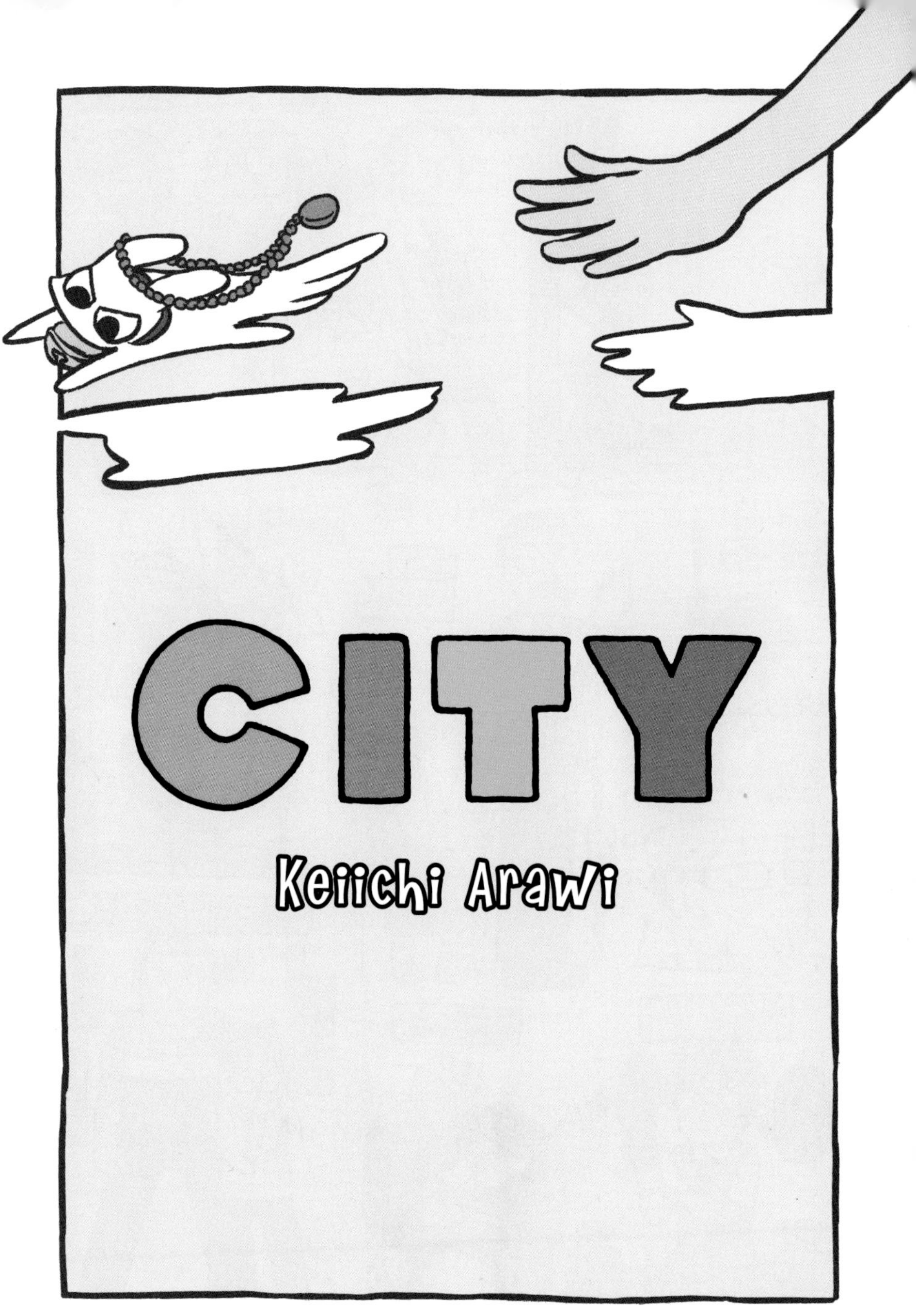

CITY

Keiichi Arawi

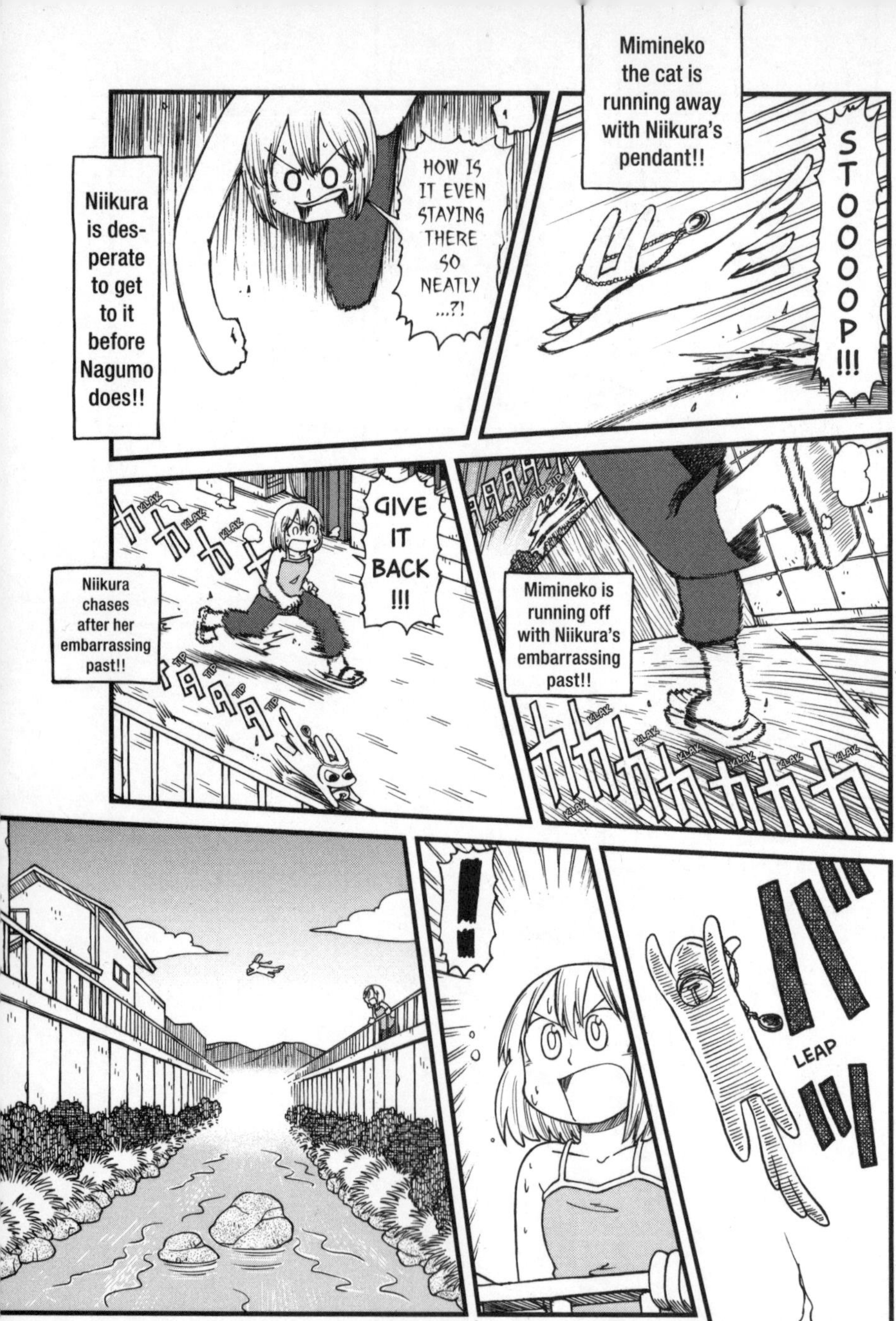
Mimineko the cat is running away with Niikura's pendant!!
STOOOOOP!!!
HOW IS IT EVEN STAYING THERE SO NEATLY ...?!
Niikura is desperate to get to it before Nagumo does!!
TIP TIP TIP
Mimineko is running off with Niikura's embarrassing past!!
KLAK KLAK KLAK KLAK KLAK KLAK
GIVE IT BACK !!!
KLAK KLAK KLAK
Niikura chases after her embarrassing past!!
TIP TIP TIP
LEAP

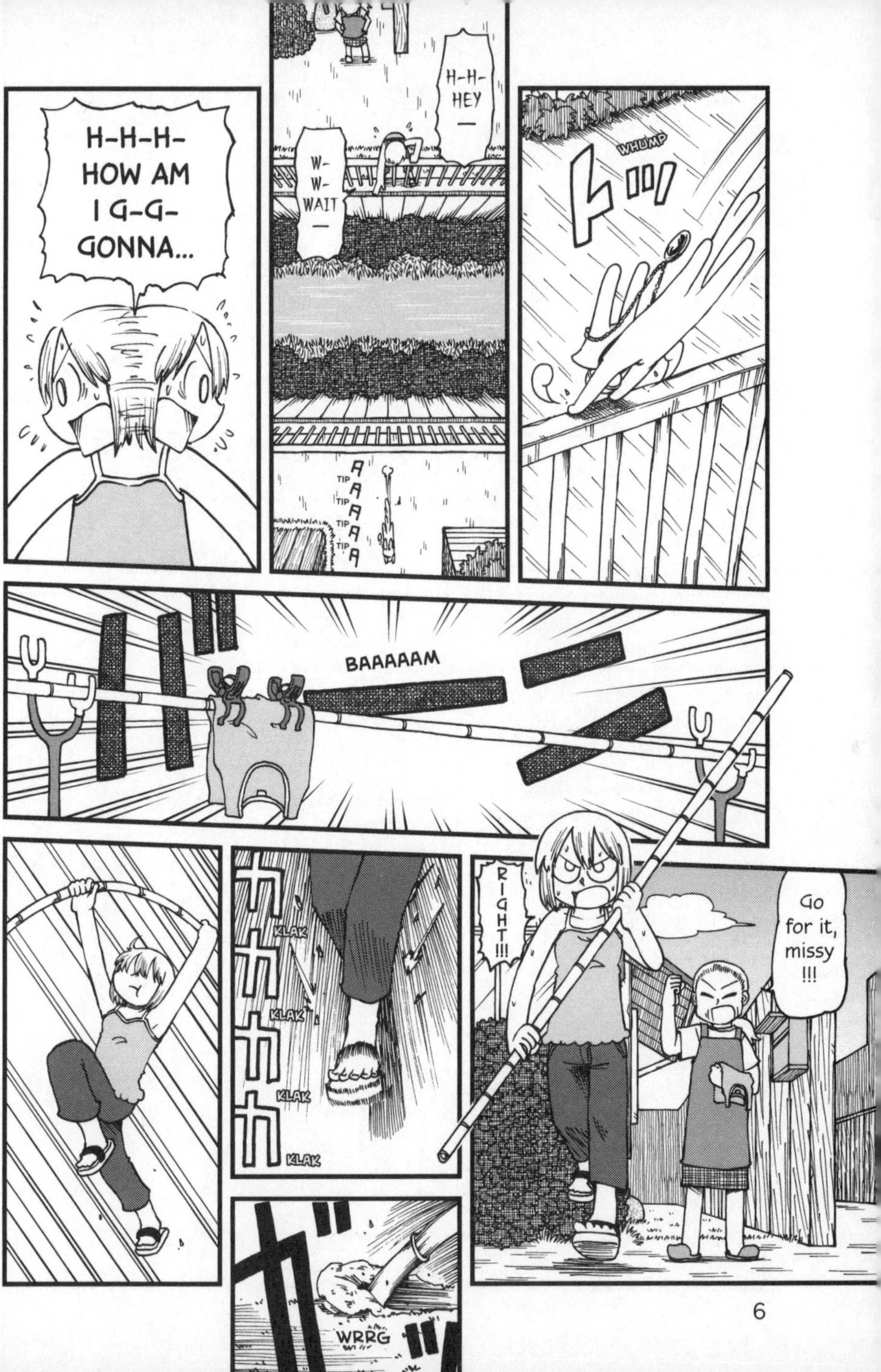
WHUMP
H-H-HEY—
W-W-WAIT—
TIP
TIP
TIP
TIP
H-H-H-HOW AM I G-G-GONNA...
BAAAAAM
Go for it, missy!!!
RIGHT!!!
KLAK
KLAK
KLAK
KLAK
WRRG

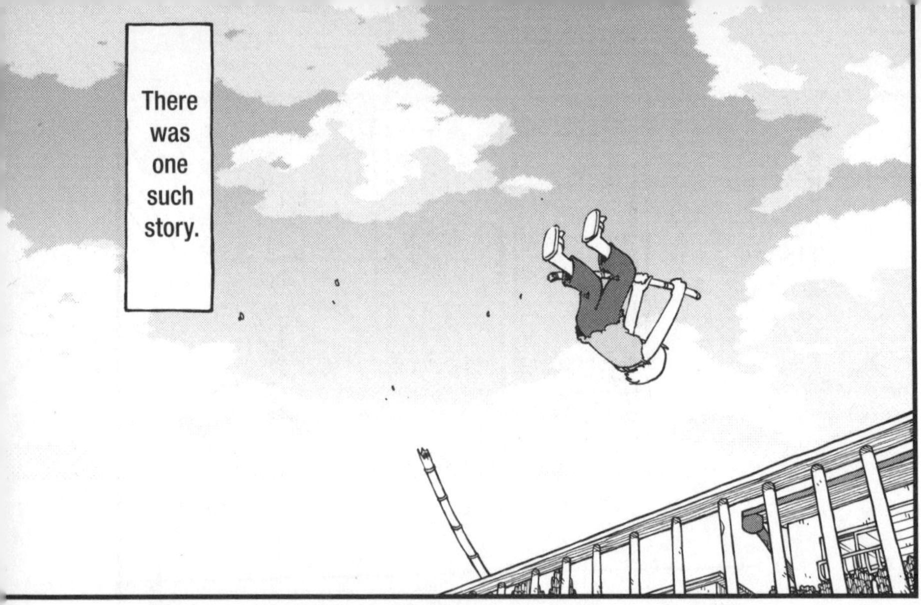
There was one such story.

Chapter 40 ◇ Human Jumble

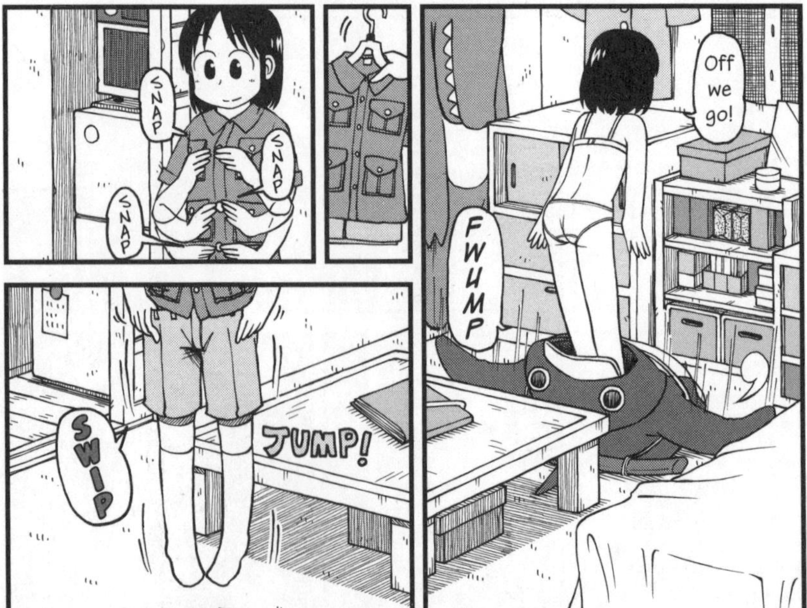
Off we go!
FWUMP
SNAP
SNAP
SNAP
JUMP!
SWIP

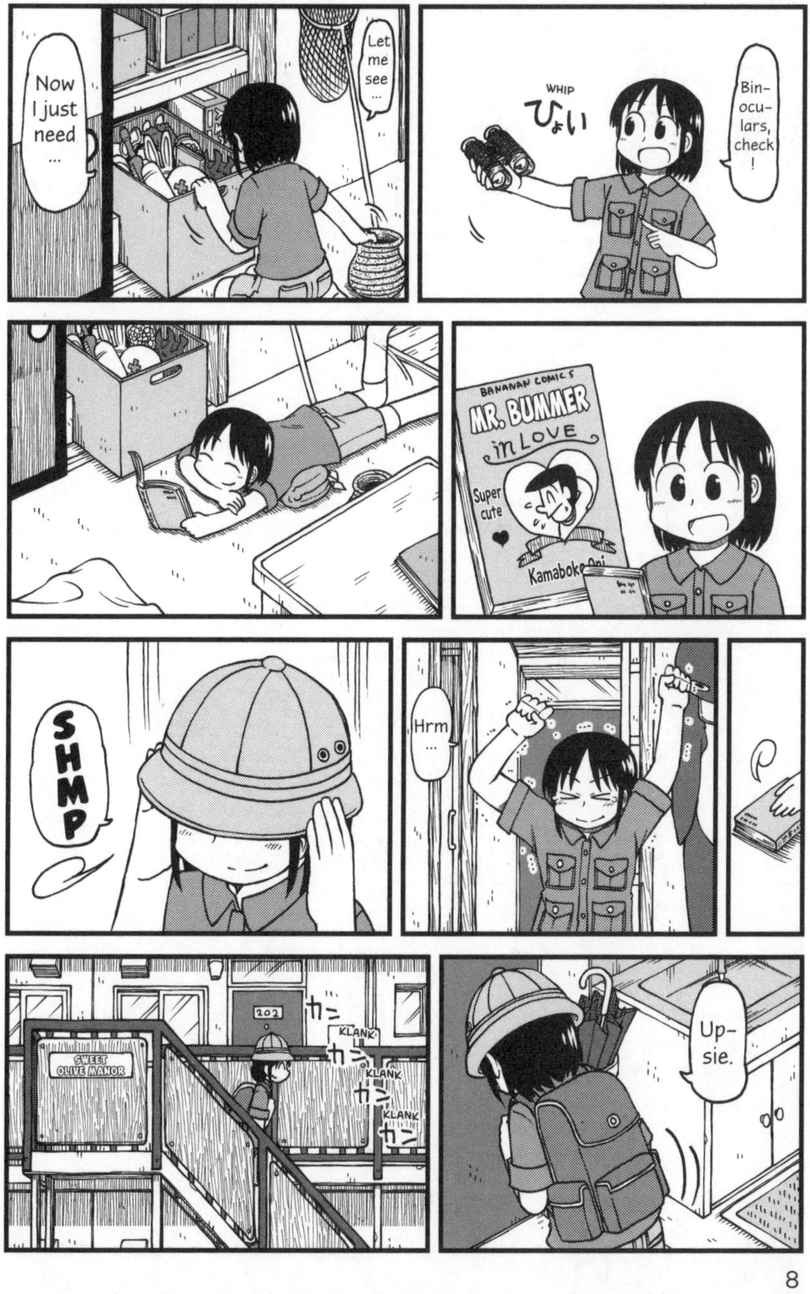
Bin-ocu-lars, check!
WHIP
ひょい
Let me see ...
Now I just need ...
BANANAN COMICS
MR. BUMMER in LOVE
Super cute
Kamaboko Oni
Hrm ...
SHMP
Up-sie.
202
カン
KLANK
カン
KLANK
カン
KLANK
カン
SWEET OLIVE MANOR

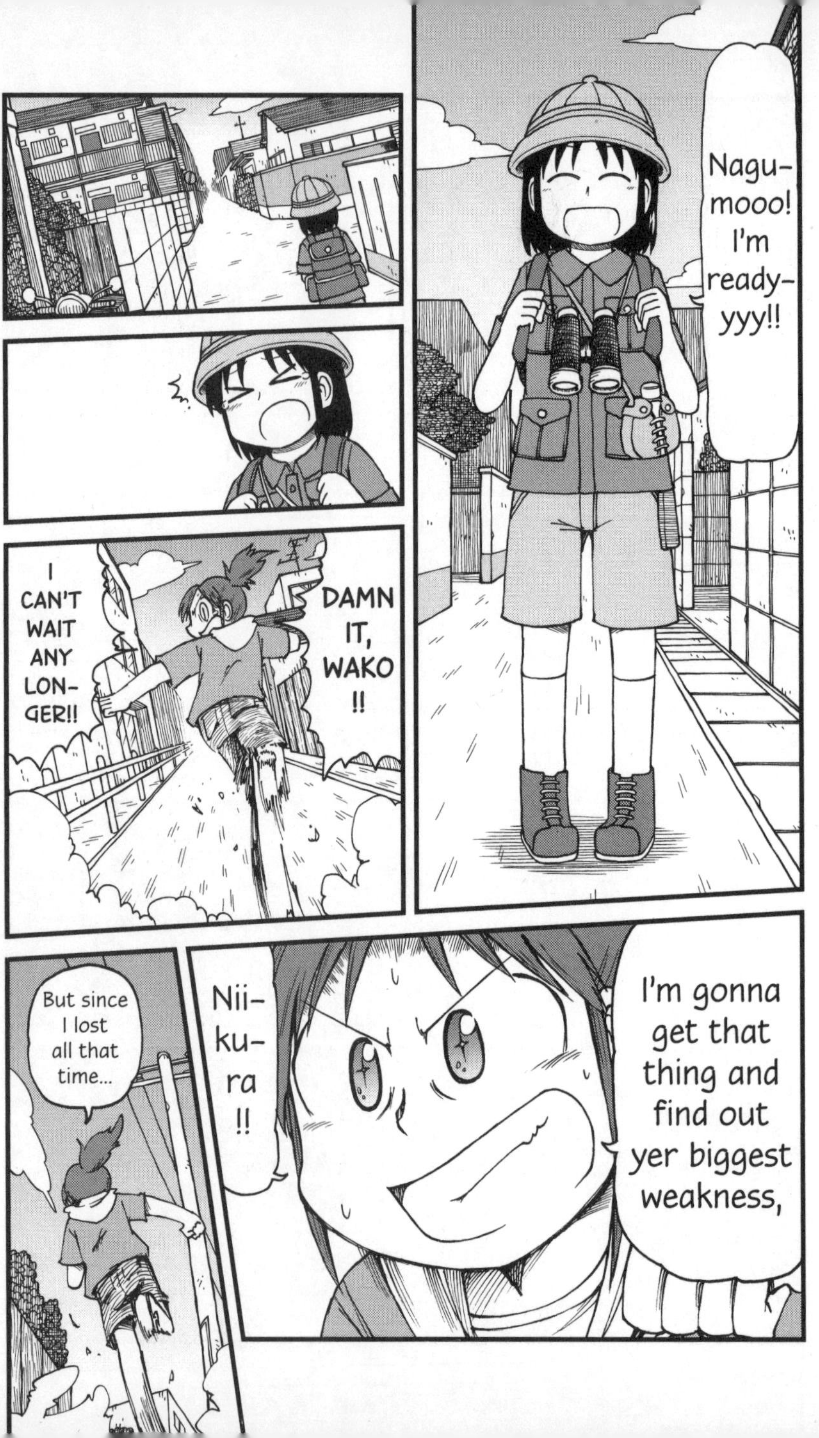
Nagu-mooo! I'm ready-yyy!!
DAMN IT, WAKO!!
I CAN'T WAIT ANY LON-GER!!
I'm gonna get that thing and find out yer biggest weakness,
Nii-ku-ra!!
But since I lost all that time...

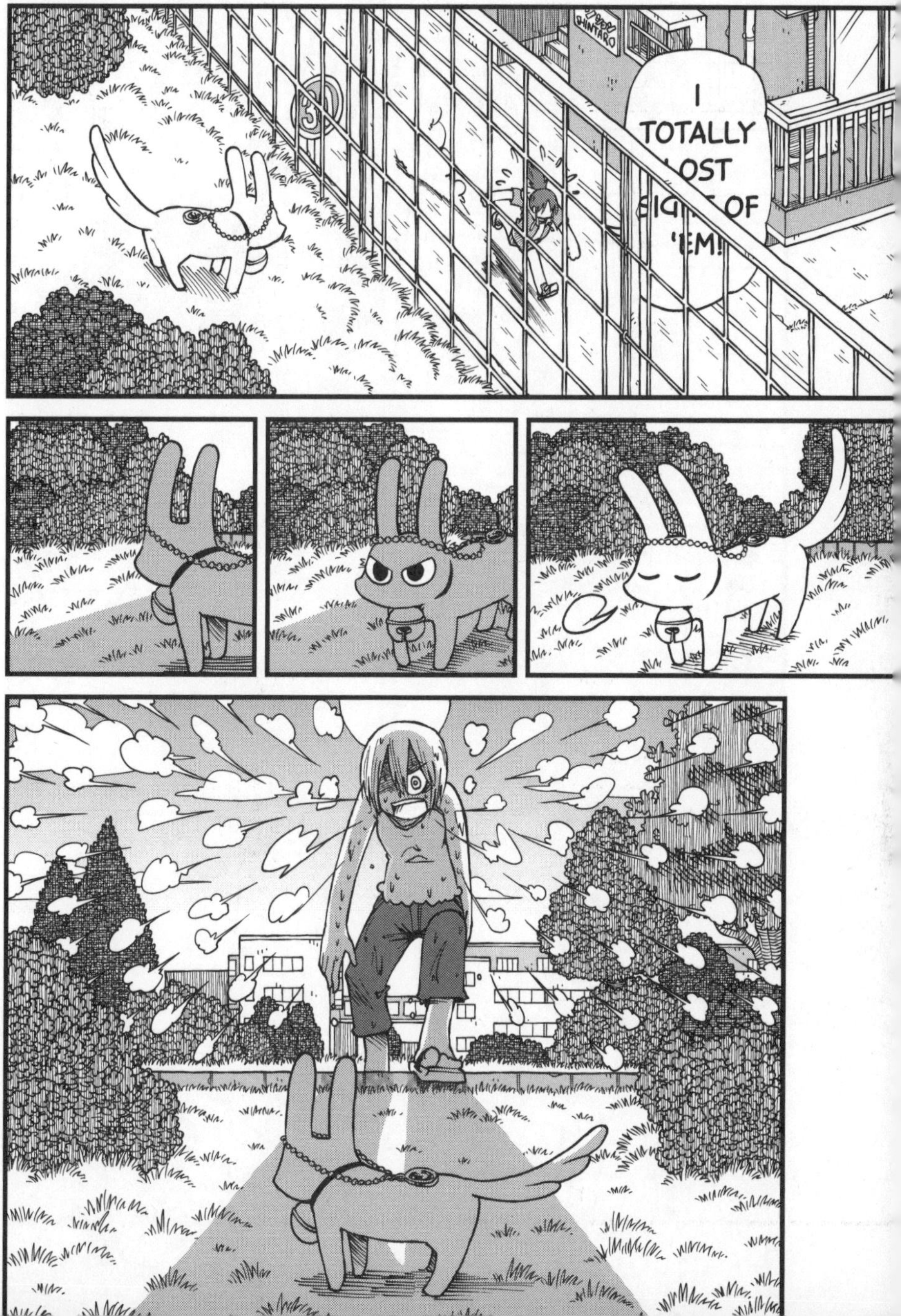
SHINTARO
30
I TOTALLY LOST SIGHT OF 'EM!

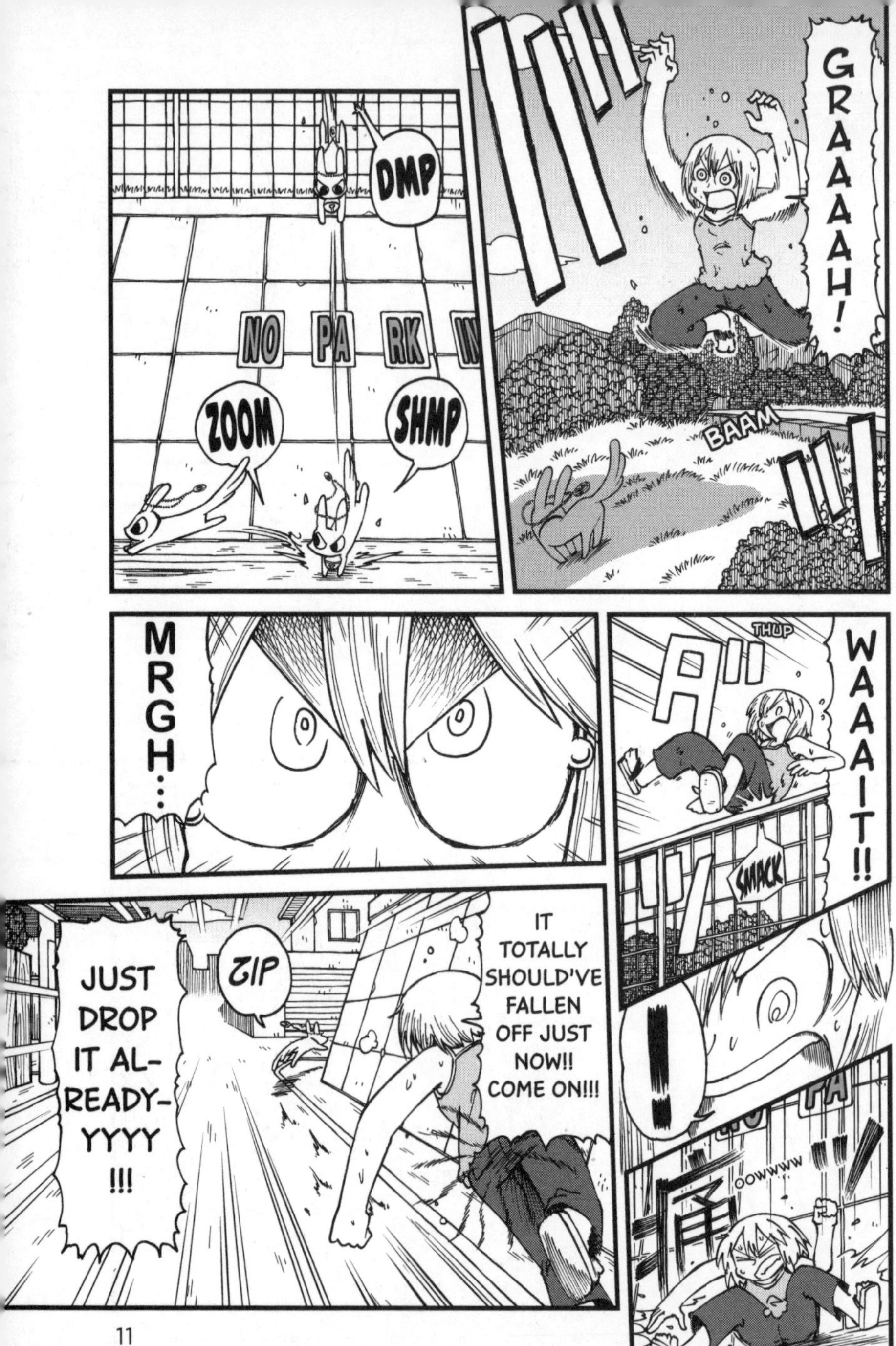
GRAAAAH!
BAAM
DMP
NO PA RK IN
ZOOM
SHMP
THUP
WAAAIT!!
SMACK
!
PA
OOWWW
MRGH...
IT TOTALLY SHOULD'VE FALLEN OFF JUST NOW!! COME ON!!!
ZIP
JUST DROP IT AL-READY-YYYY !!!

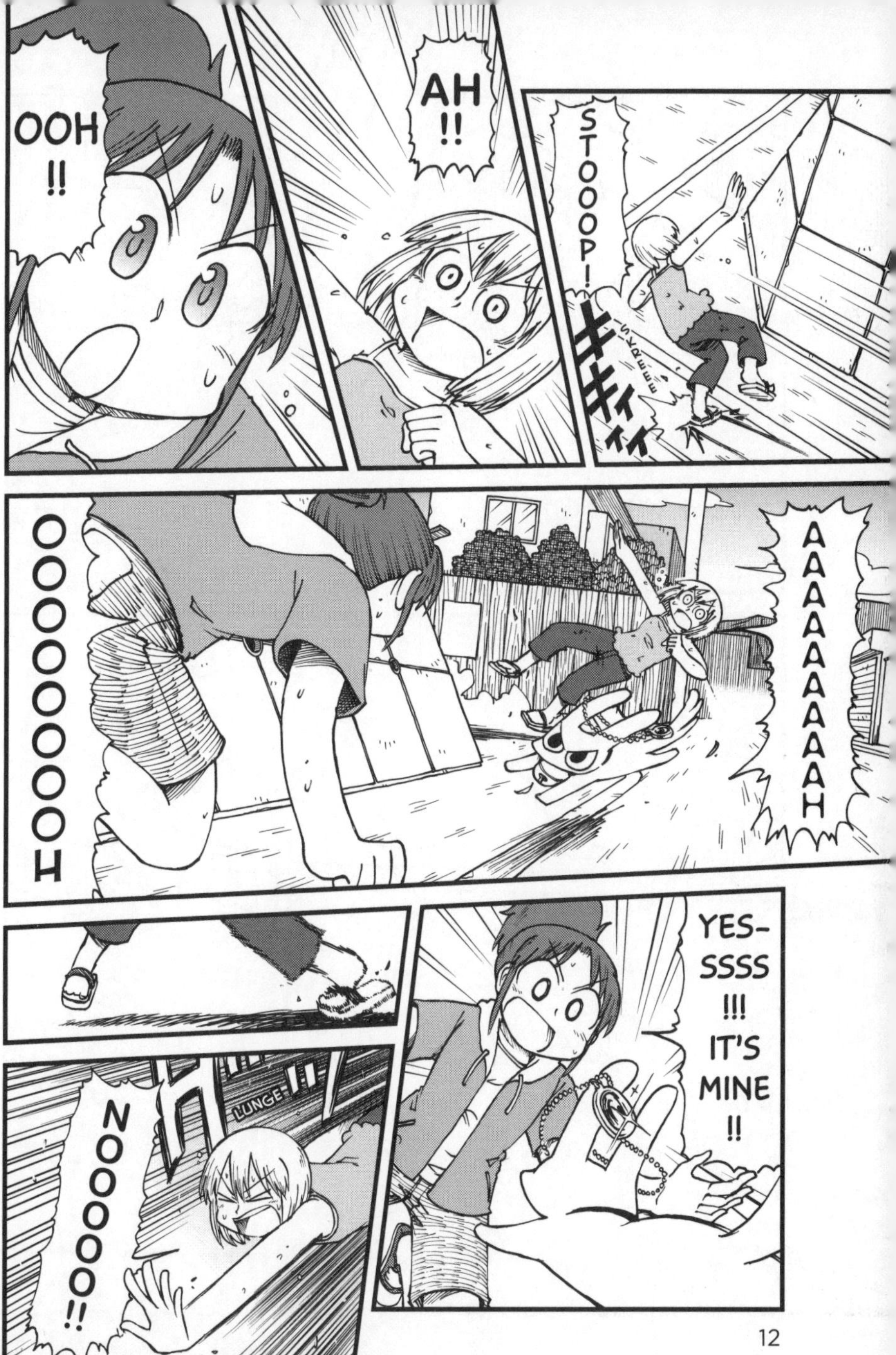
STOOOP!
キキィイ
SKREEEE
AH!!
OOH!!
AAAAAAAAAAAH
OOOOOOOOOOOH
YES-SSSS!!! IT'S MINE!!
LUNGE
NOOOOOO!!

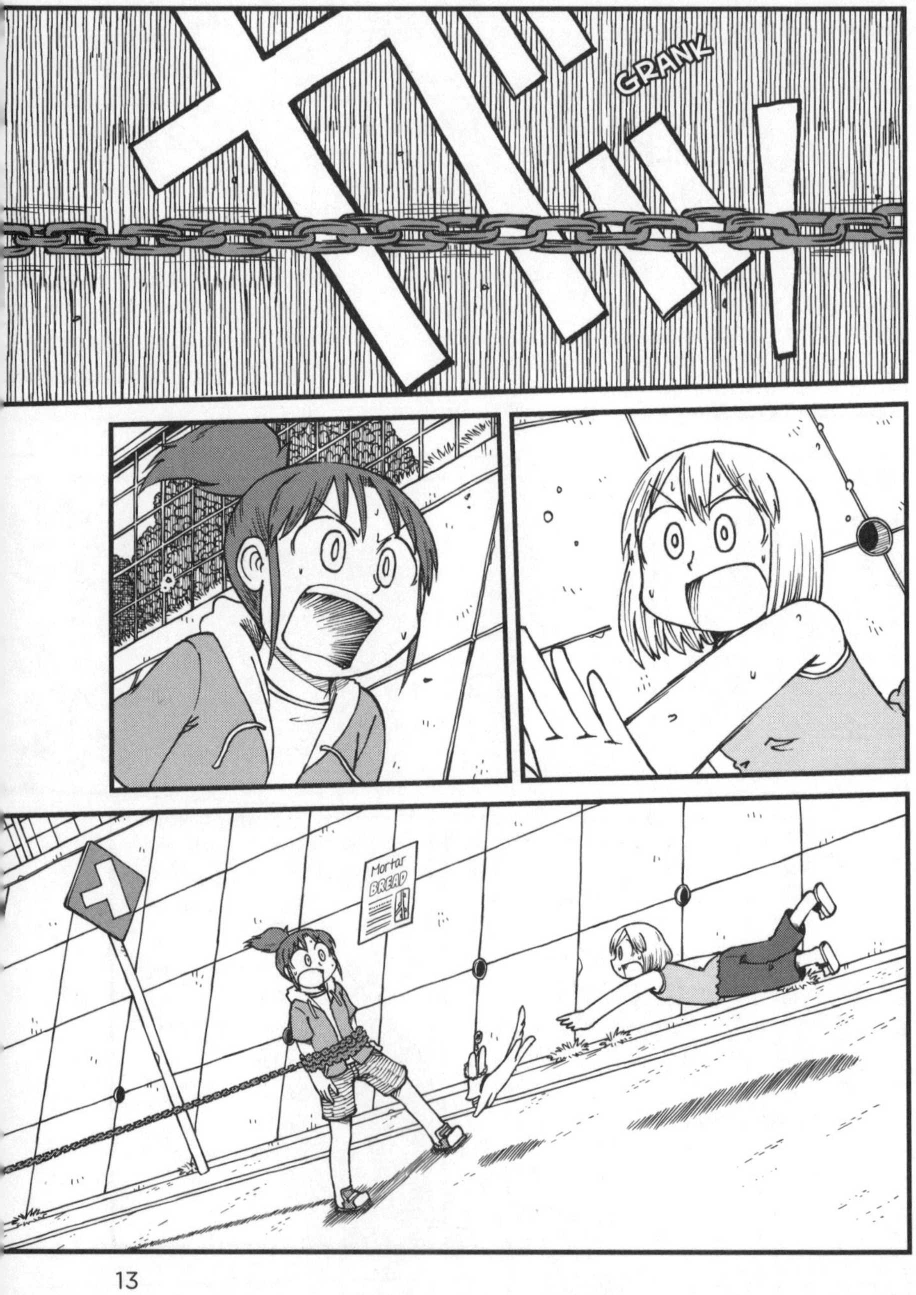
GRANK
Mortar
BREAD

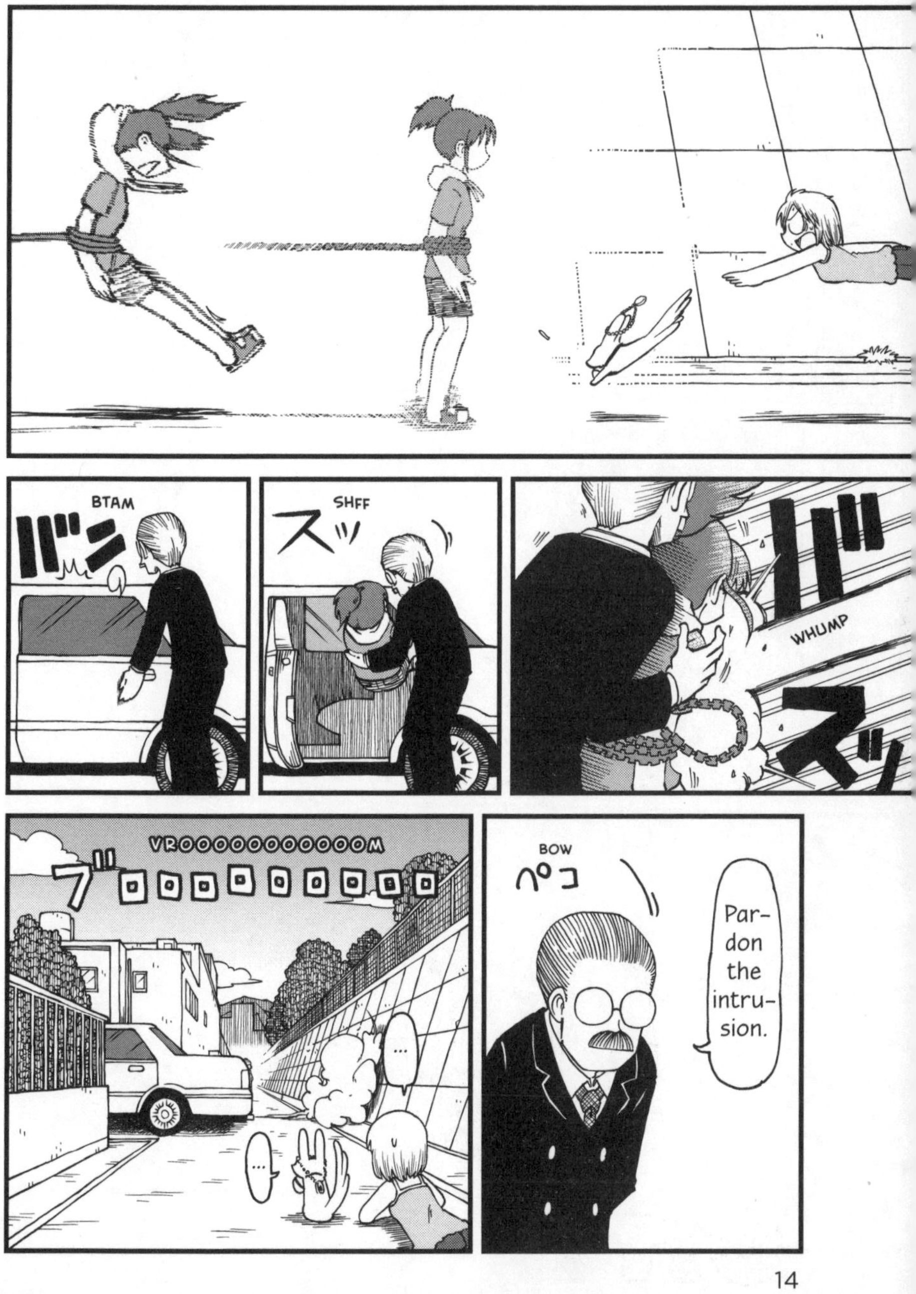
WHUMP
スッ
SHFF
バン
BTAM
ペコ
BOW
Pardon the intrusion.
VROOOOOOOOOOOOM
...
...

CITY

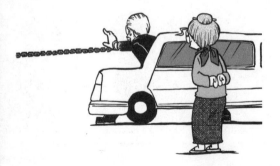

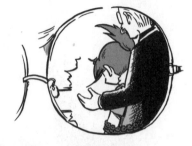

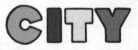

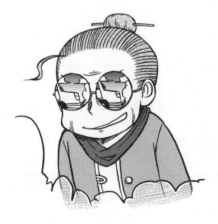

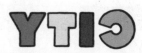

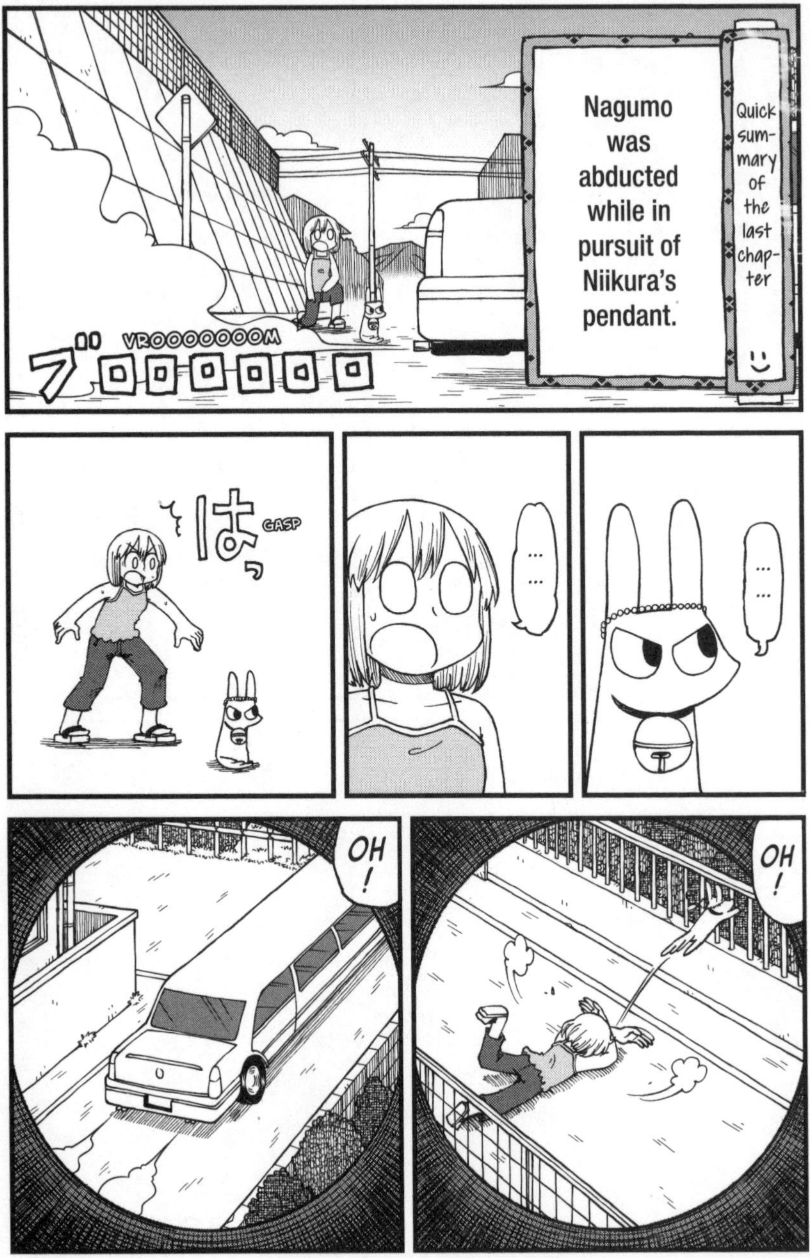

Quick summary of the last chapter :)
Nagumo was abducted while in pursuit of Niikura's pendant.
ブロロロロロロロ
VROOOOOOOM
……
……
はっ
GASP
OH!
OH!

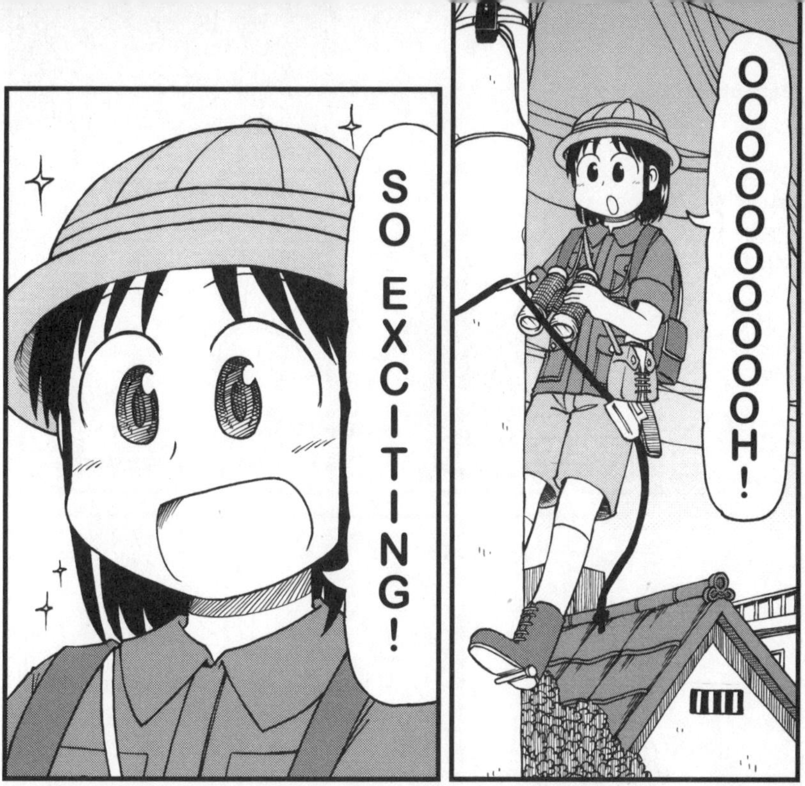
OOOOOOOOOOH!
SO EXCITING!

Chapter 41 Tower

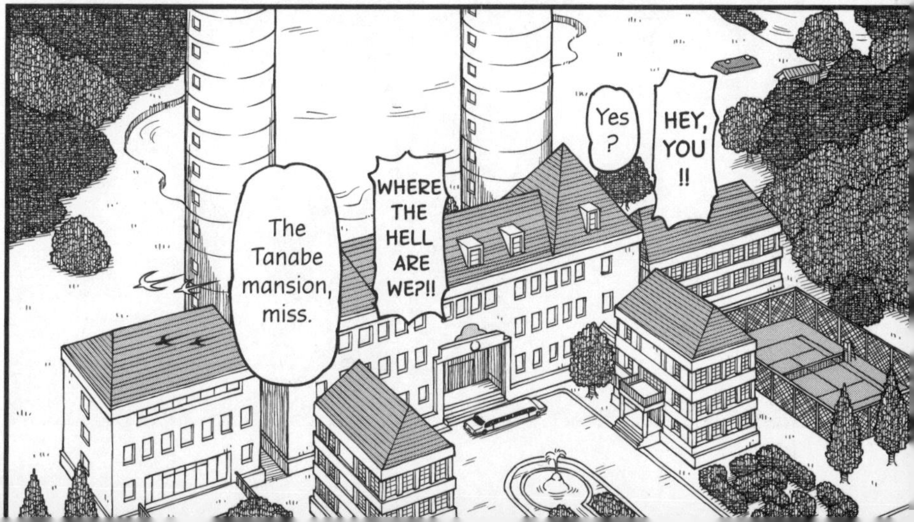
HEY, YOU !!
Yes ?
WHERE THE HELL ARE WE?!!
The Tanabe mansion, miss.

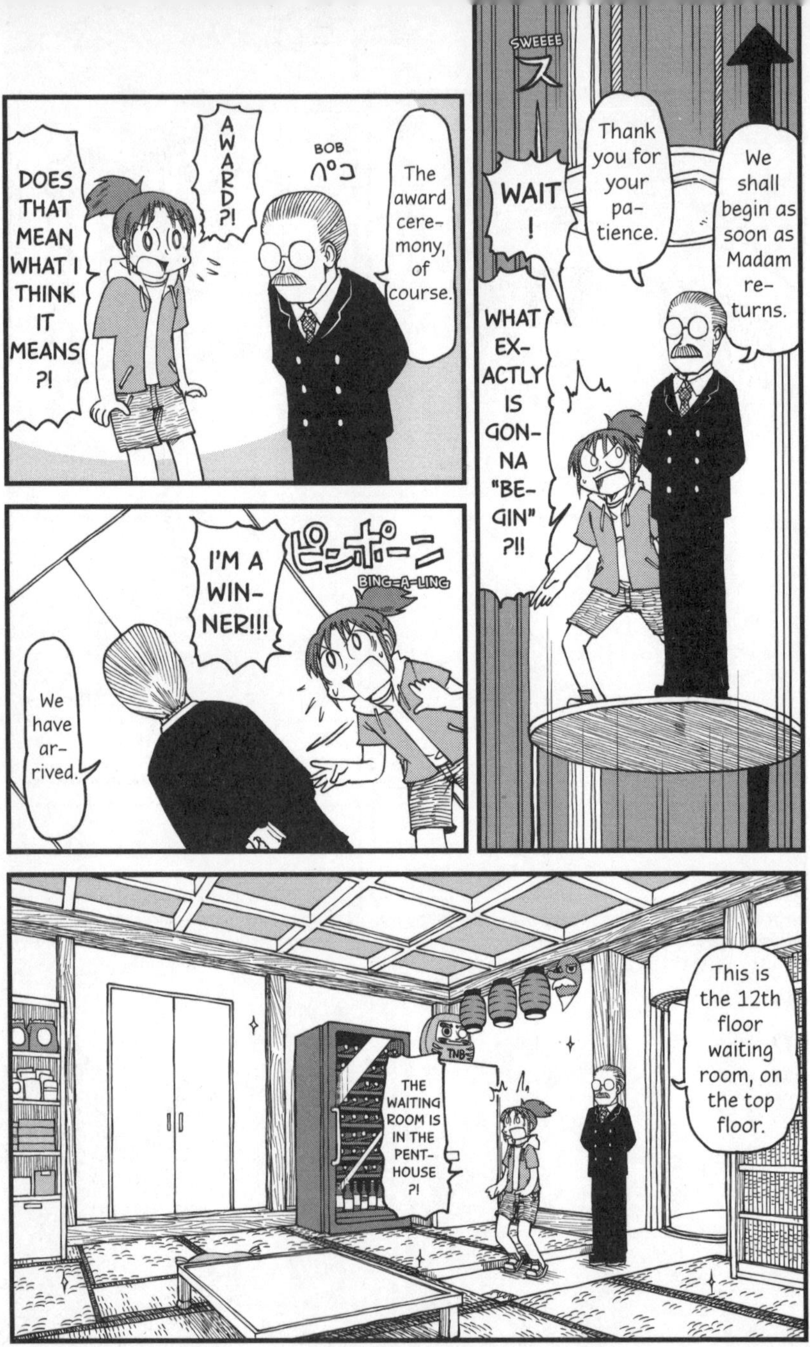
SWEEEE
ス
We shall begin as soon as Madam returns.
Thank you for your patience.
WAIT!
WHAT EXACTLY IS GONNA "BEGIN"?!!
BOB
ペコ
The award ceremony, of course.
AWARD?!
DOES THAT MEAN WHAT I THINK IT MEANS?!
ピンポーン
BING-A-LING
I'M A WINNER!!!
We have arrived.
This is the 12th floor waiting room, on the top floor.
TNB
THE WAITING ROOM IS IN THE PENTHOUSE?!

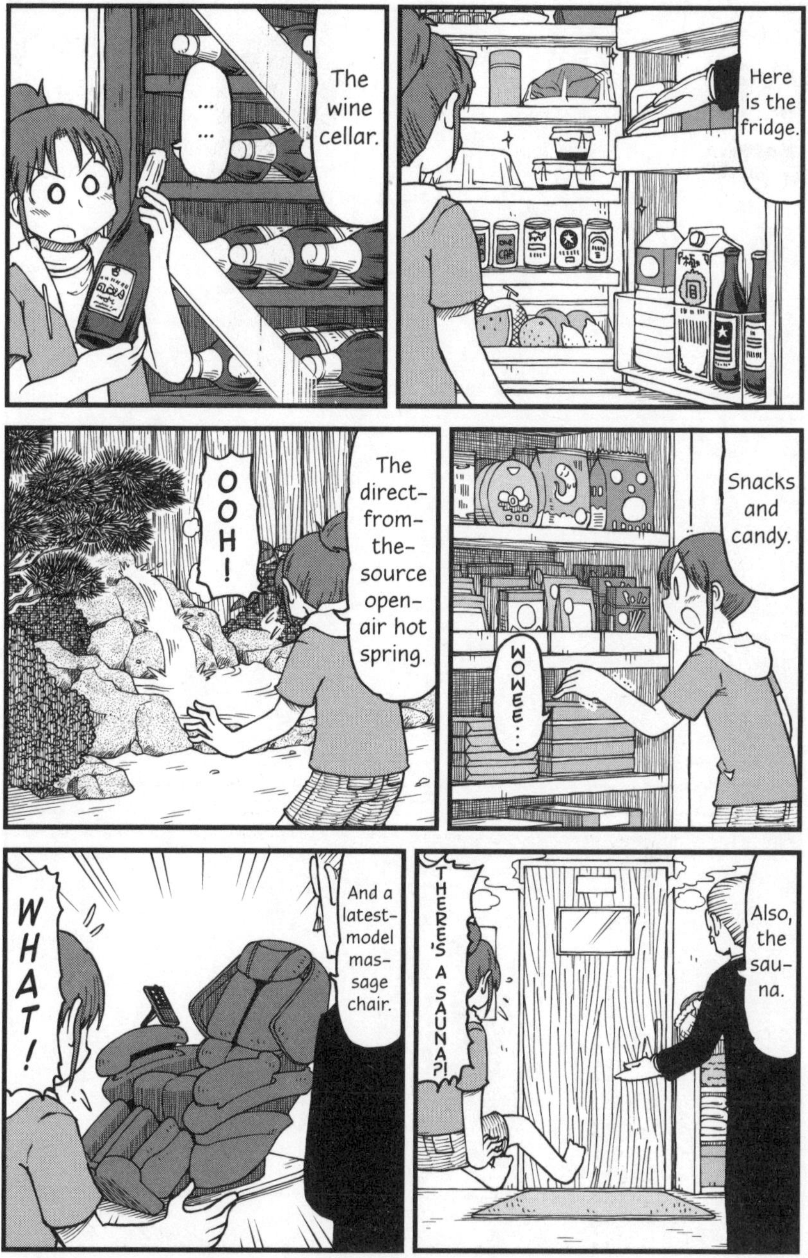
Here is the fridge.
The wine cellar.
... ...
Snacks and candy.
WOWEE...
The direct-from-the-source open-air hot spring.
OOH!
Also, the sauna.
THERE'S A SAUNA?!
And a latest-model massage chair.
WHAT!

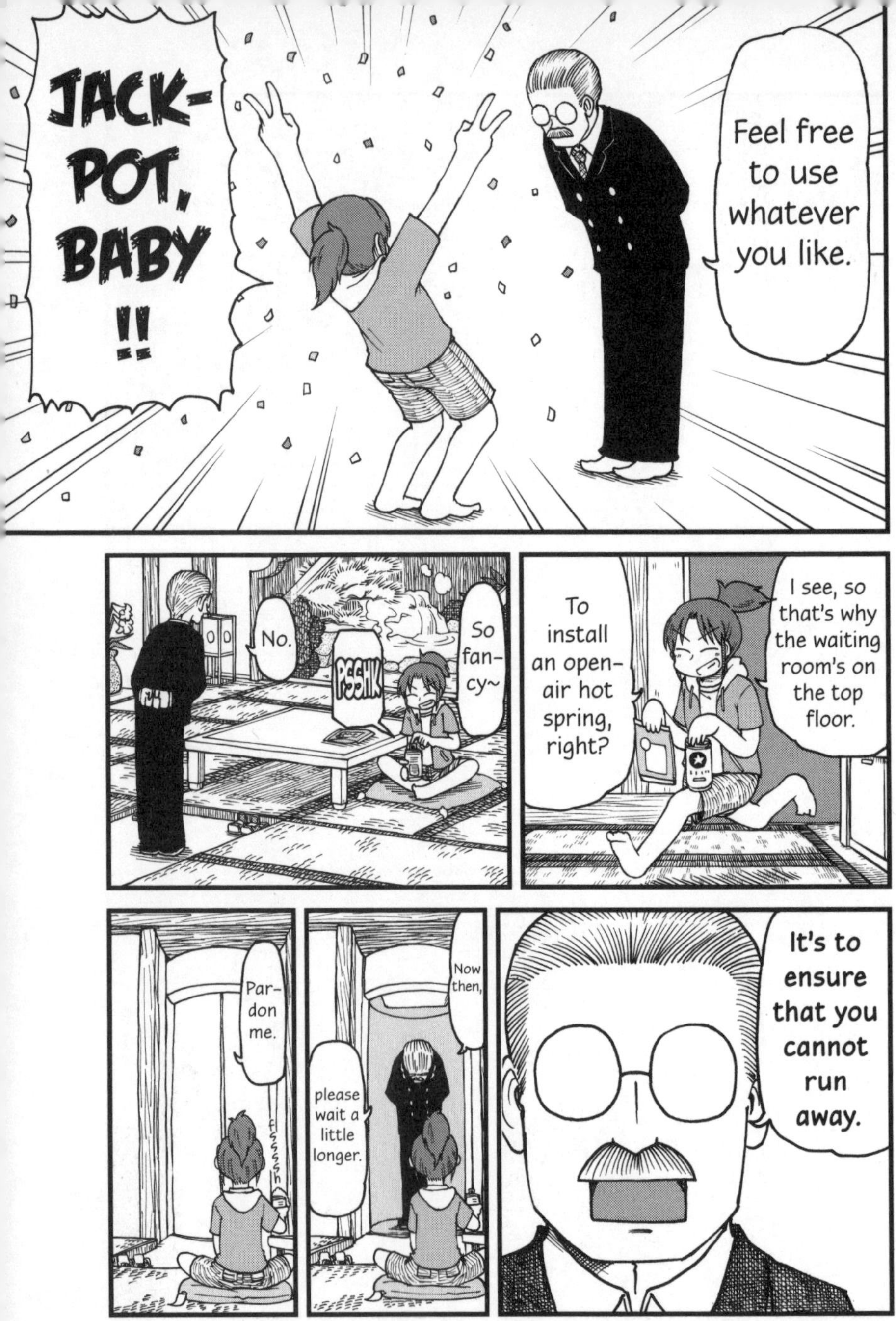
Feel free to use whatever you like.
JACK-POT, BABY!!
I see, so that's why the waiting room's on the top floor.
To install an open-air hot spring, right?
So fancy~
PSSHK
No.
It's to ensure that you cannot run away.
Now then,
please wait a little longer.
Pardon me.
fssssh

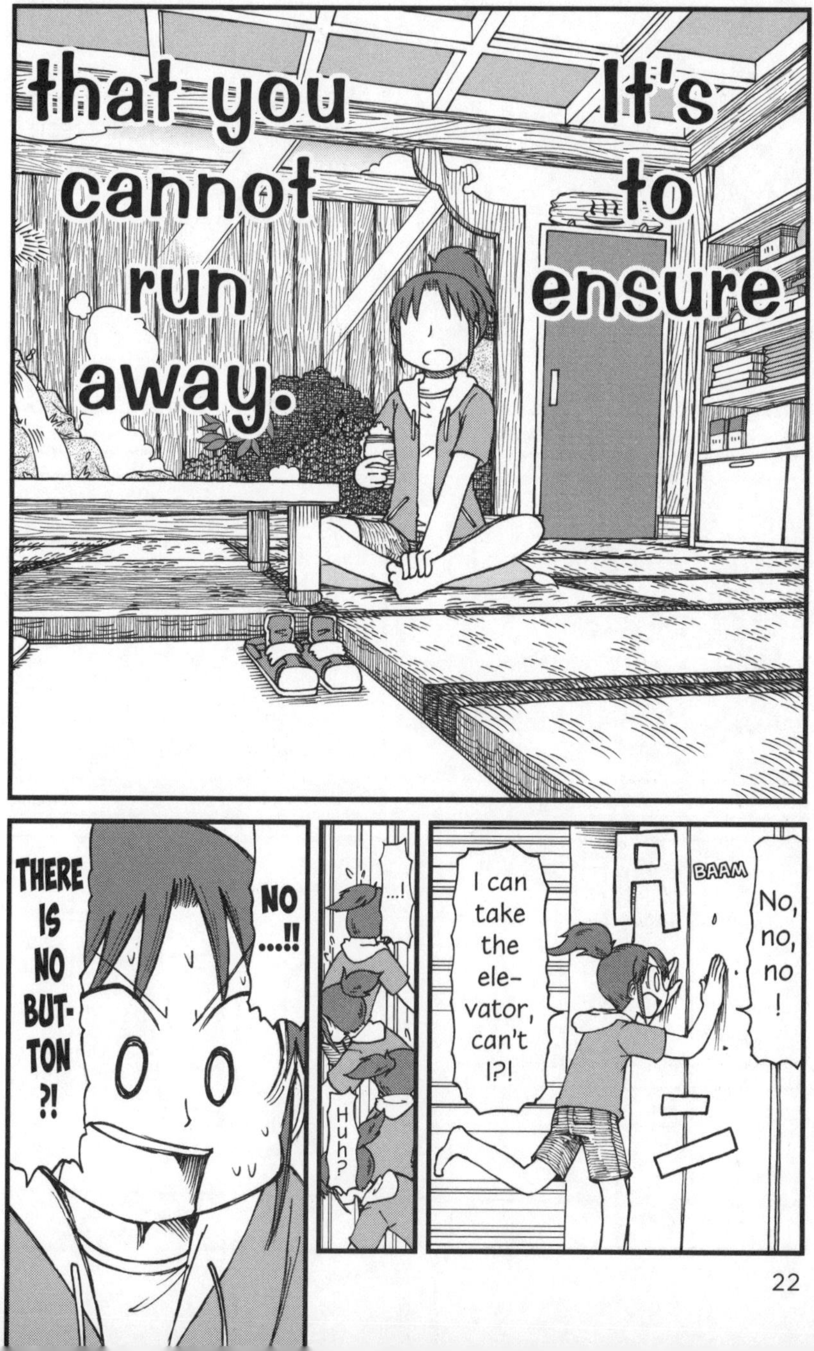
It's to ensure
that you cannot run away.
No, no, no!
BAAM
I can take the elevator, can't I?!
...!
Huh?
NO ....!!
THERE IS NO BUTTON ?!

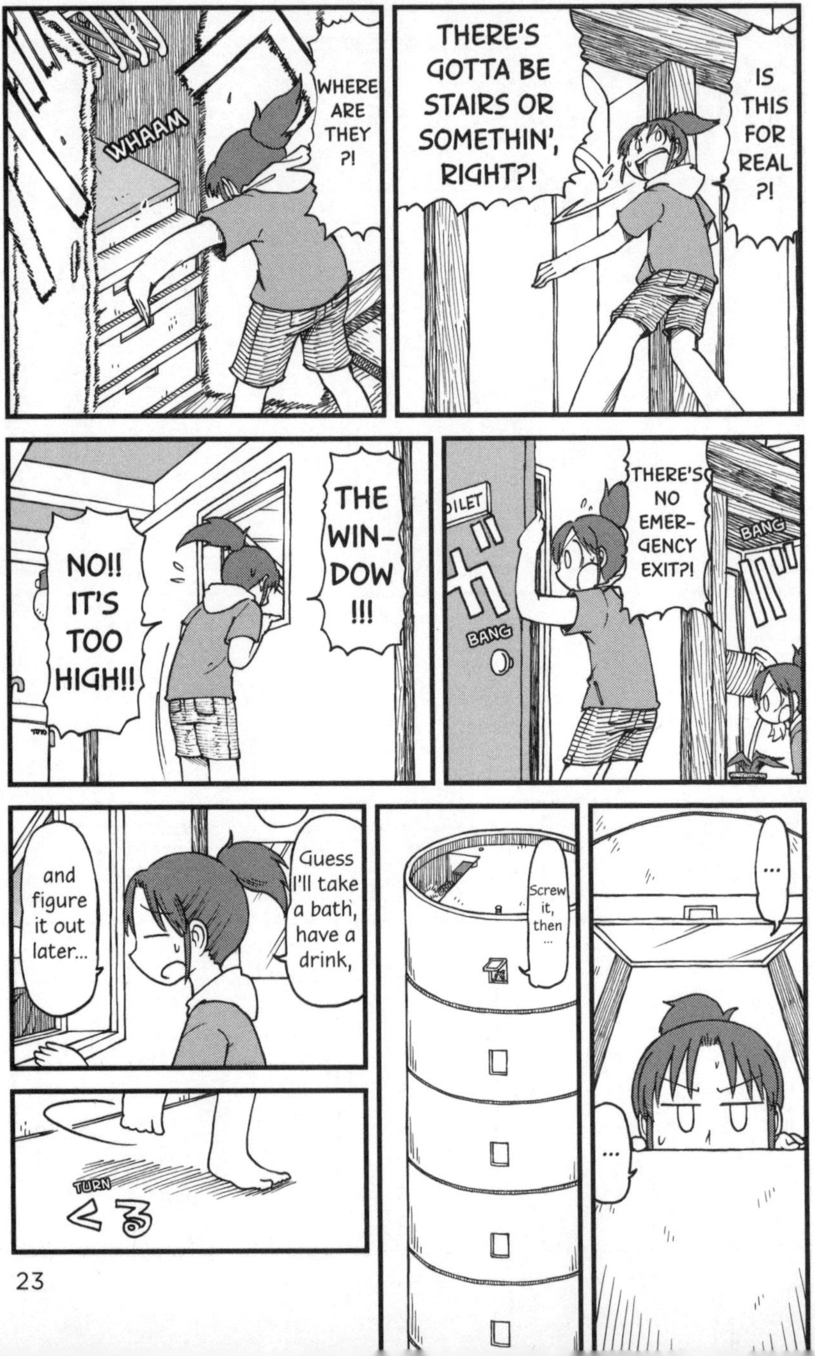
IS THIS FOR REAL ?!
THERE'S GOTTA BE STAIRS OR SOMETHIN', RIGHT?!
WHERE ARE THEY ?!
WHAAM
THERE'S NO EMER-GENCY EXIT?!
BANG
OILET
BANG
THE WIN-DOW !!!
NO!! IT'S TOO HIGH!!
...
...
Screw it, then ...
Guess I'll take a bath, have a drink,
and figure it out later...
TURN
くる

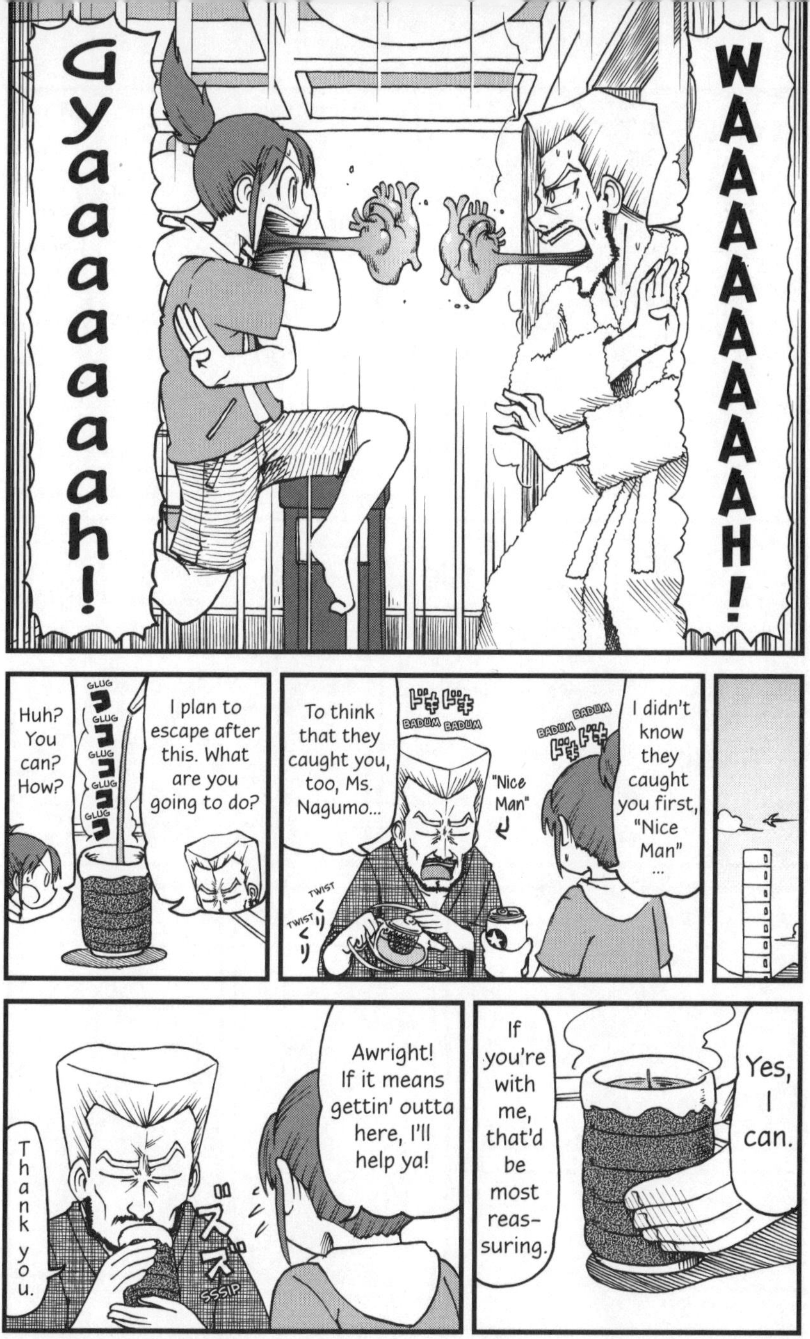
WAAAAAAAAH!
Gyaaaaaaah!
BADUM BADUM
I didn't know they caught you first, "Nice Man" ...
"Nice Man"
BADUM BADUM
To think that they caught you, too, Ms. Nagumo...
TWIST TWIST
I plan to escape after this. What are you going to do?
GLUG GLUG GLUG GLUG GLUG
Huh? You can? How?
Yes, I can.
If you're with me, that'd be most reassuring.
Awright! If it means gettin' outta here, I'll help ya!
SSSIP
Thank you.

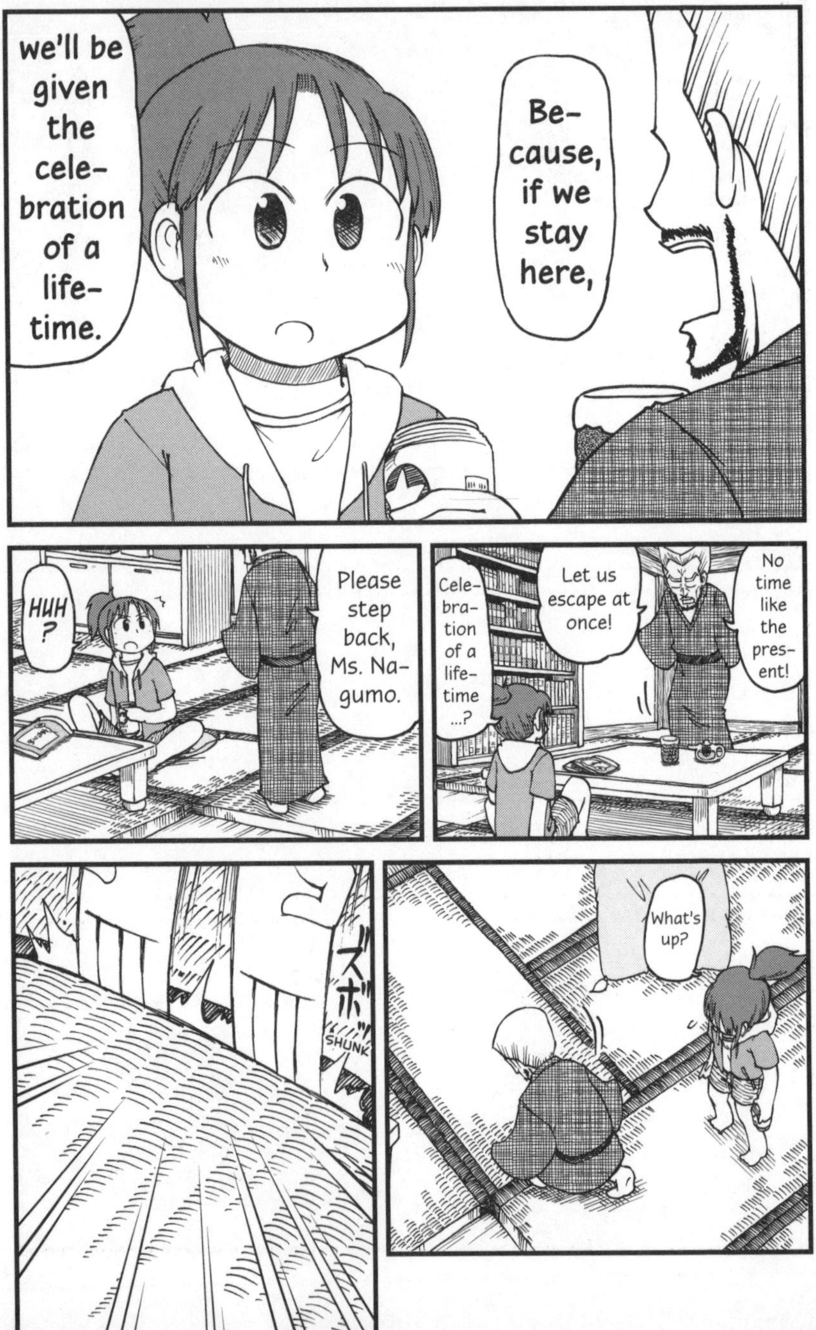
Be-cause, if we stay here,
we'll be given the cele-bration of a life-time.
No time like the pres-ent!
Let us escape at once!
Cele-bra-tion of a life-time ...?
Please step back, Ms. Na-gumo.
HUH?
What's up?
ズボッ
SHUNK

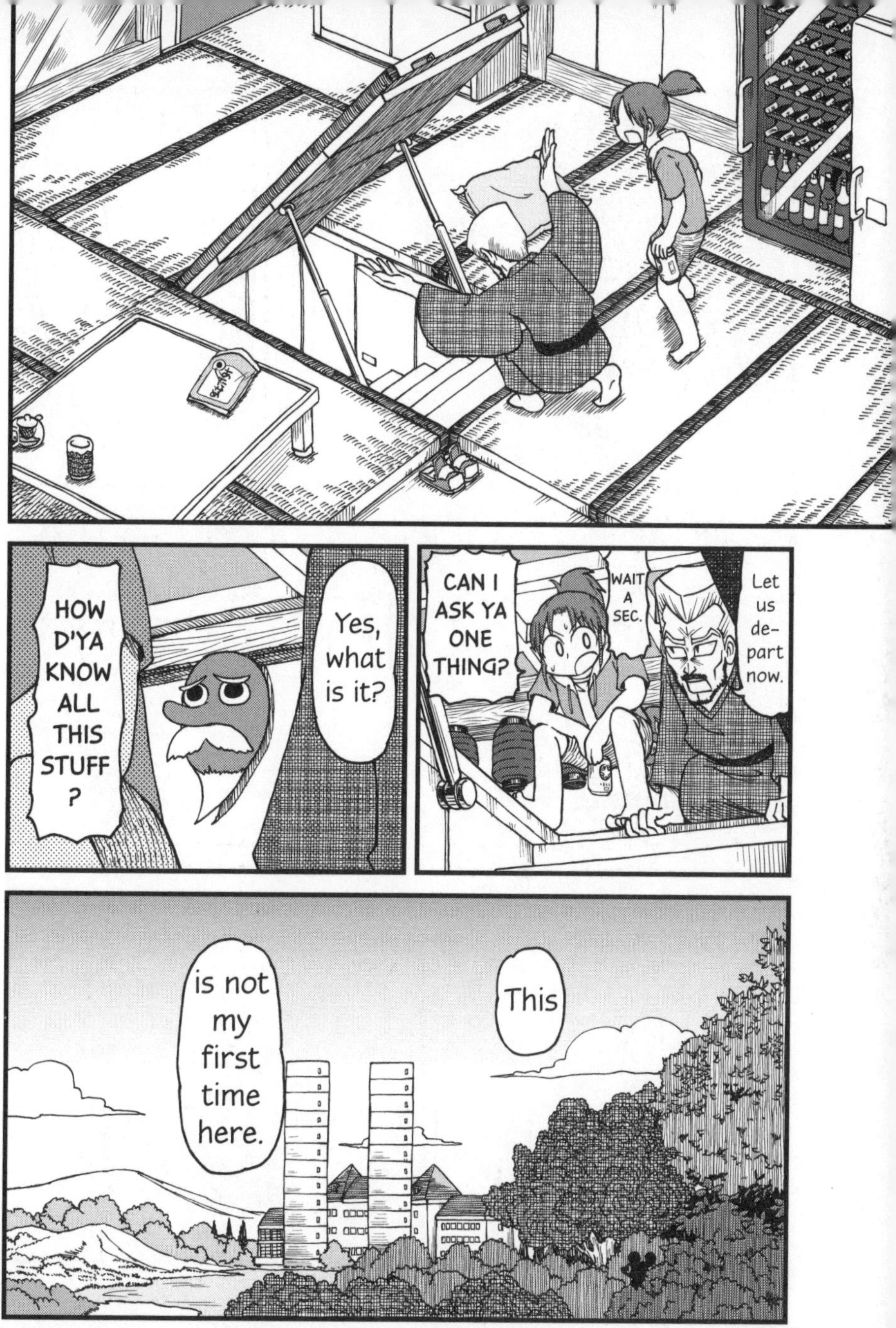
Let us de-part now.
WAIT A SEC.
CAN I ASK YA ONE THING?
Yes, what is it?
HOW D'YA KNOW ALL THIS STUFF?
This
is not my first time here.

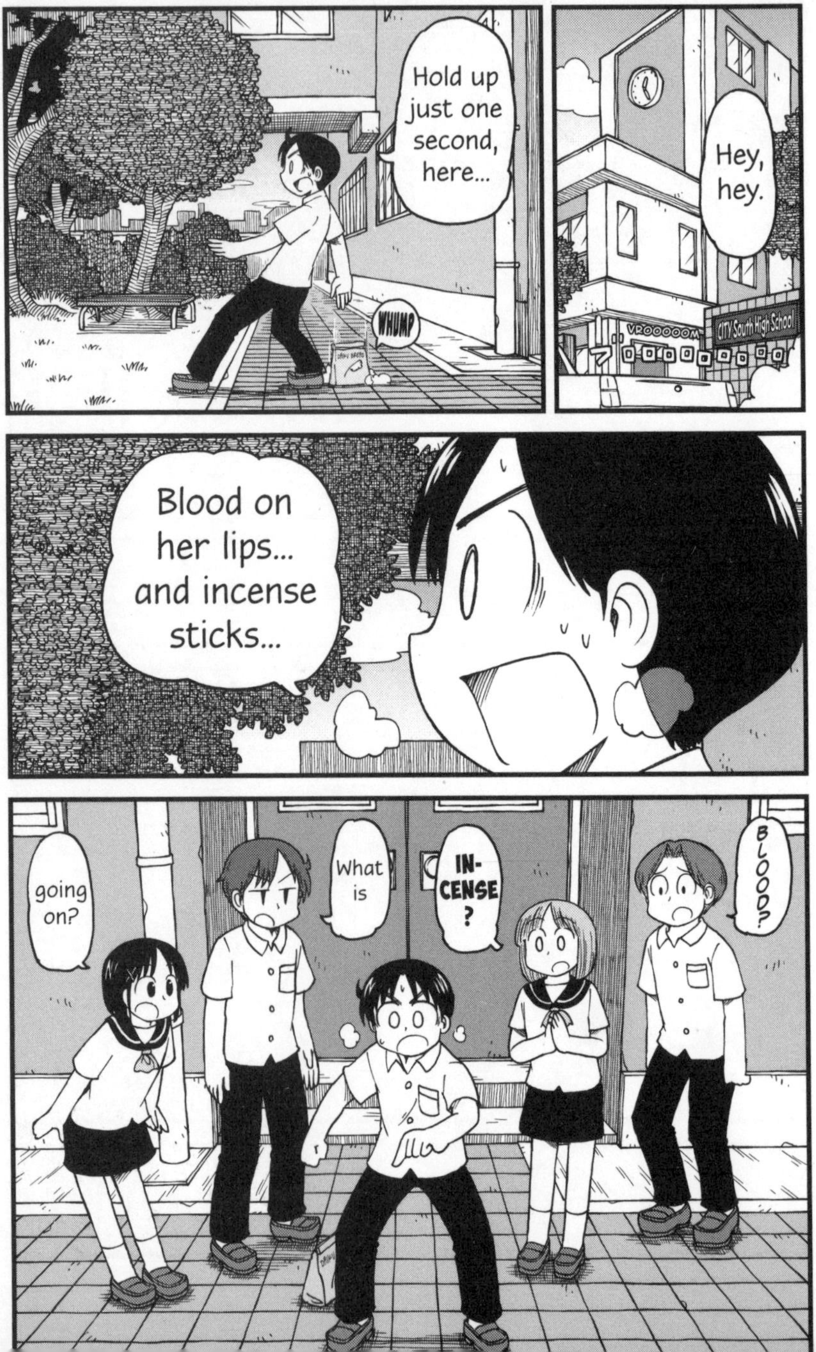
Hey, hey.
CITY South High School
VROOOOOM
Hold up just one second, here...
WHUMP
Blood on her lips... and incense sticks...
BLOOD?
IN-CENSE?
What is
going on?

Izumiii!!
PIIIIIIING
Adatara Wines

Chapter 42

zzzzzzzzzzzz
There it is! A snot bubble!!
BWOOOP

~ Kindness Incident ~

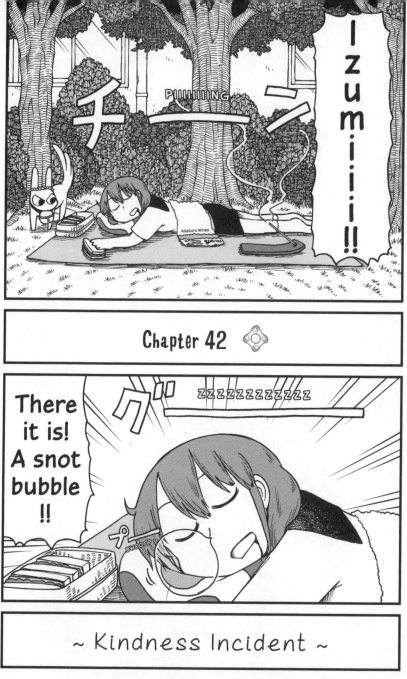

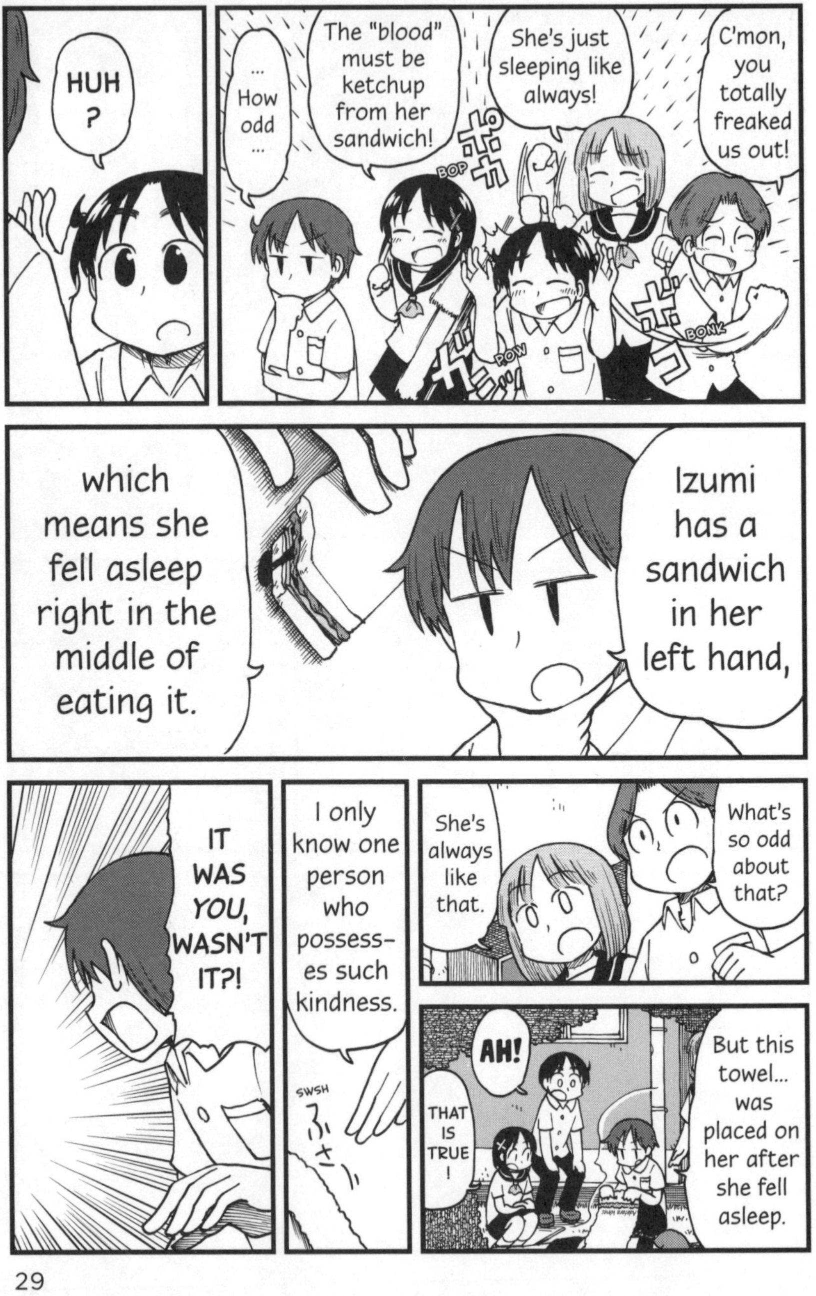
C'mon, you totally freaked us out!
BONK
She's just sleeping like always!
BOP
POW
The "blood" must be ketchup from her sandwich!
... How odd ...
HUH ?
Izumi has a sandwich in her left hand,
which means she fell asleep right in the middle of eating it.
What's so odd about that?
She's always like that.
But this towel... was placed on her after she fell asleep.
AH!
THAT IS TRUE!
I only know one person who possesses such kindness.
SWSH
IT WAS *YOU*, WASN'T IT?!

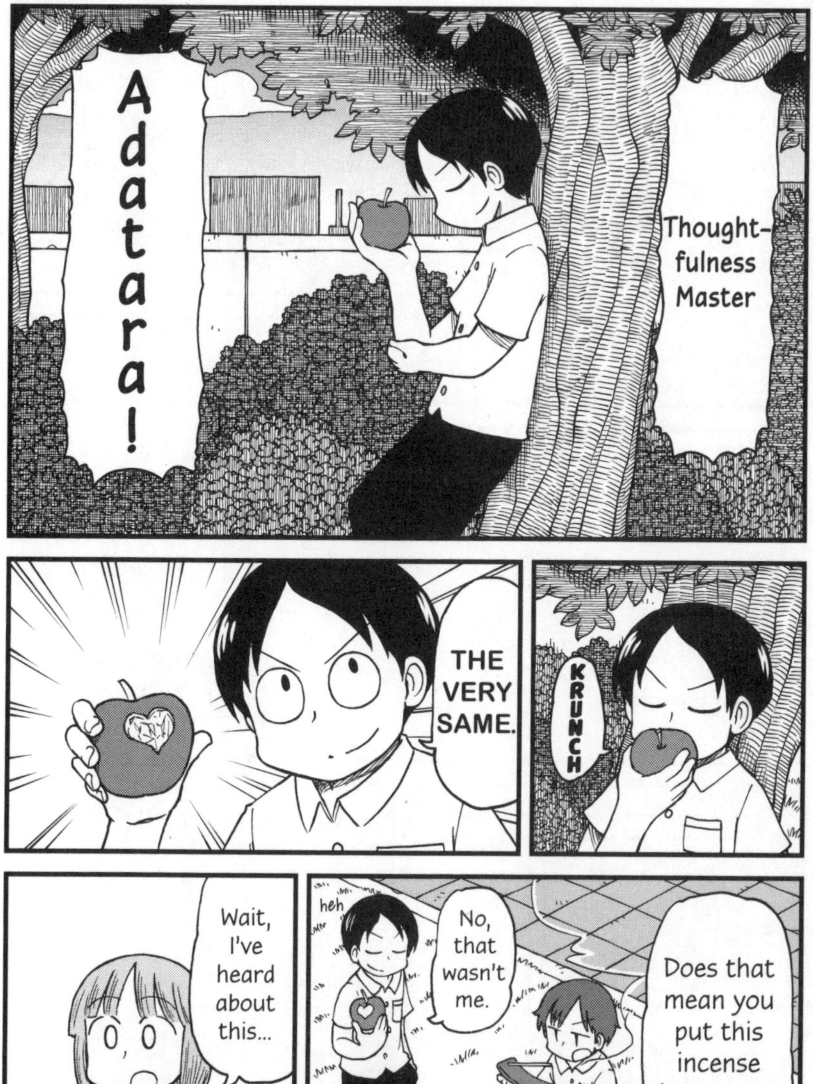
Thought-fulness Master
Adatara!
KRUNCH
THE VERY SAME.
Does that mean you put this incense here, too?
No, that wasn't me.
heh
Wait, I've heard about this...

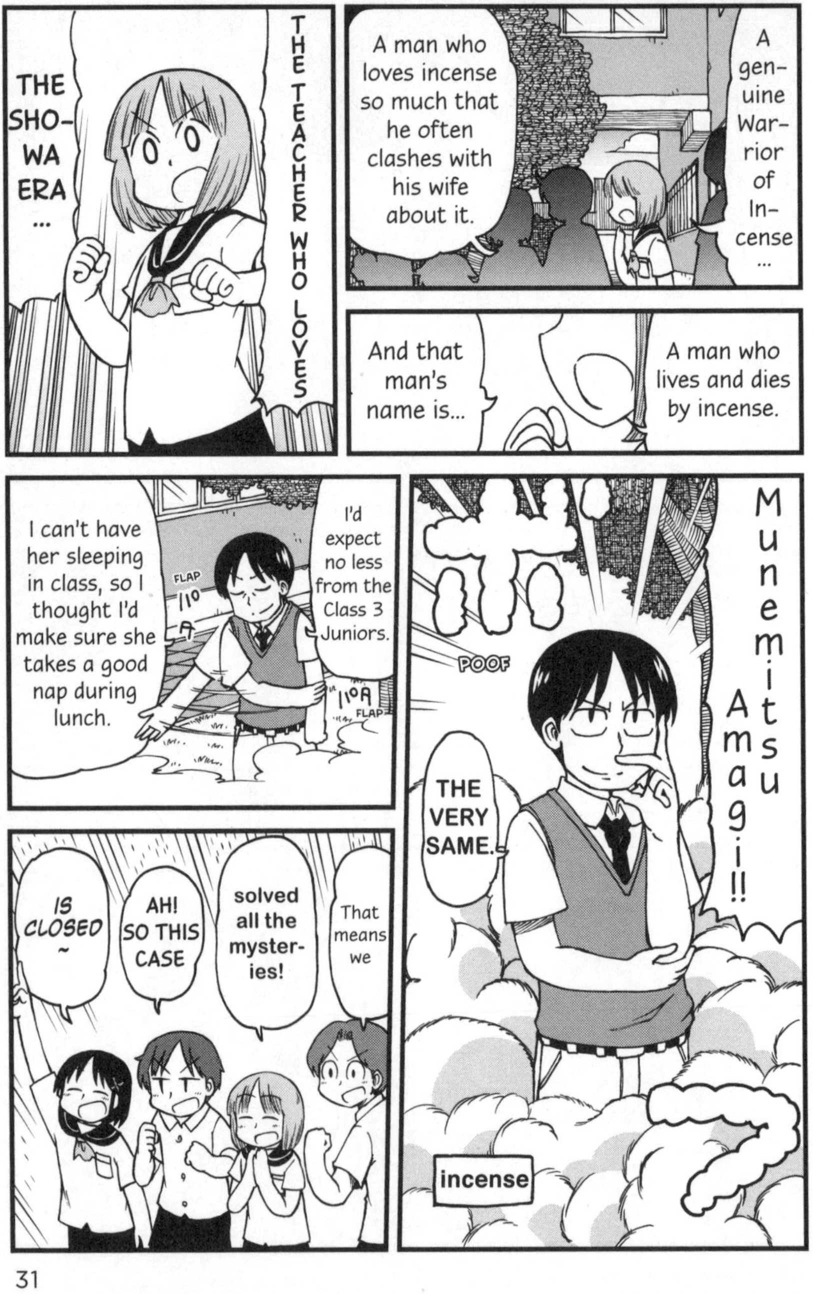
A genuine Warrior of Incense ...
A man who loves incense so much that he often clashes with his wife about it.
A man who lives and dies by incense.
And that man's name is...
THE TEACHER WHO LOVES
THE SHOWA ERA ...
Munemitsu Amagi!!
POOF
THE VERY SAME.
incense
I'd expect no less from the Class 3 Juniors.
FLAP
FLAP
I can't have her sleeping in class, so I thought I'd make sure she takes a good nap during lunch.
That means we
solved all the mysteries!
AH! SO THIS CASE
IS CLOSED ~

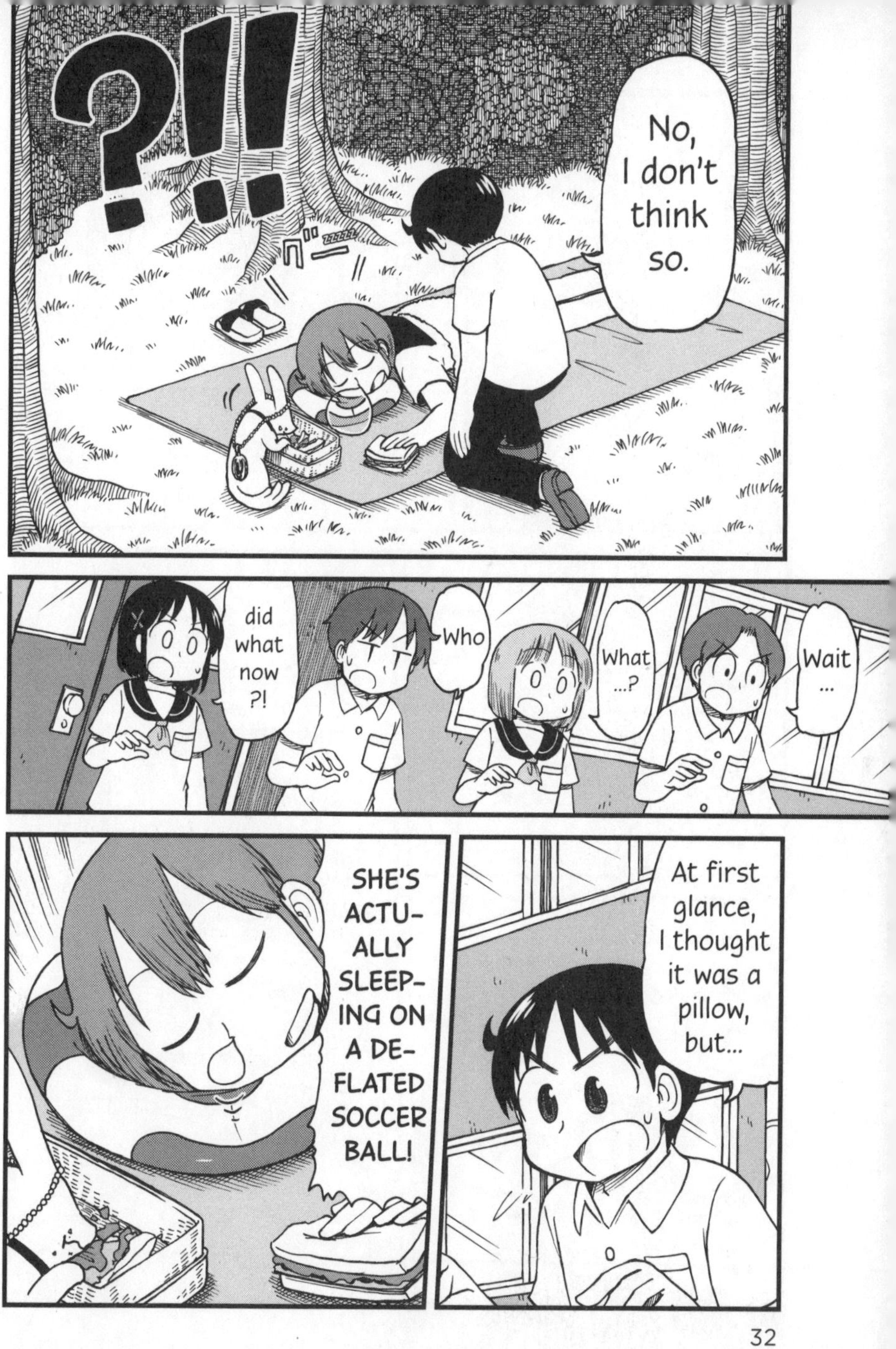

No, I don't think so.
?!!
Wait ...
What ...?
Who
did what now ?!
At first glance, I thought it was a pillow, but...
SHE'S ACTU-ALLY SLEEP-ING ON A DE-FLATED SOCCER BALL!

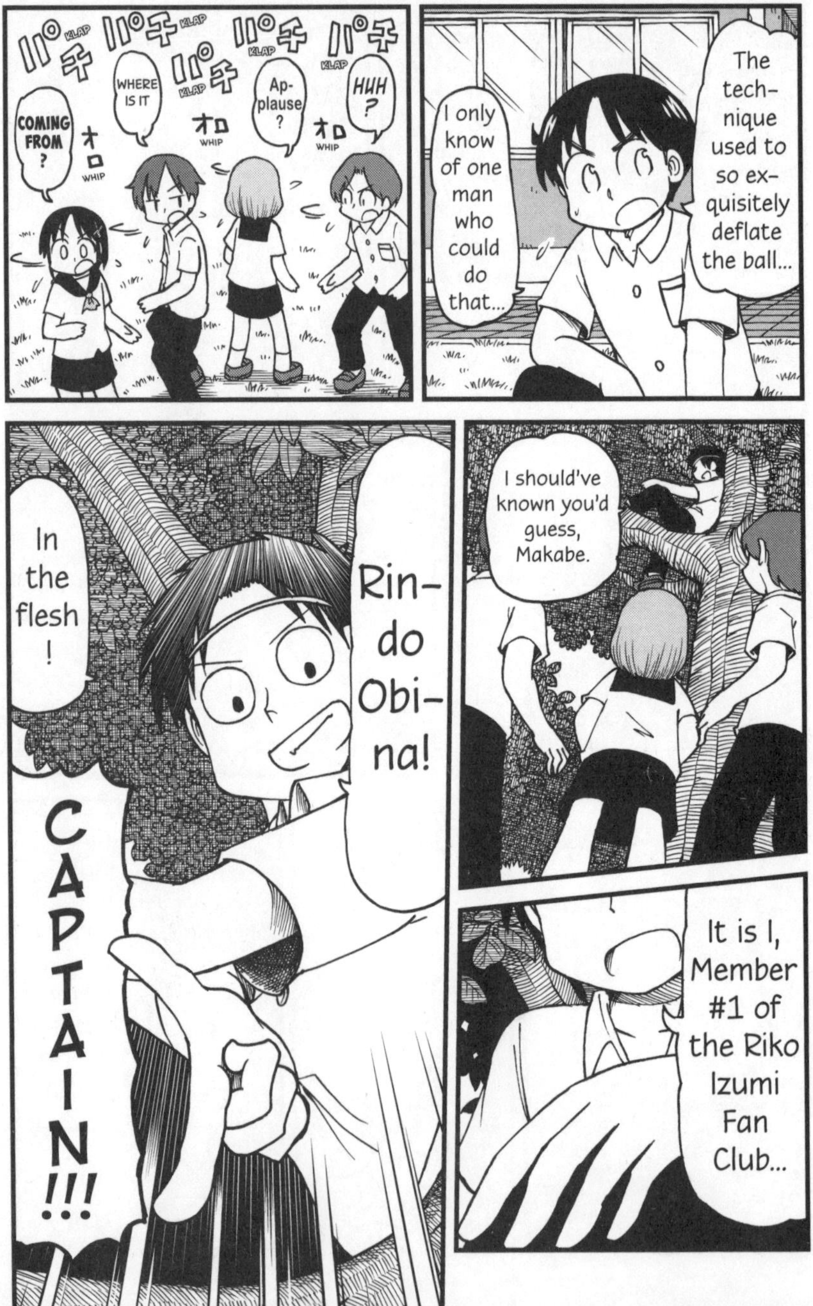
The tech-nique used to so ex-quisitely deflate the ball...
I only know of one man who could do that...
パチ KLAP
HUH?
オロ WHIP
Ap-plause?
WHERE IS IT
COMING FROM?
I should've known you'd guess, Makabe.
It is I, Member #1 of the Riko Izumi Fan Club...
Rin-do Obi-na!
In the flesh!
CAPTAIN!!!

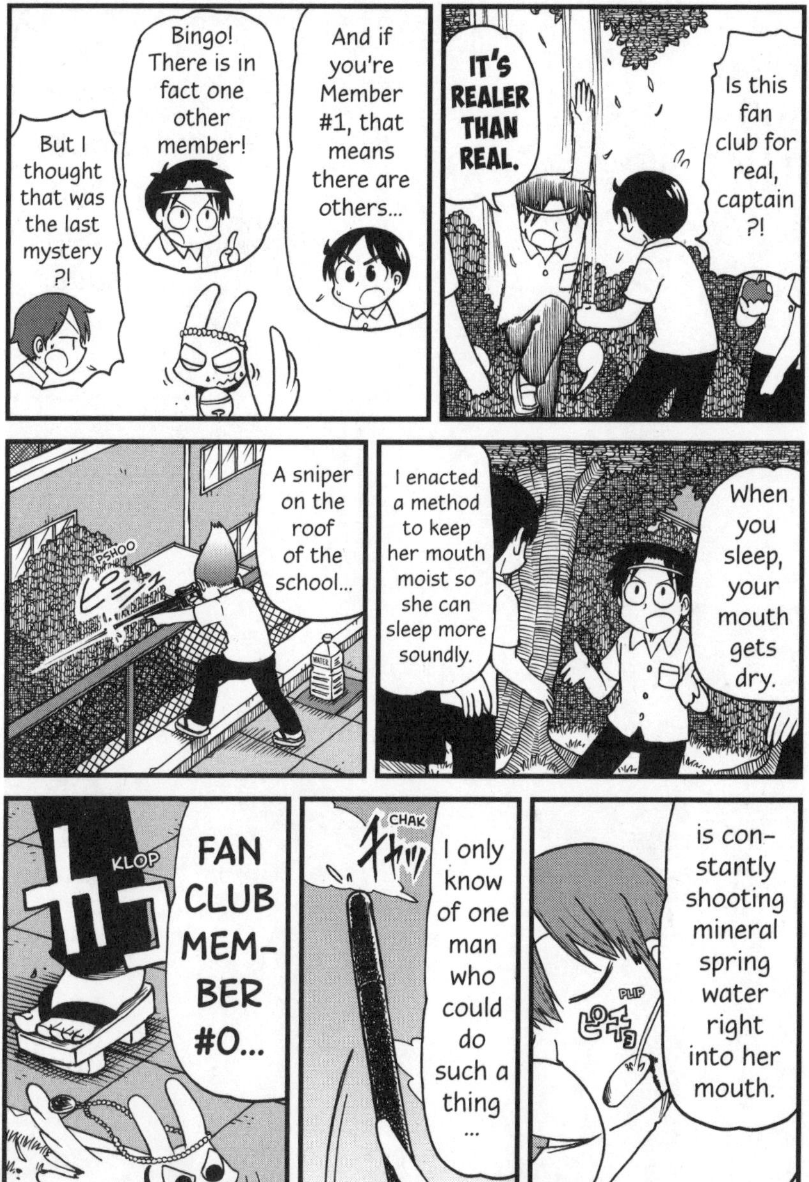
Is this fan club for real, captain?!
IT'S REALER THAN REAL.
And if you're Member #1, that means there are others...
Bingo! There is in fact one other member!
But I thought that was the last mystery?!
When you sleep, your mouth gets dry.
I enacted a method to keep her mouth moist so she can sleep more soundly.
A sniper on the roof of the school...
PSHOO
WATER
is con-stantly shooting mineral spring water right into her mouth.
PLIP
CHAK
I only know of one man who could do such a thing...
KLOP
FAN CLUB MEM-BER #0...

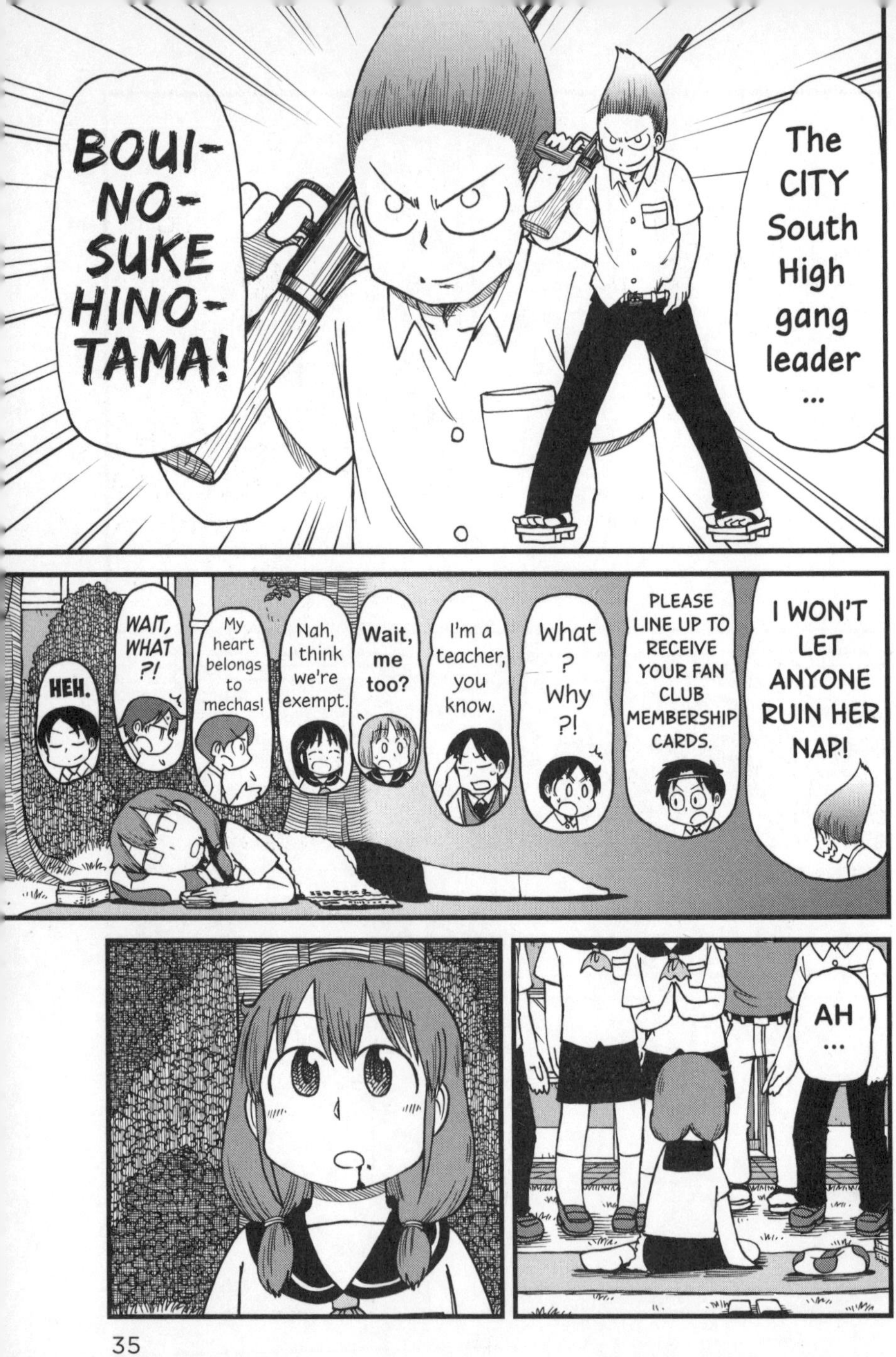
The CITY South High gang leader ...
BOUI-NO-SUKE HINO-TAMA!
I WON'T LET ANYONE RUIN HER NAP!
PLEASE LINE UP TO RECEIVE YOUR FAN CLUB MEMBERSHIP CARDS.
What? Why?!
I'm a teacher, you know.
Wait, me too?
Nah, I think we're exempt.
My heart belongs to mechas!
WAIT, WHAT?!
HEH.
AH ...

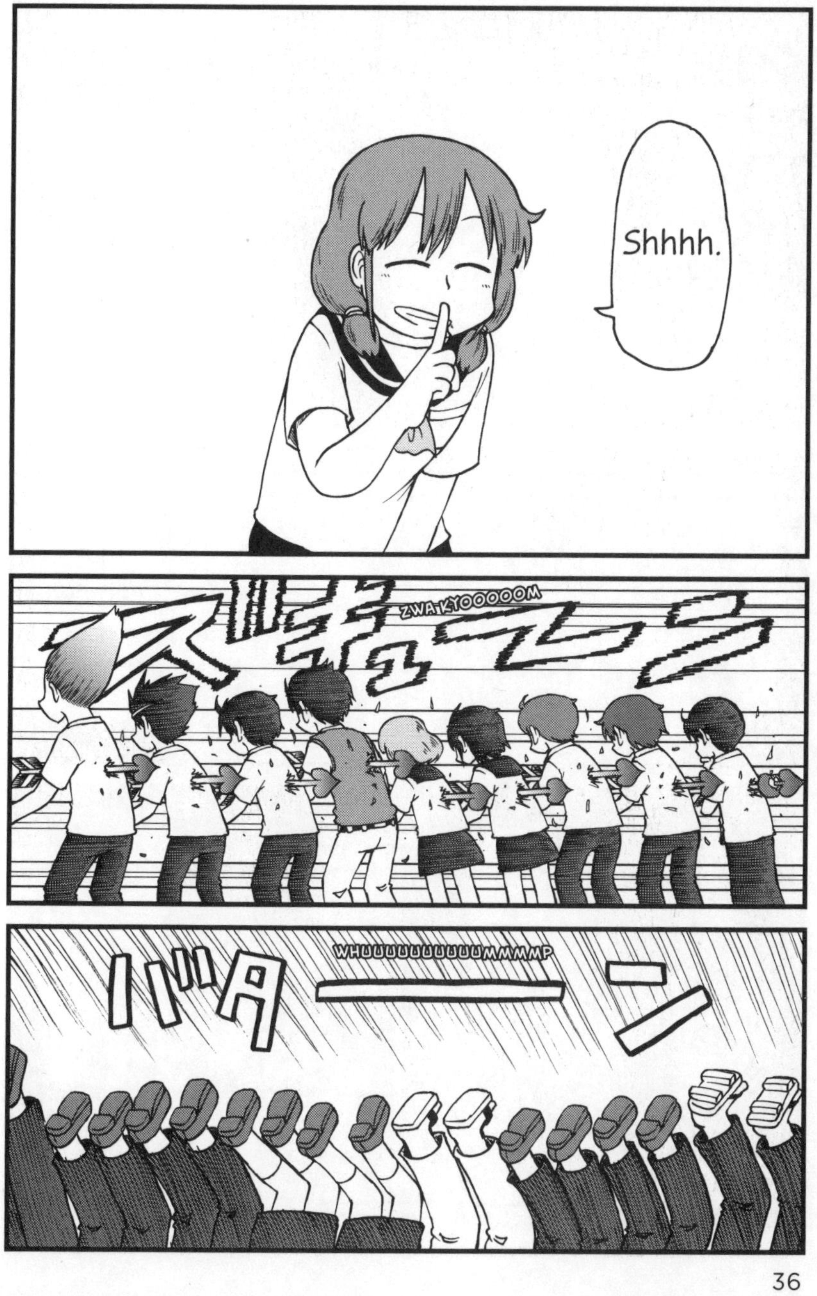
Shhhh.
ZWA-KYOOOOOM
WHUUUUUUUUUUMMMMP

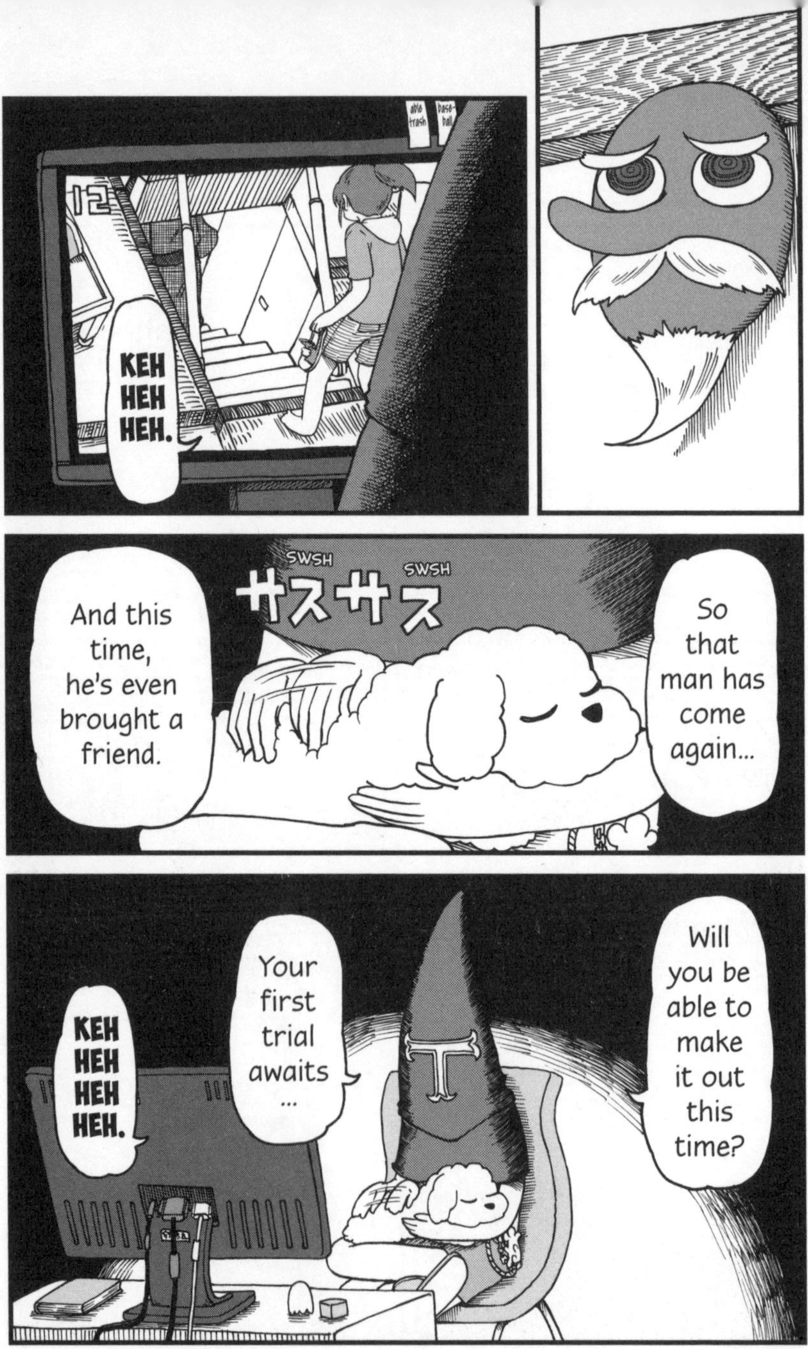
able trash
base-ball
12
KEH HEH HEH.
SWSH SWSH
サスサス
So that man has come again...
And this time, he's even brought a friend.
Will you be able to make it out this time?
Your first trial awaits ...
KEH HEH HEH HEH.

Chapter 43 Tower G

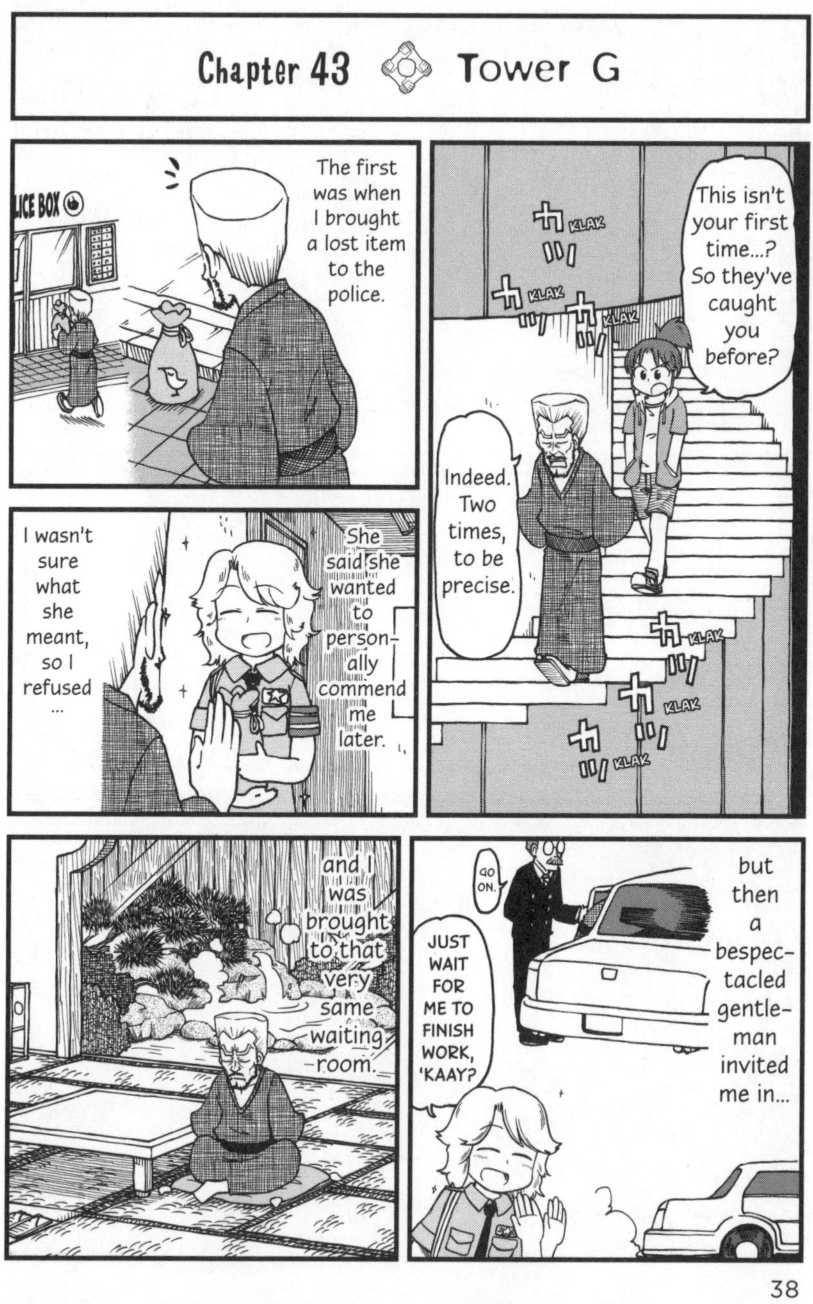
This isn't your first time...? So they've caught you before?
KLAK
KLAK
KLAK
Indeed. Two times, to be precise.
KLAK
KLAK
KLAK
The first was when I brought a lost item to the police.
LICE BOX
She said she wanted to personally commend me later.
I wasn't sure what she meant, so I refused ...
but then a bespectacled gentleman invited me in...
GO ON.
JUST WAIT FOR ME TO FINISH WORK, 'KAAY?
and I was brought to that very same waiting room.

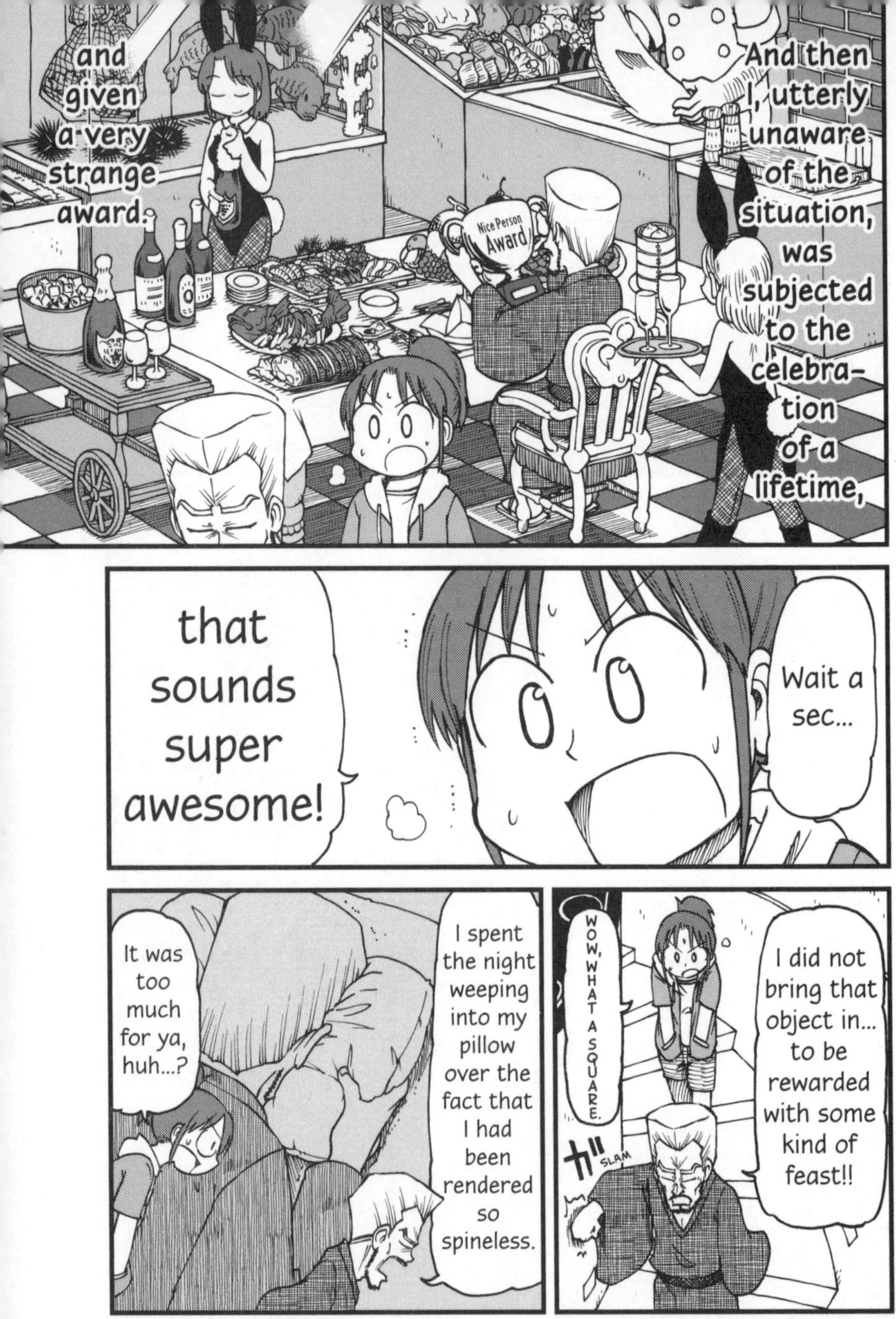
And then I, utterly unaware of the situation, was subjected to the celebration of a lifetime,
Nice Person Award
and given a very strange award.
Wait a sec...
that sounds super awesome!
I did not bring that object in... to be rewarded with some kind of feast!!
WOW, WHAT A SQUARE.
SLAM
I spent the night weeping into my pillow over the fact that I had been rendered so spineless.
It was too much for ya, huh...?

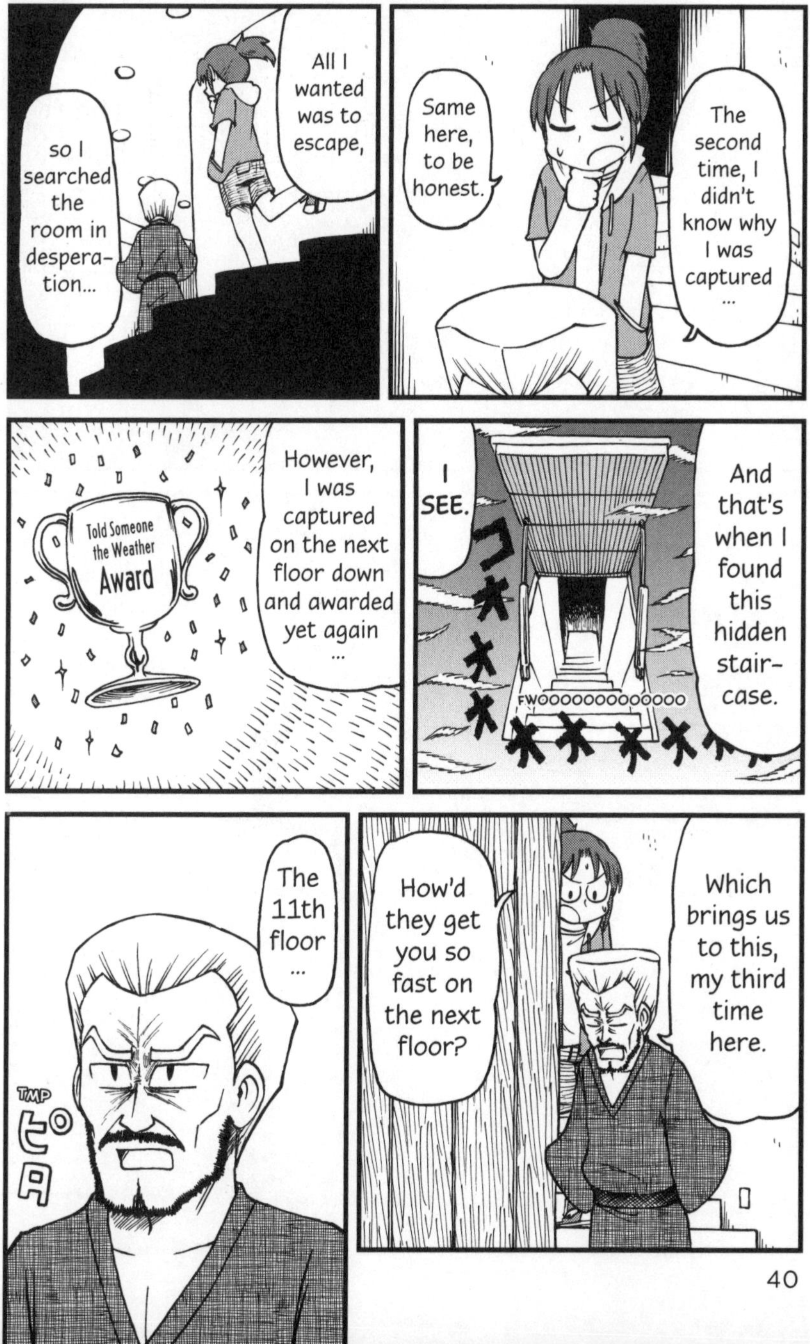

The second time, I didn't know why I was captured ...
Same here, to be honest.
All I wanted was to escape,
so I searched the room in desperation...
And that's when I found this hidden staircase.
I SEE.
FWOOOOOOOOOOOOO
However, I was captured on the next floor down and awarded yet again ...
Told Someone the Weather Award
Which brings us to this, my third time here.
How'd they get you so fast on the next floor?
The 11th floor ...
TMP

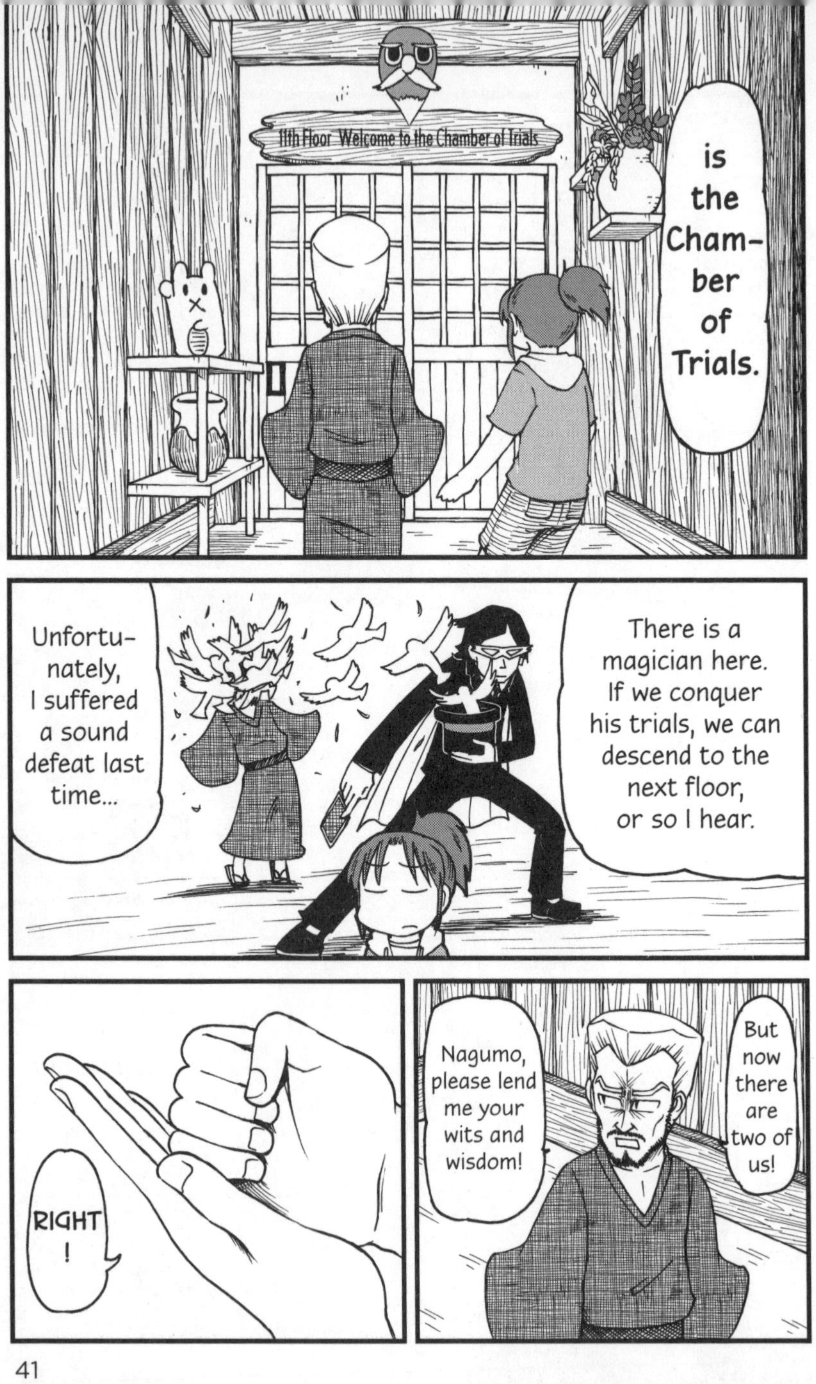
11th Floor Welcome to the Chamber of Trials
is the Chamber of Trials.
There is a magician here. If we conquer his trials, we can descend to the next floor, or so I hear.
Unfortunately, I suffered a sound defeat last time...
But now there are two of us!
Nagumo, please lend me your wits and wisdom!
RIGHT!

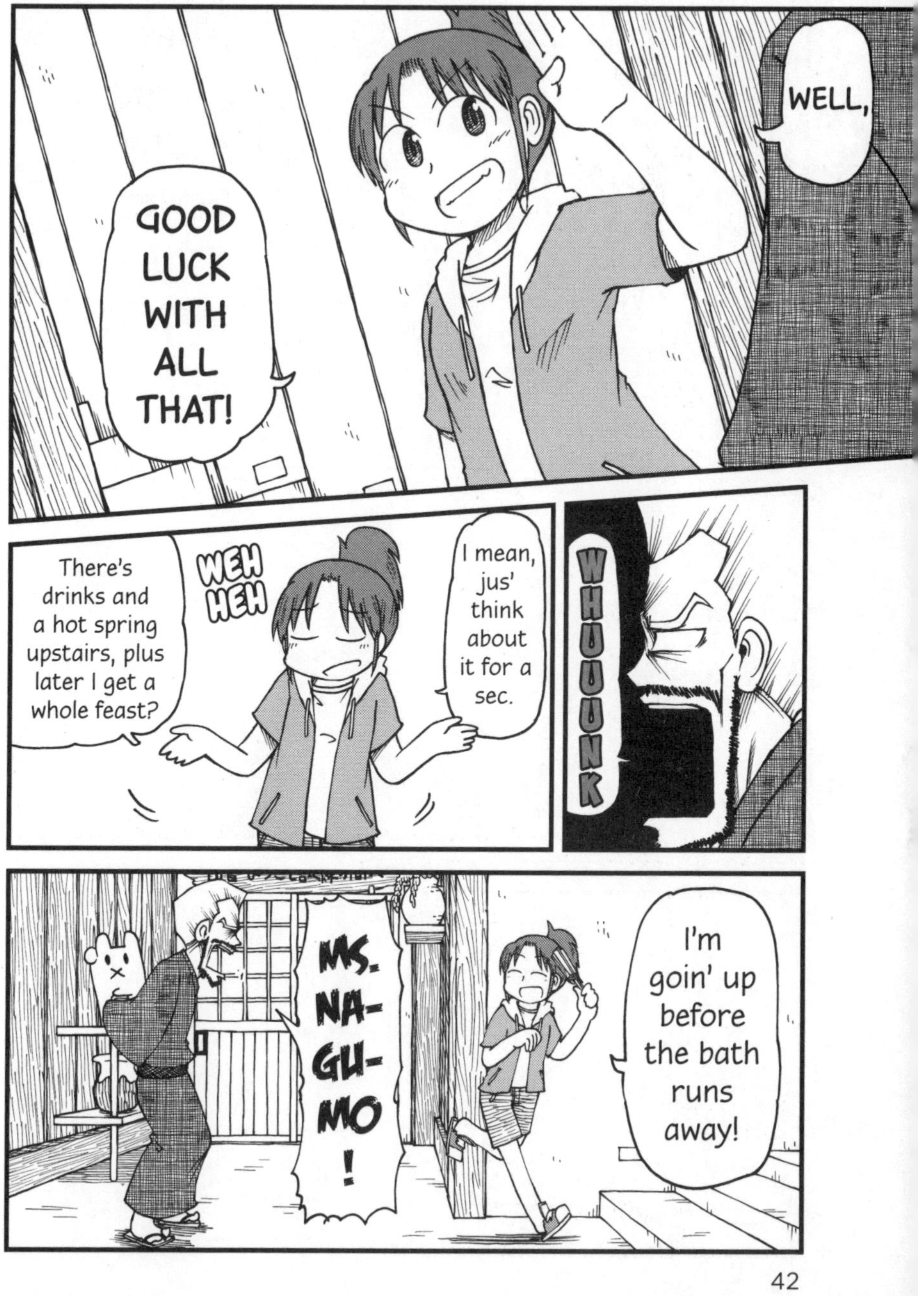
WELL,
GOOD LUCK WITH ALL THAT!
WHUUUUNK
I mean, jus' think about it for a sec.
WEH HEH
There's drinks and a hot spring upstairs, plus later I get a whole feast?
I'm goin' up before the bath runs away!
MS. NA-GU-MO!

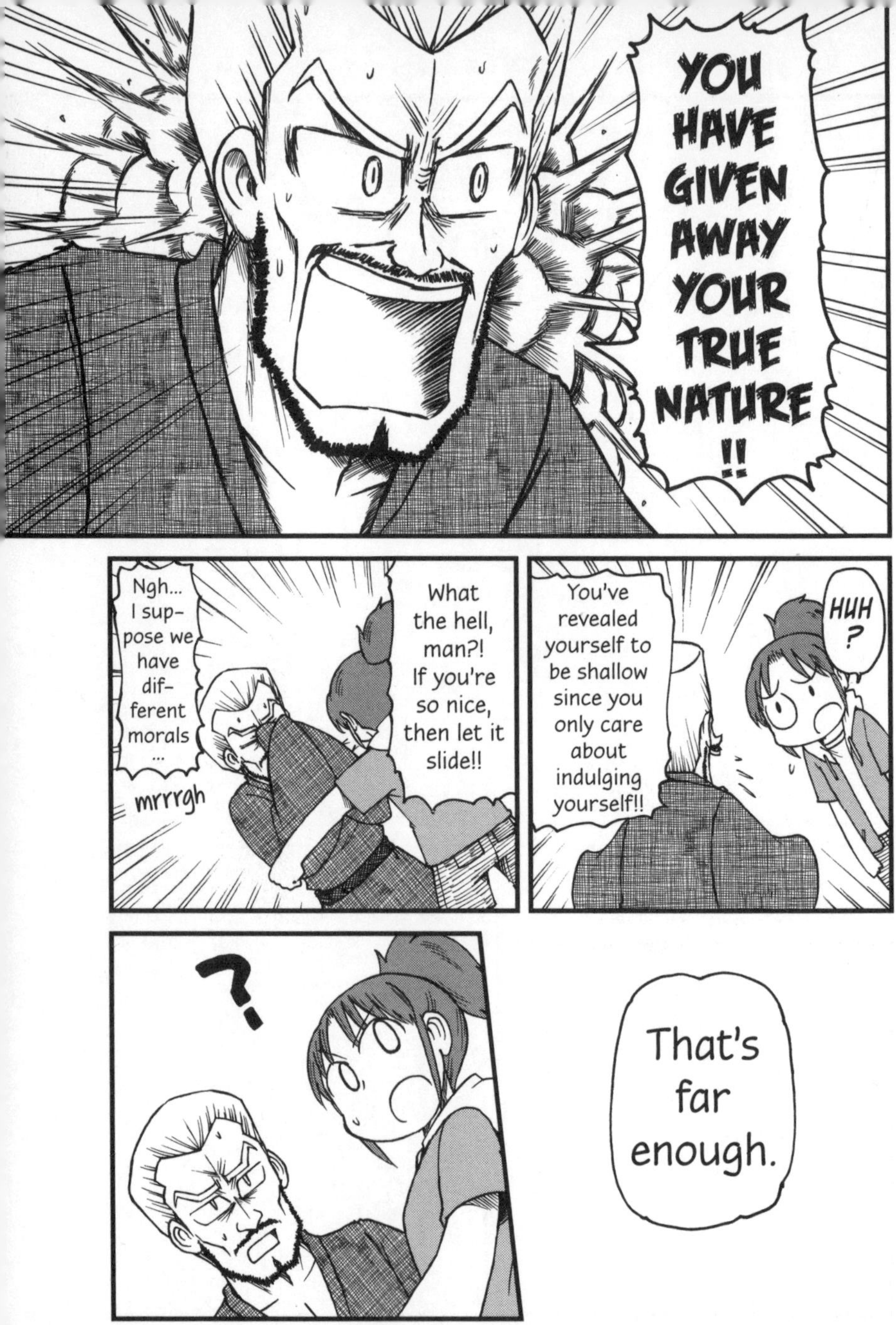
YOU HAVE GIVEN AWAY YOUR TRUE NATURE !!
HUH ?
You've revealed yourself to be shallow since you only care about indulging yourself!!
What the hell, man?! If you're so nice, then let it slide!!
Ngh... I suppose we have different morals ...
mrrrgh
That's far enough.
?

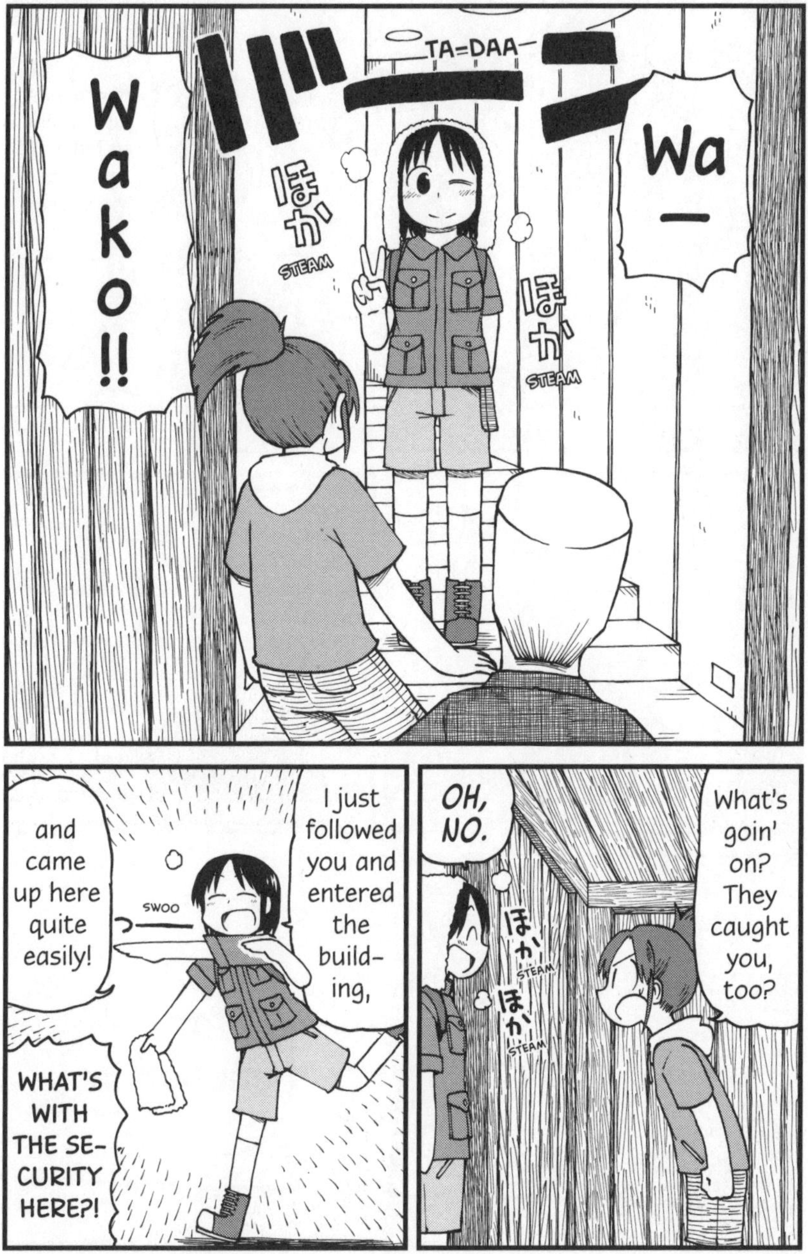
Wa—
バーン
TA=DAA
ほか
STEAM
ほか
STEAM
Wako!!
What's goin' on? They caught you, too?
OH, NO.
ほか
STEAM
ほか
STEAM
I just followed you and entered the build-ing,
and came up here quite easily!
SWOO
WHAT'S WITH THE SE-CURITY HERE?!

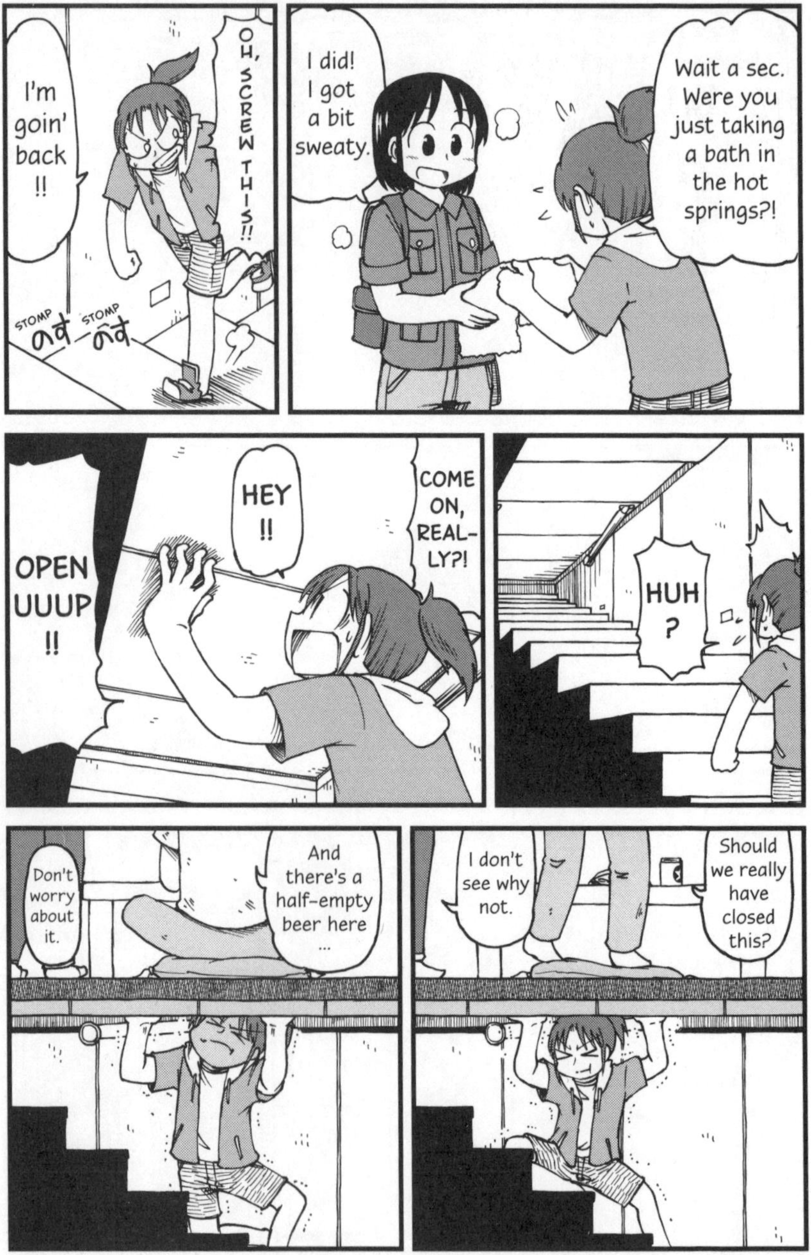
Wait a sec. Were you just taking a bath in the hot springs?!
I did! I got a bit sweaty.
OH, SCREW THIS!!
I'm goin' back !!
STOMP
のす
STOMP
のす
HUH ?
COME ON, REAL-LY?!
HEY !!
OPEN UUUP !!
Should we really have closed this?
I don't see why not.
And there's a half-empty beer here ...
Don't worry about it.

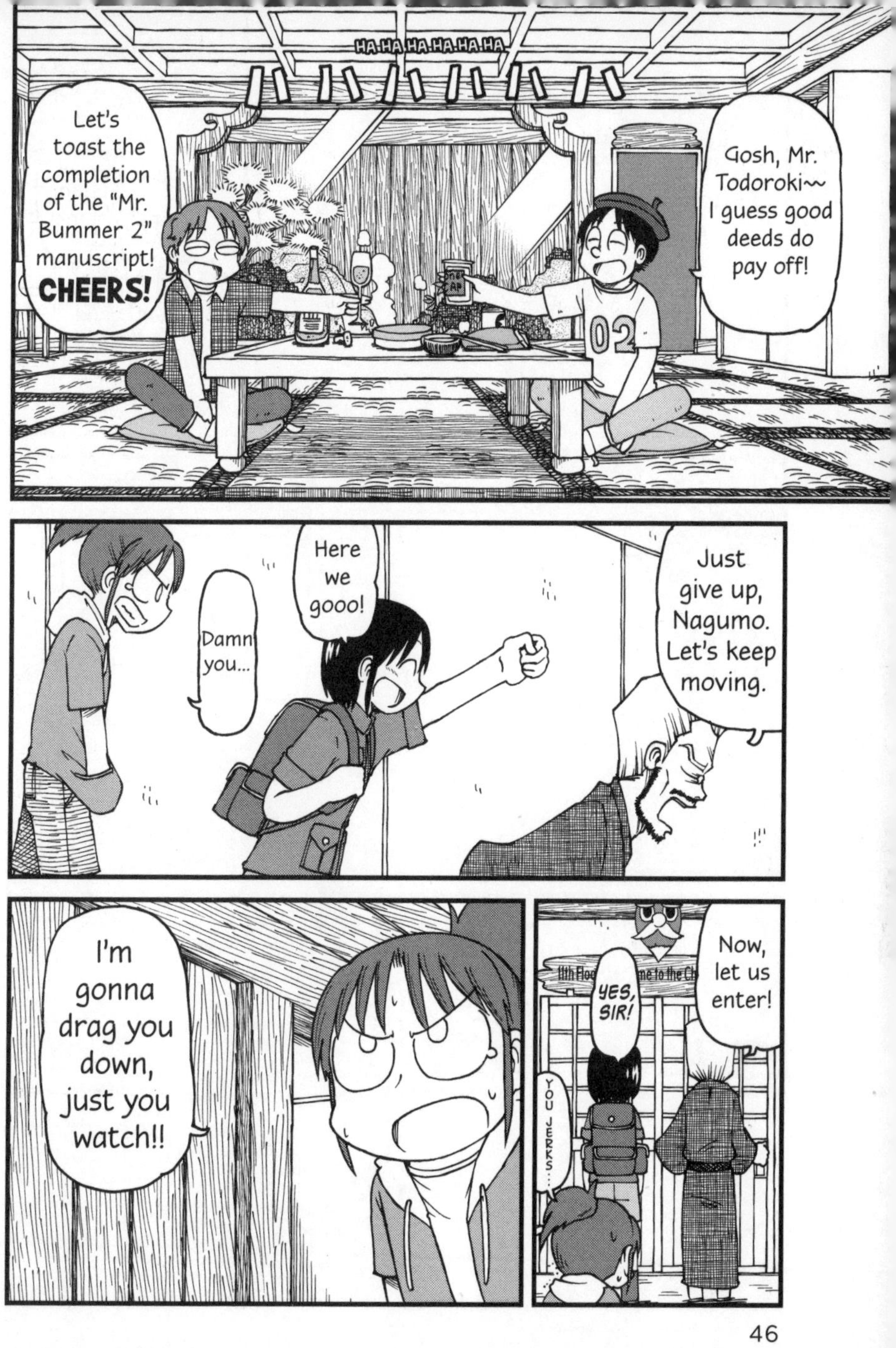
HA HA HA HA HA HA
Gosh, Mr. Todoroki~ I guess good deeds do pay off!
Let's toast the completion of the "Mr. Bummer 2" manuscript! CHEERS!
Just give up, Nagumo. Let's keep moving.
Here we gooo!
Damn you...
Now, let us enter!
YES, SIR!
YOU JERKS...
I'm gonna drag you down, just you watch!!

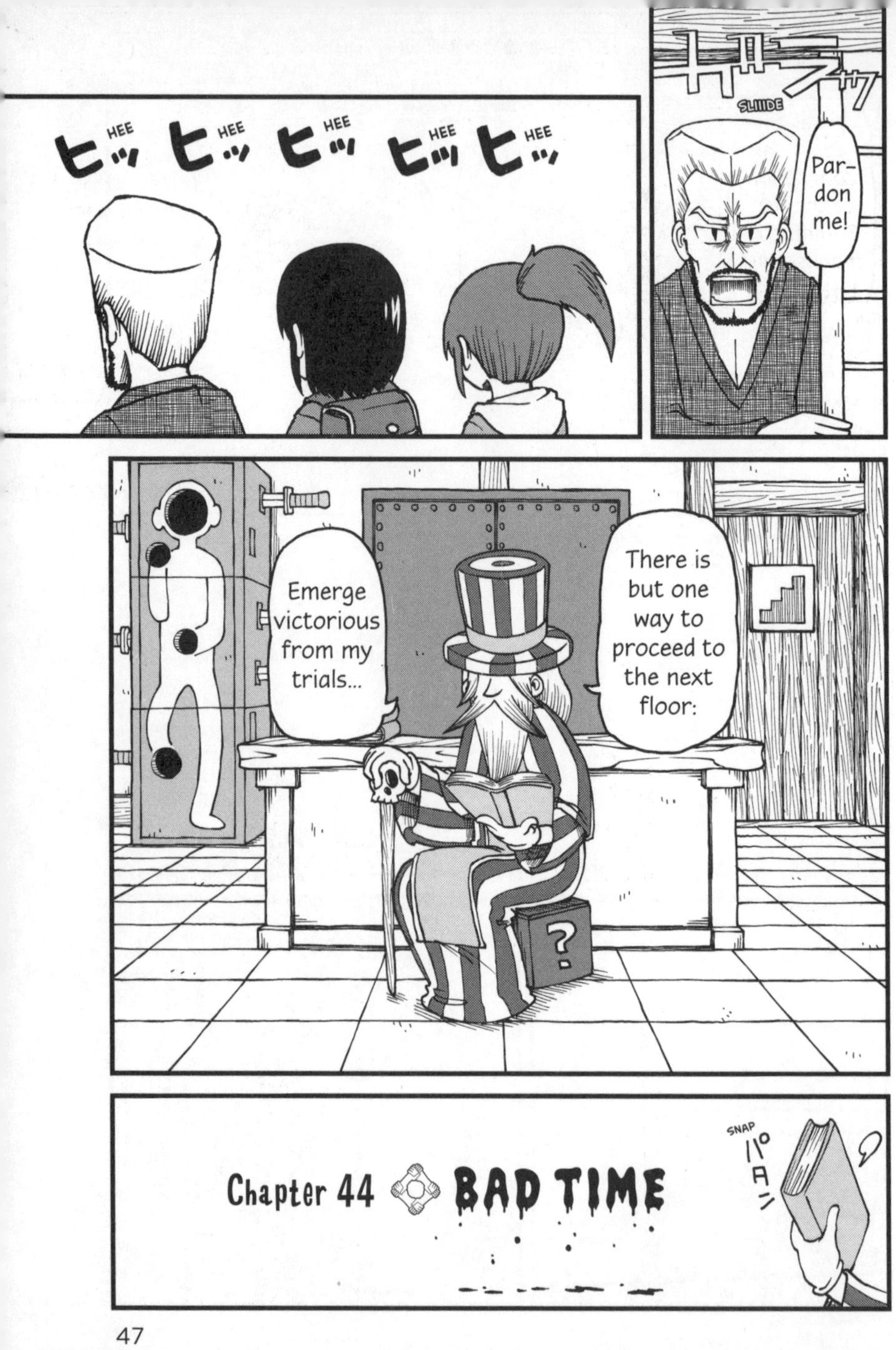
SLIIDE
Pardon me!
HEE HEE HEE HEE HEE
There is but one way to proceed to the next floor:
Emerge victorious from my trials...
SNAP
パタン
Chapter 44 BAD TIME

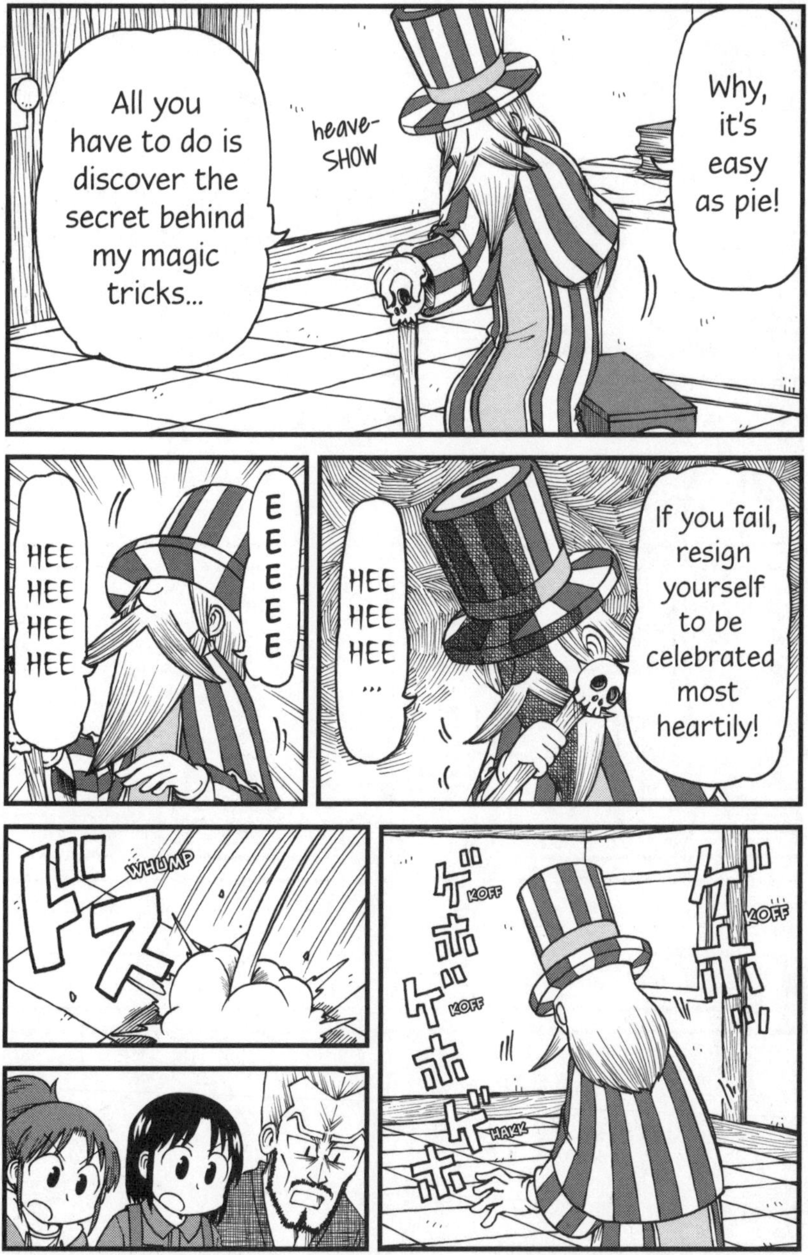
Why, it's easy as pie!
heave-SHOW
All you have to do is discover the secret behind my magic tricks...
If you fail, resign yourself to be celebrated most heartily!
HEE HEE HEE ...
EEEEEE
HEE HEE HEE HEE
ゲホッ
KOFF
ゲホゲホゲホ
KOFF
KOFF
HAKK
ドス
WHUMP

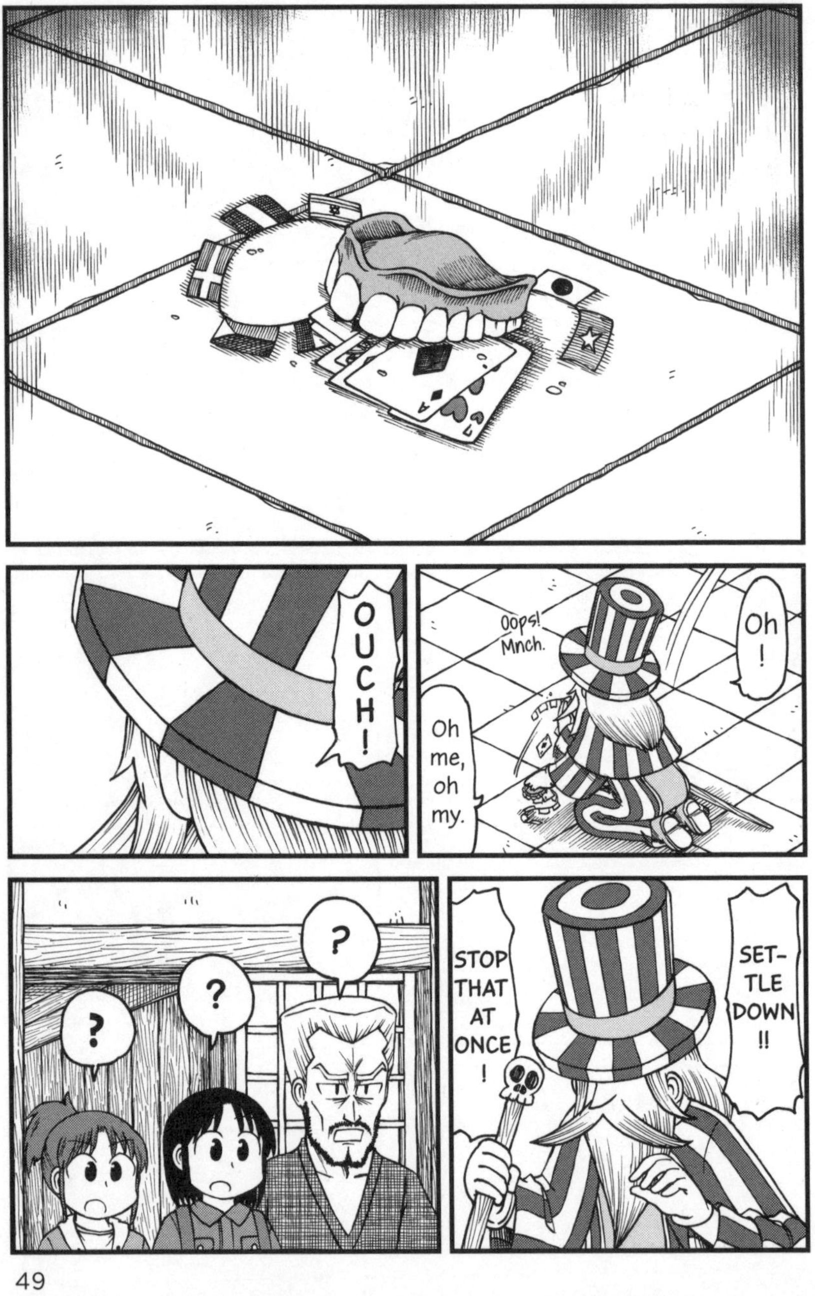
Oh!
Oops! Mnch.
Oh me, oh my.
OUCH!
SET-TLE DOWN!!
STOP THAT AT ONCE!
?
?
?

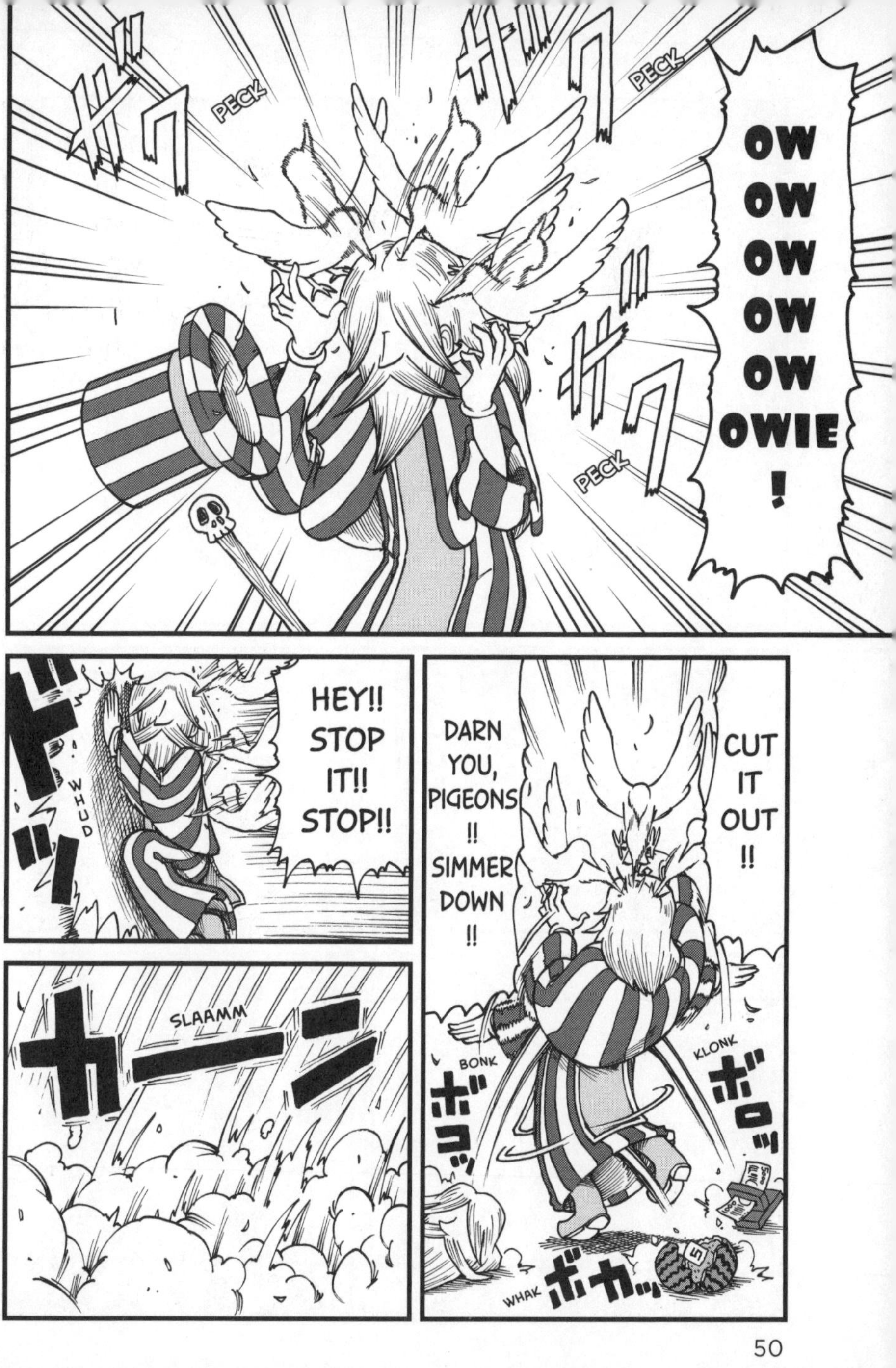
OW OW OW OW OW OWIE !
PECK
PECK
PECK
CUT IT OUT !!
DARN YOU, PIGEONS !! SIMMER DOWN !!
KLONK
BONK
WHAK
HEY!! STOP IT!! STOP!!
WHUD
SLAAMM

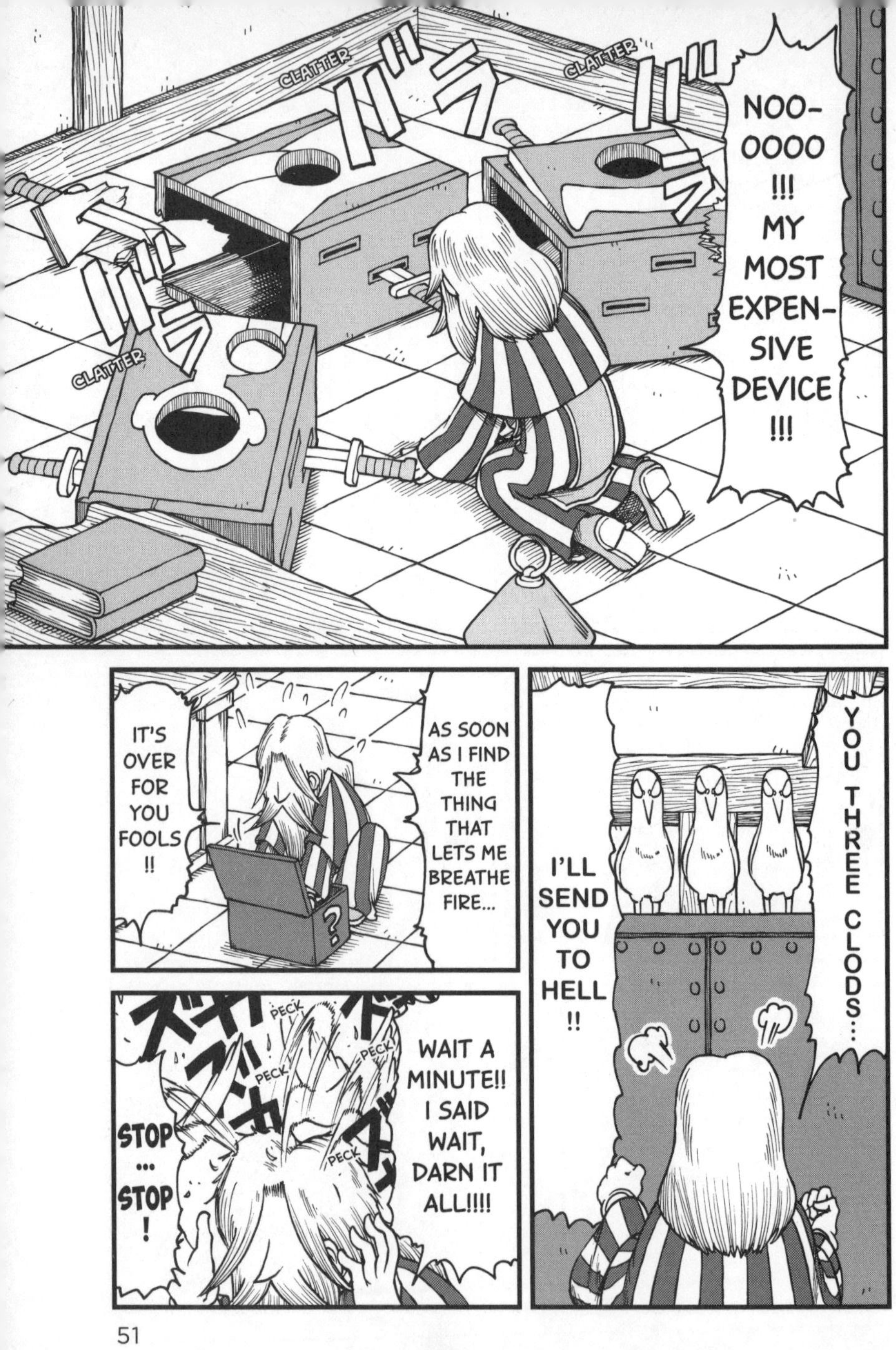
CLATTER
CLATTER
NOO-OOOO!!! MY MOST EXPENSIVE DEVICE!!!
CLATTER
YOU THREE CLODS...
I'LL SEND YOU TO HELL!!
AS SOON AS I FIND THE THING THAT LETS ME BREATHE FIRE...
IT'S OVER FOR YOU FOOLS!!
WAIT A MINUTE!! I SAID WAIT, DARN IT ALL!!!!
PECK
PECK
PECK
PECK
STOP... STOP!

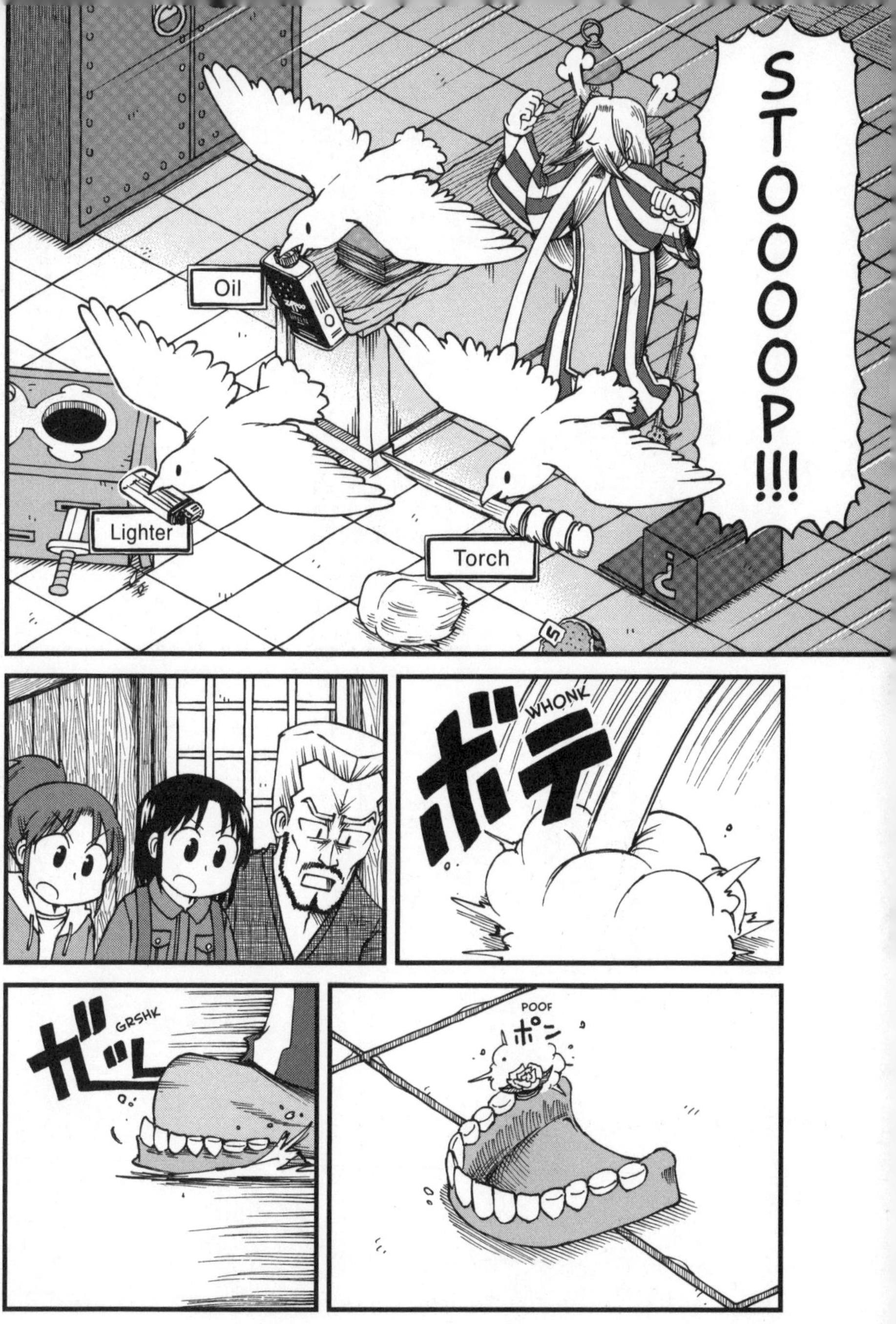
STOOOOP!!!
Oil
Torch
Lighter
ボテ
WHONK
POOF
ポン
ガッ
GRSHK

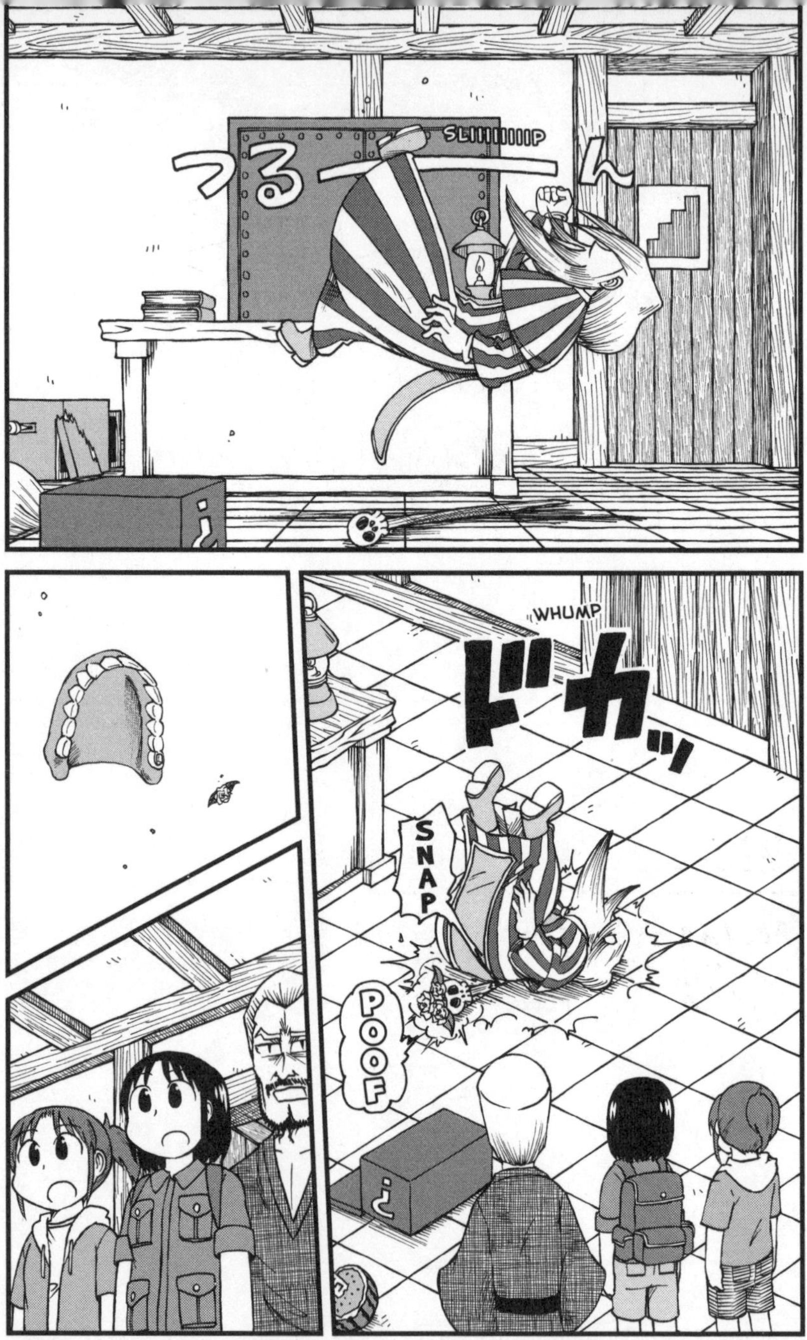
つるーーん
SLIIIIIIIIP
ドカッ
WHUMP
SNAP
POOF

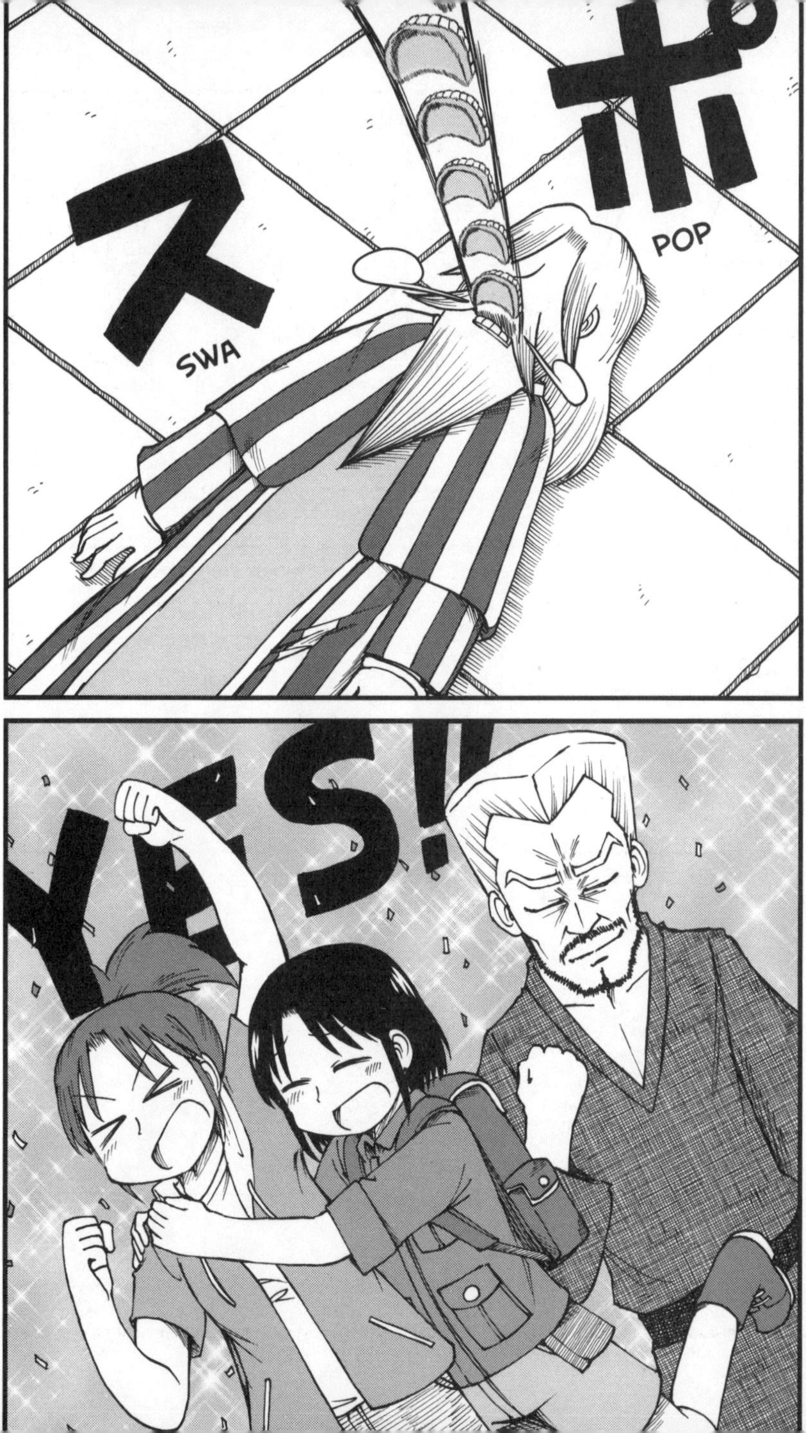
ポ
POP
ス
SWA
YES!!

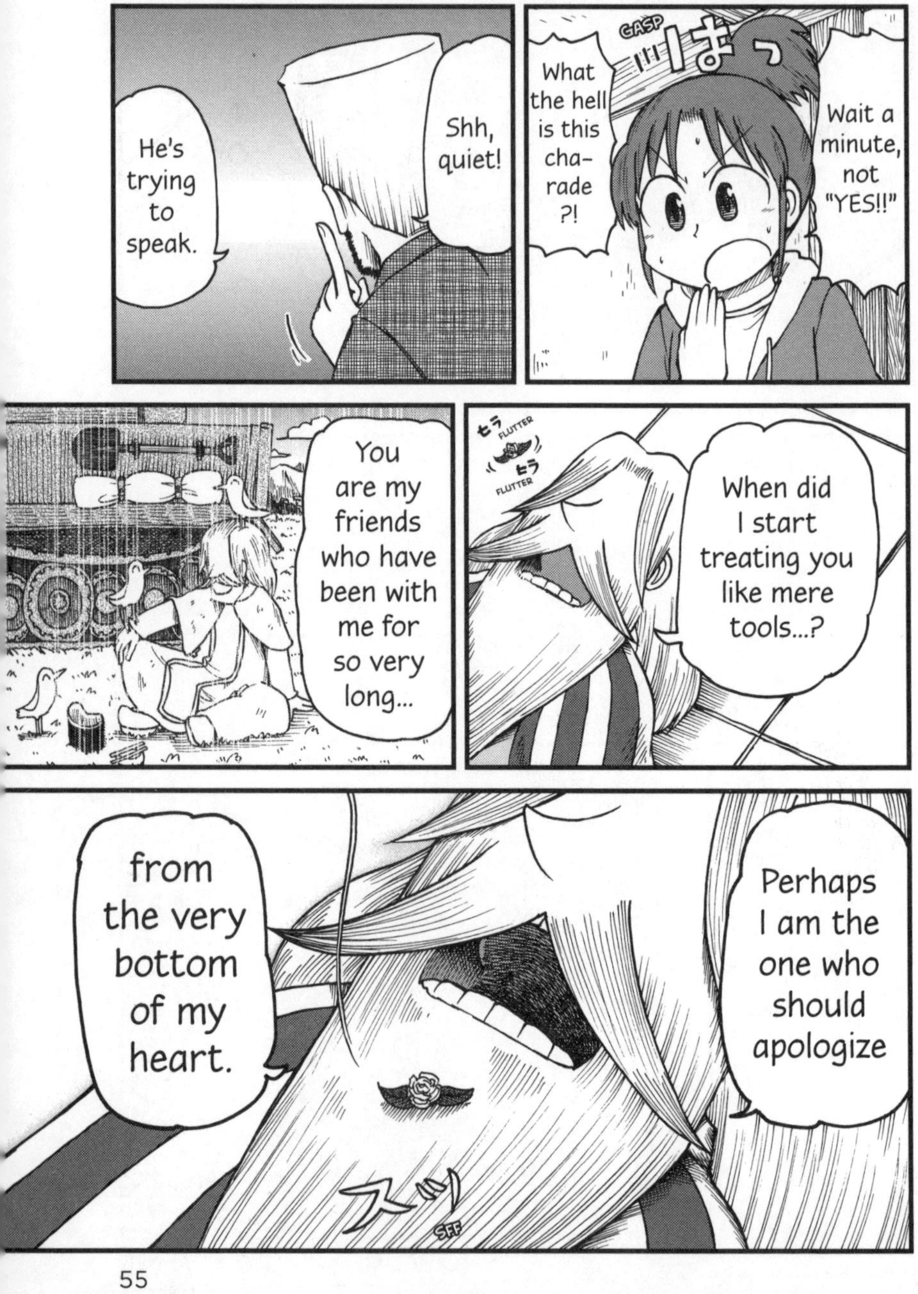
GASP
Wait a minute, not "YES!!"
What the hell is this charade?!
Shh, quiet!
He's trying to speak.
FLUTTER
FLUTTER
When did I start treating you like mere tools...?
You are my friends who have been with me for so very long...
Perhaps I am the one who should apologize
from the very bottom of my heart.
SFF

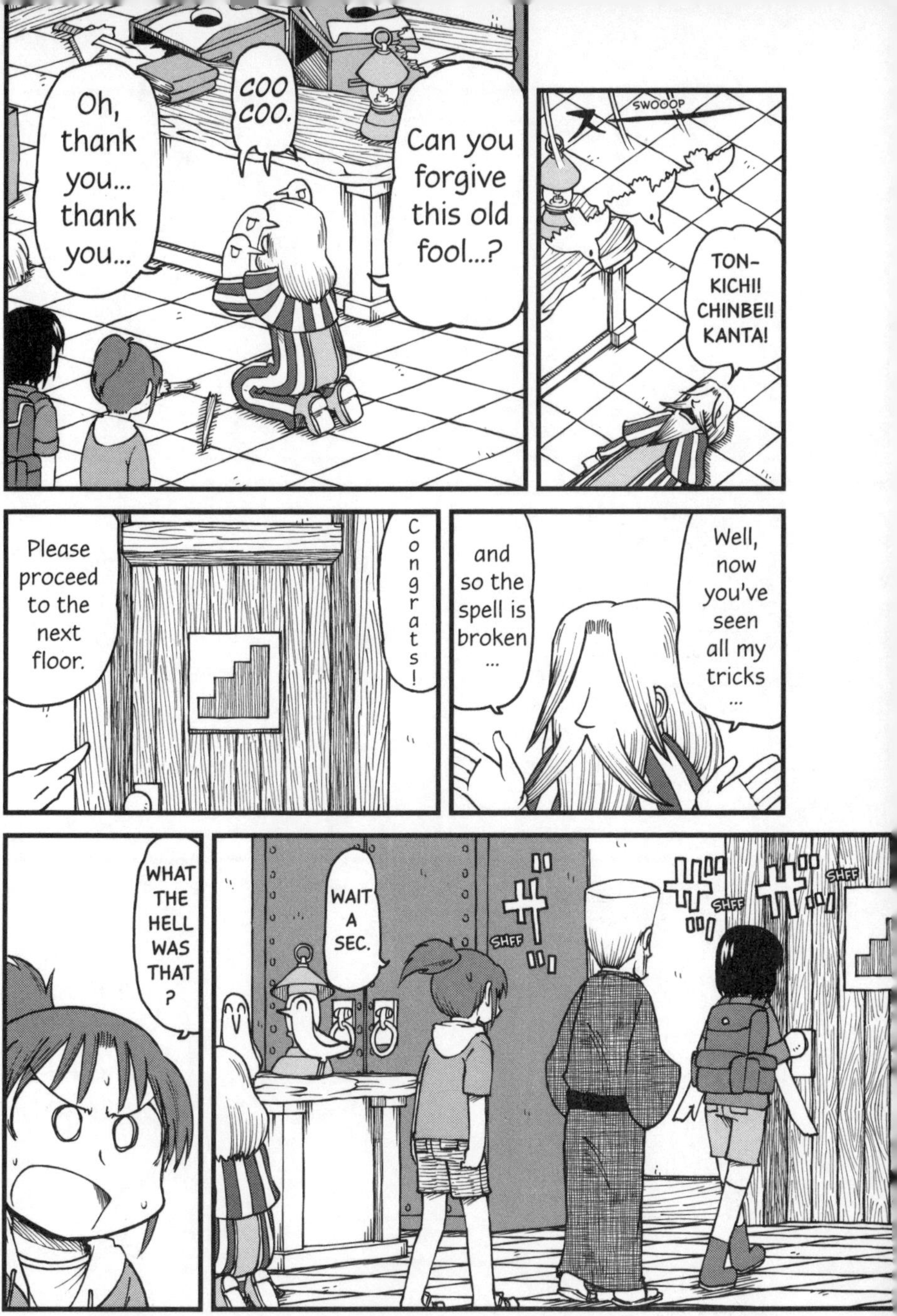
SWOOOP
TON-KICHI! CHINBEI! KANTA!
Can you forgive this old fool...?
COO COO.
Oh, thank you... thank you...
Well, now you've seen all my tricks...
and so the spell is broken...
Congrats!
Please proceed to the next floor.
SHFF
SHFF
SHFF
WAIT A SEC.
WHAT THE HELL WAS THAT?

CITY

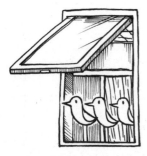

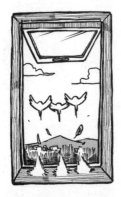

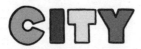

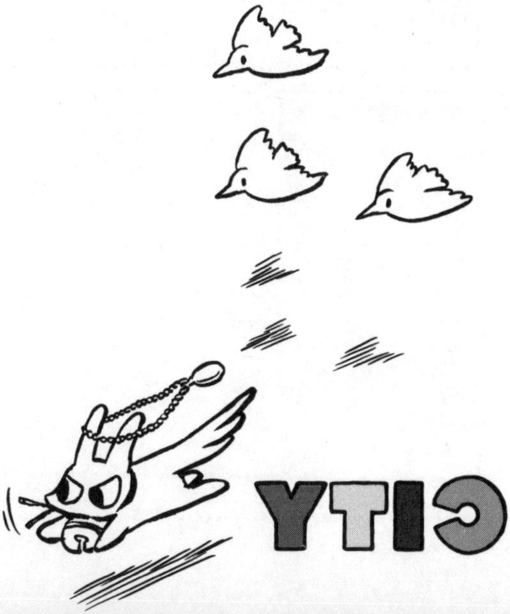

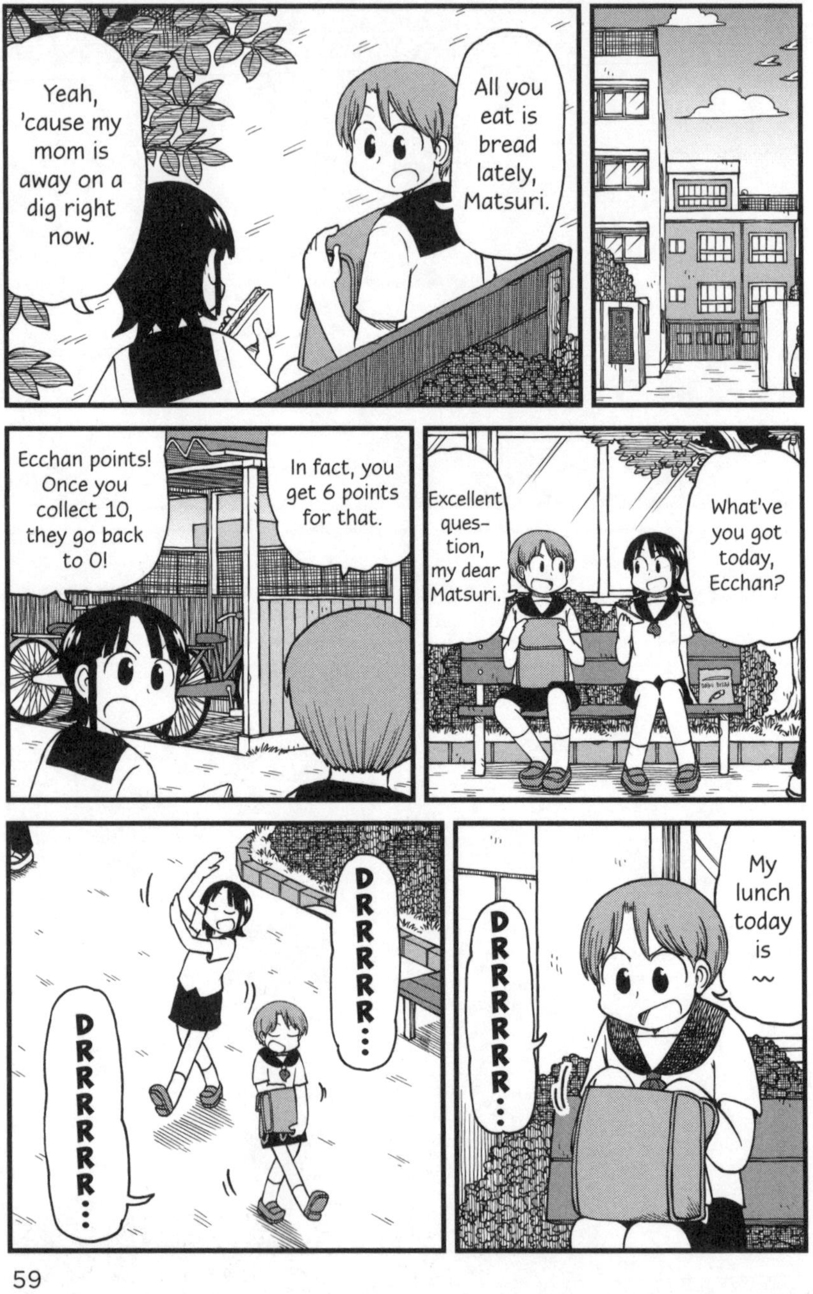
All you eat is bread lately, Matsuri.
Yeah, 'cause my mom is away on a dig right now.
What've you got today, Ecchan?
Excellent ques-tion, my dear Matsuri.
In fact, you get 6 points for that.
Ecchan points! Once you collect 10, they go back to 0!
My lunch today is ~
DRRRRRR...
DRRRRR...
DRRRRRR...

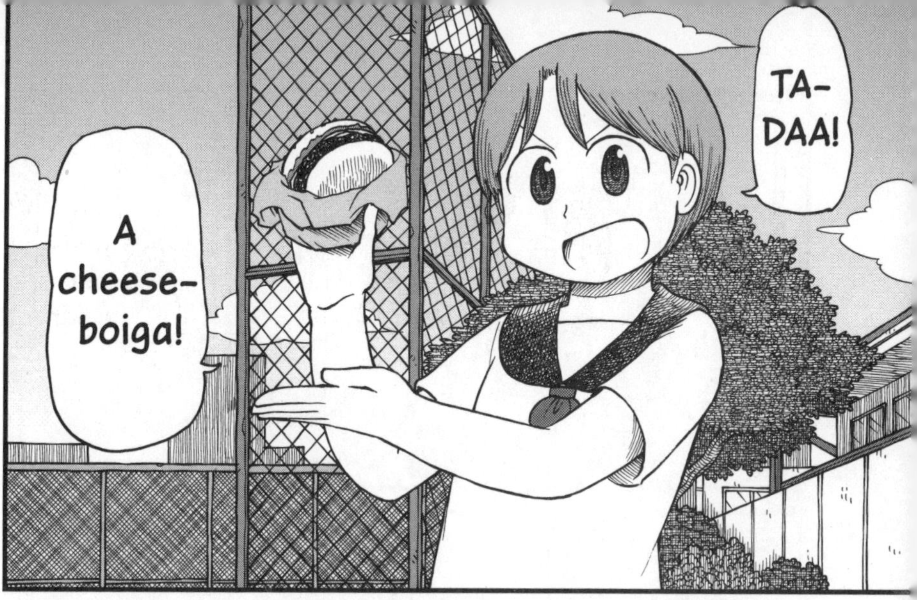
TA-DAA!
A cheese-boiga!

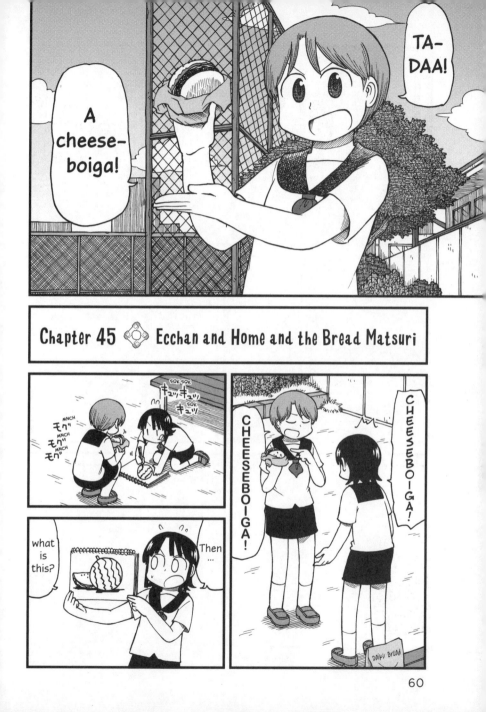

Chapter 45 ◇ Ecchan and Home and the Bread Matsuri

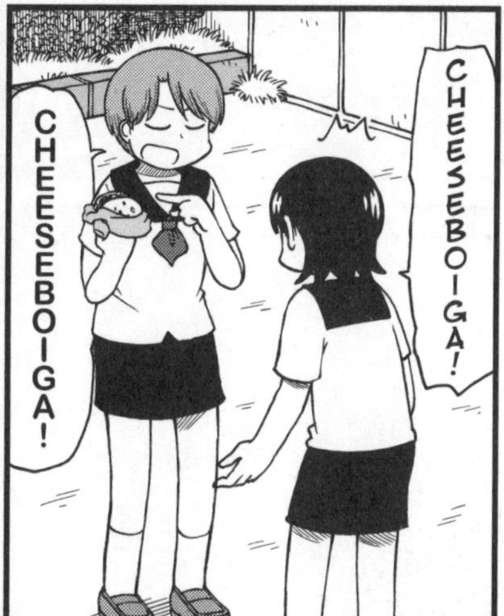
CHEESEBOIGA!
CHEESEBOIGA!
Daiku Bread

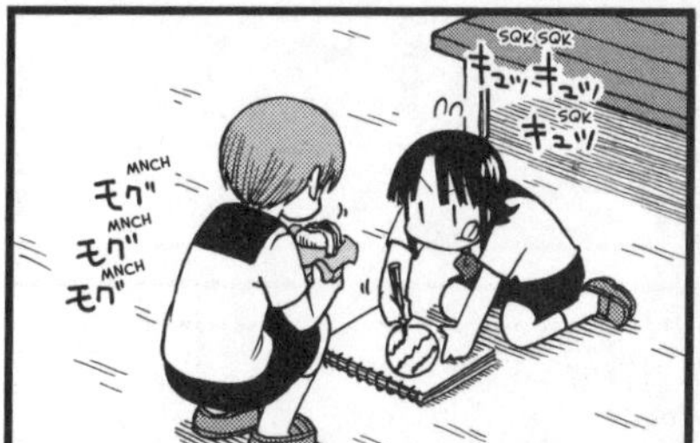
キュッ SQK キュッ SQK
キュッ SQK
モグ MNCH
モグ MNCH
モグ MNCH

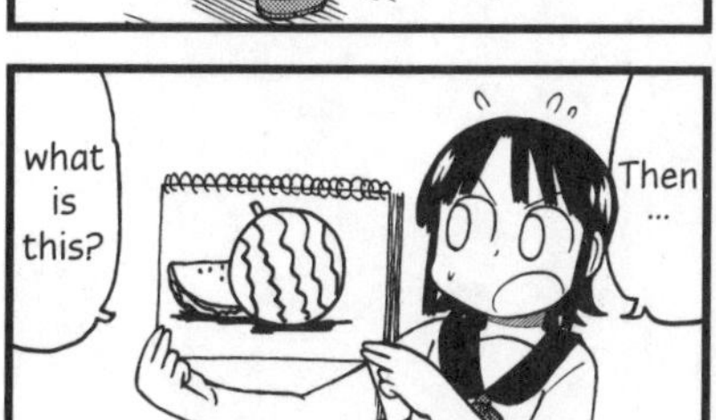
Then ...
what is this?

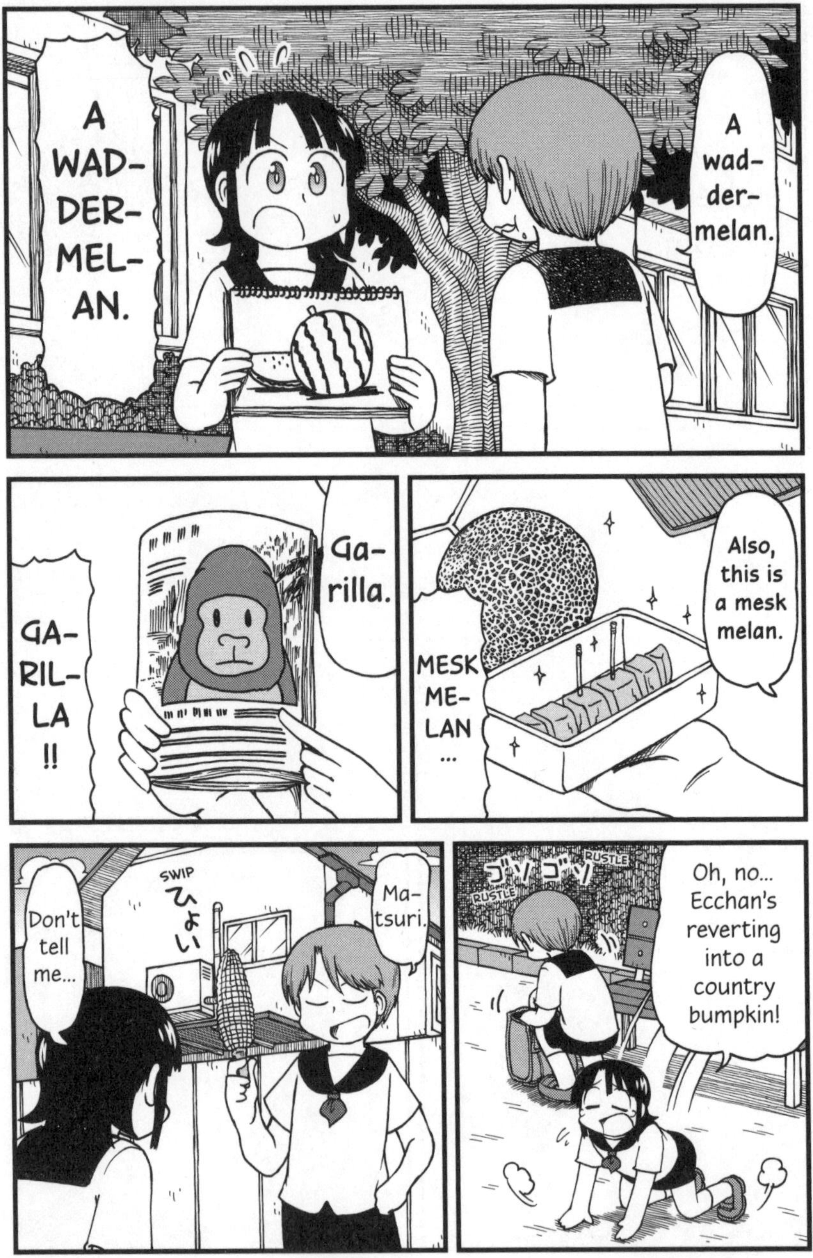
A wad-der-melan.
A WAD-DER-MEL-AN.
Also, this is a mesk melan.
MESK ME-LAN ...
Ga-rilla.
GA-RIL-LA !!
ゴソゴソ
RUSTLE RUSTLE
Oh, no... Ecchan's reverting into a country bumpkin!
Ma-tsuri.
ひょい
SWIP
Don't tell me...

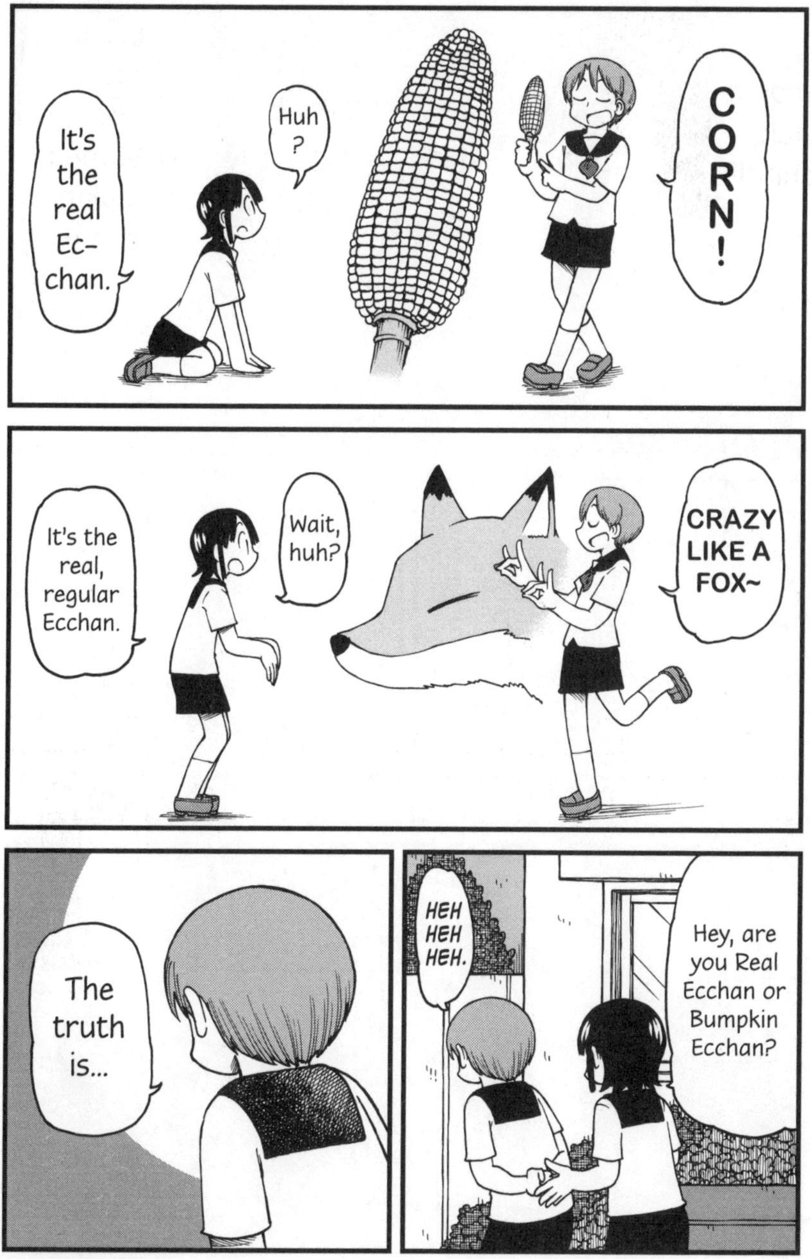
CORN!
Huh?
It's the real Ec-chan.
CRAZY LIKE A FOX~
Wait, huh?
It's the real, regular Ecchan.
Hey, are you Real Ecchan or Bumpkin Ecchan?
HEH HEH HEH.
The truth is...

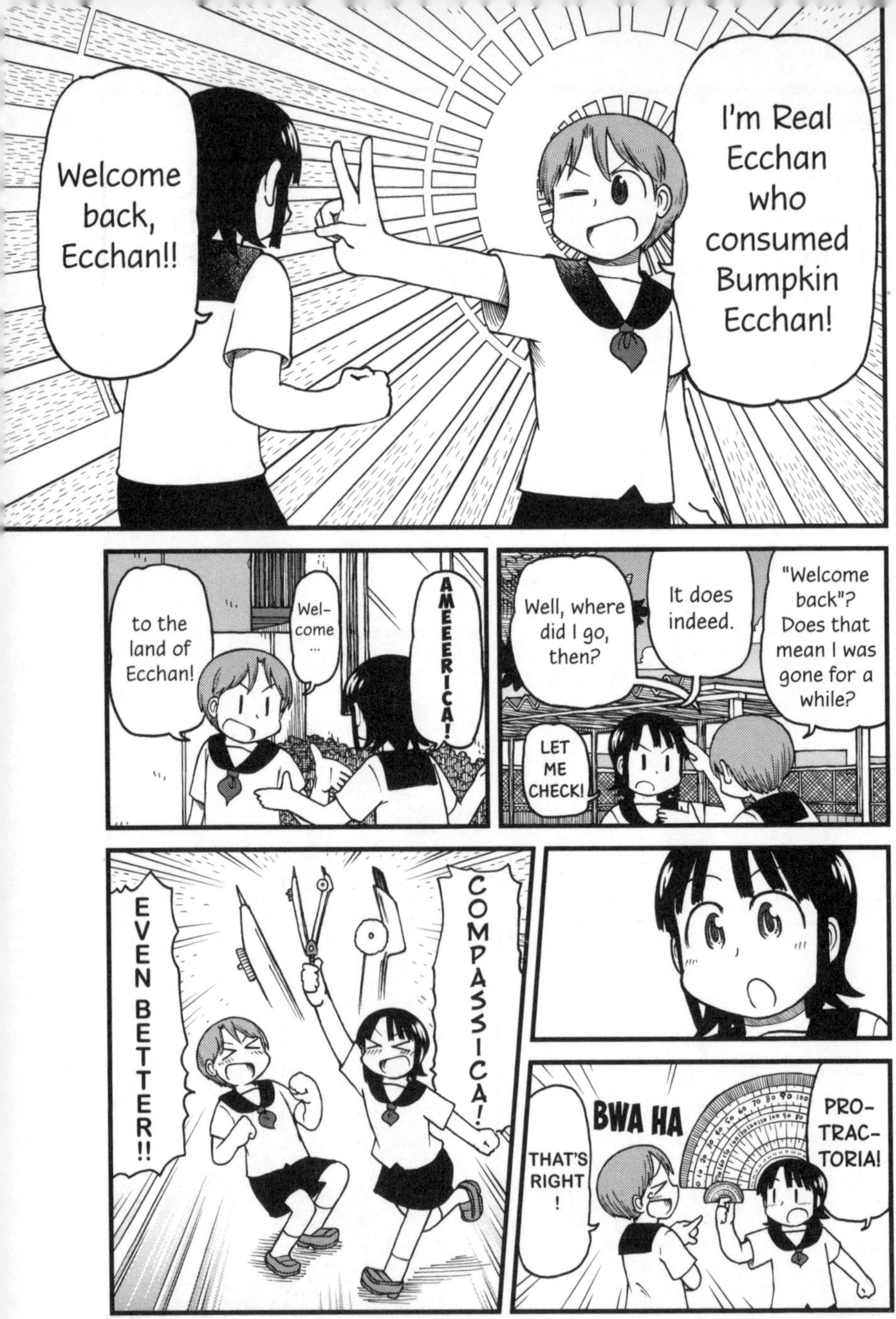
I'm Real Ecchan who consumed Bumpkin Ecchan!
Welcome back, Ecchan!!
"Welcome back"? Does that mean I was gone for a while?
It does indeed.
Well, where did I go, then?
LET ME CHECK!
AMEEERICA!
Wel-come ...
to the land of Ecchan!
PRO-TRAC-TORIA!
BWA HA
THAT'S RIGHT!
COMPASSICA!
EVEN BETTER!!

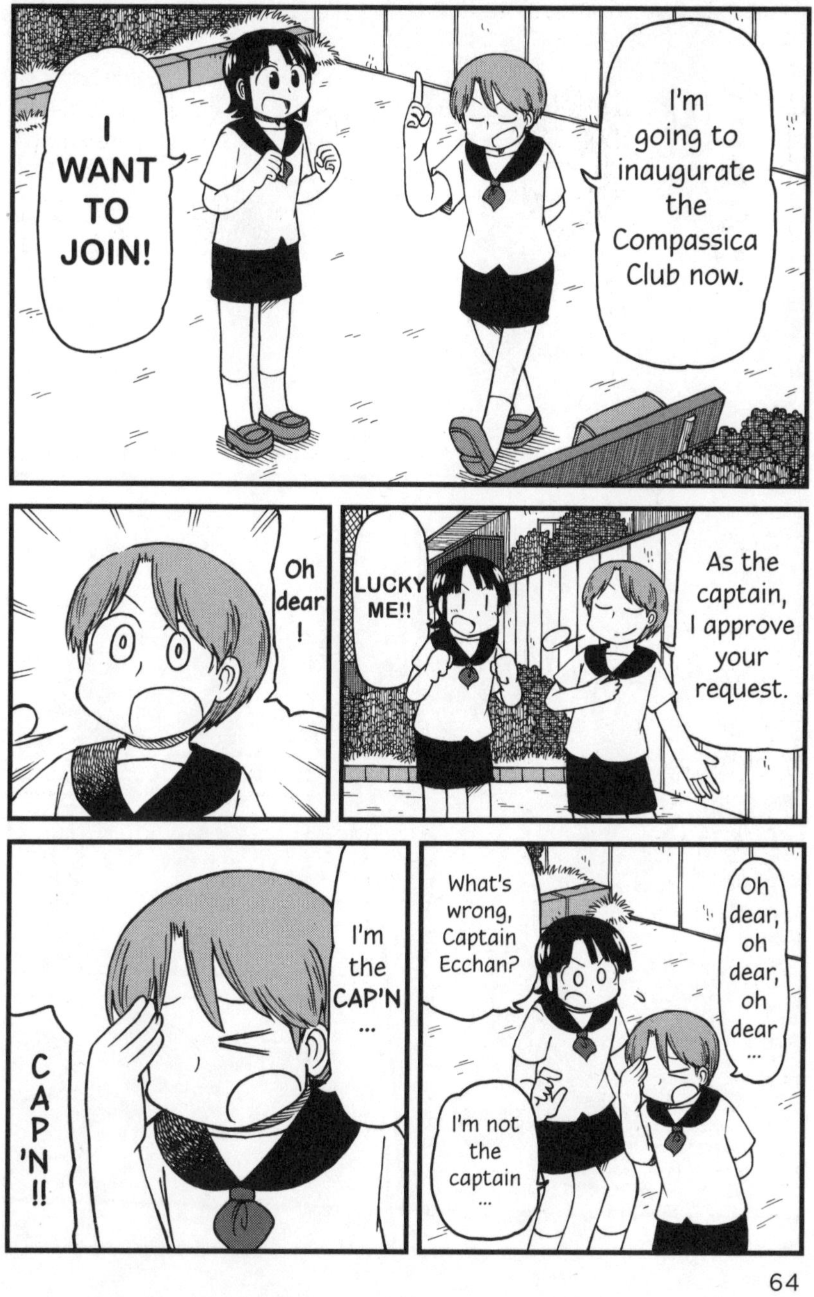
I'm going to inaugurate the Compassica Club now.
I WANT TO JOIN!
As the captain, I approve your request.
LUCKY ME!!
Oh dear!
Oh dear, oh dear, oh dear...
What's wrong, Captain Ecchan?
I'm not the captain...
I'm the CAP'N...
CAP'N!!

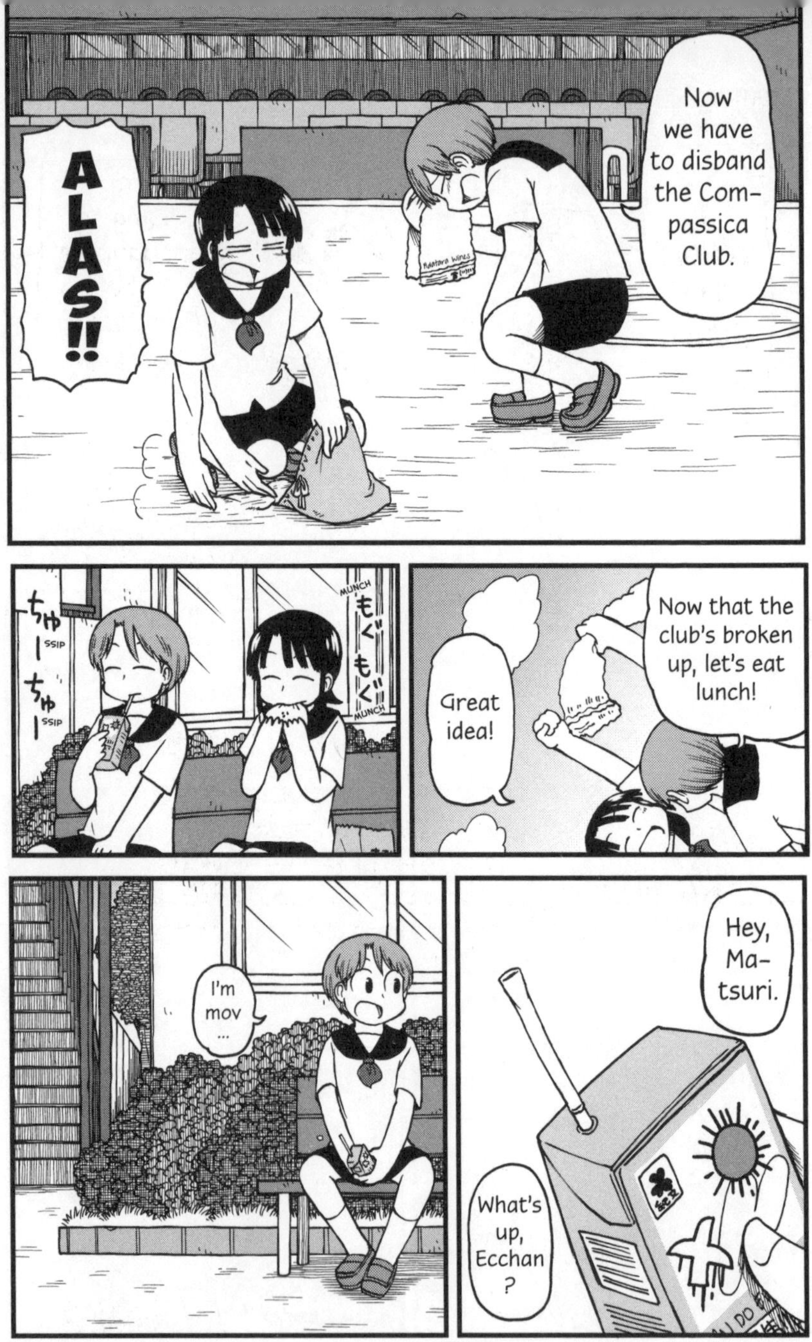

Now we have to disband the Com-passica Club.
ALAS!!
Now that the club's broken up, let's eat lunch!
Great idea!
MUNCH もぐもぐ MUNCH
ちゅー SSIP ちゅー SSIP
Hey, Ma-tsuri.
What's up, Ecchan?
I'm mov ...

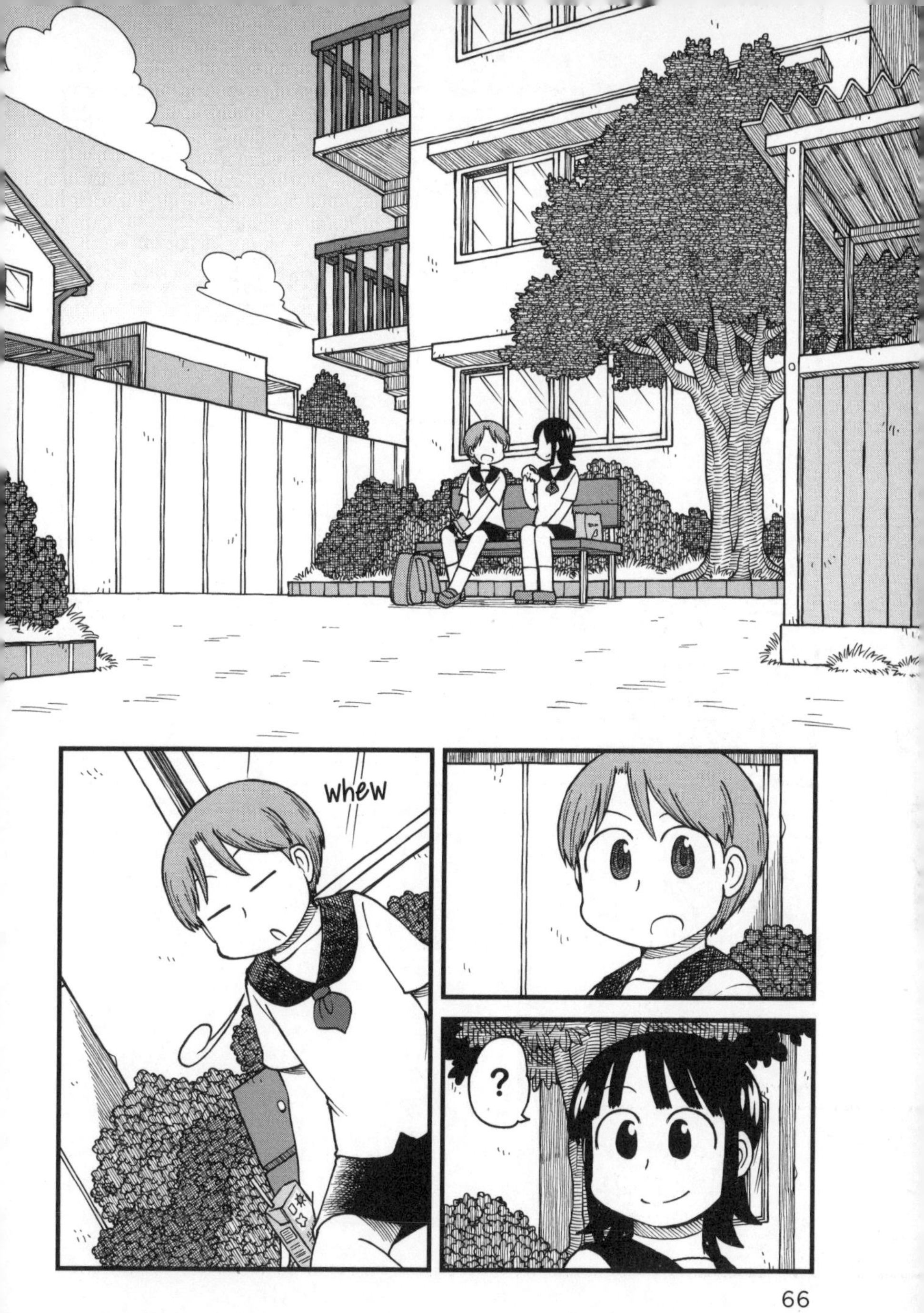
?
whew

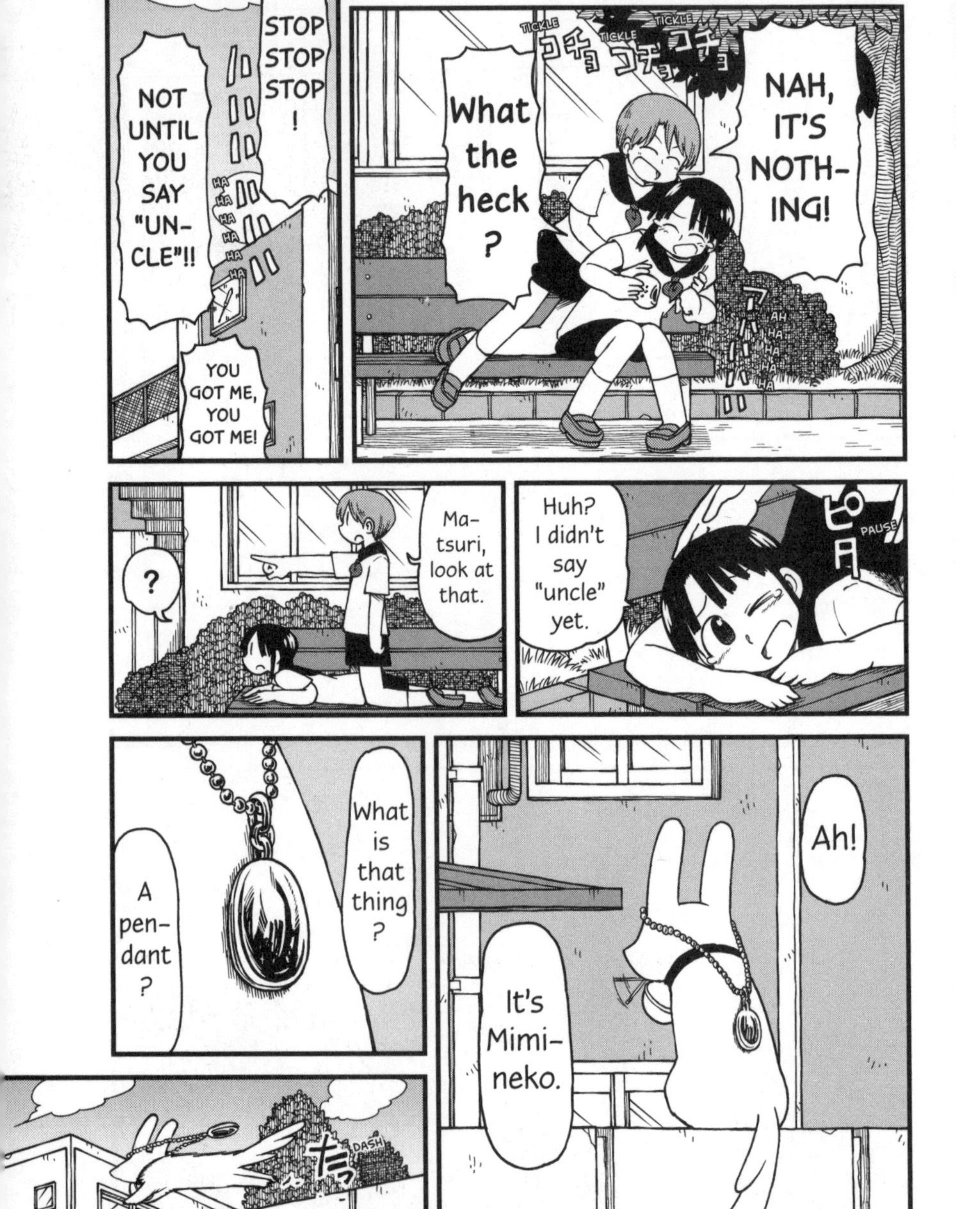
NAH, IT'S NOTHING!
TICKLE TICKLE TICKLE
What the heck?
AH HA HA HA HA HA
STOP STOP STOP!
NOT UNTIL YOU SAY "UNCLE"!!
HA HA HA HA HA HA
YOU GOT ME, YOU GOT ME!
PAUSE
Huh? I didn't say "uncle" yet.
Matsuri, look at that.
?
Ah!
It's Mimineko.
What is that thing?
A pendant?
DASH

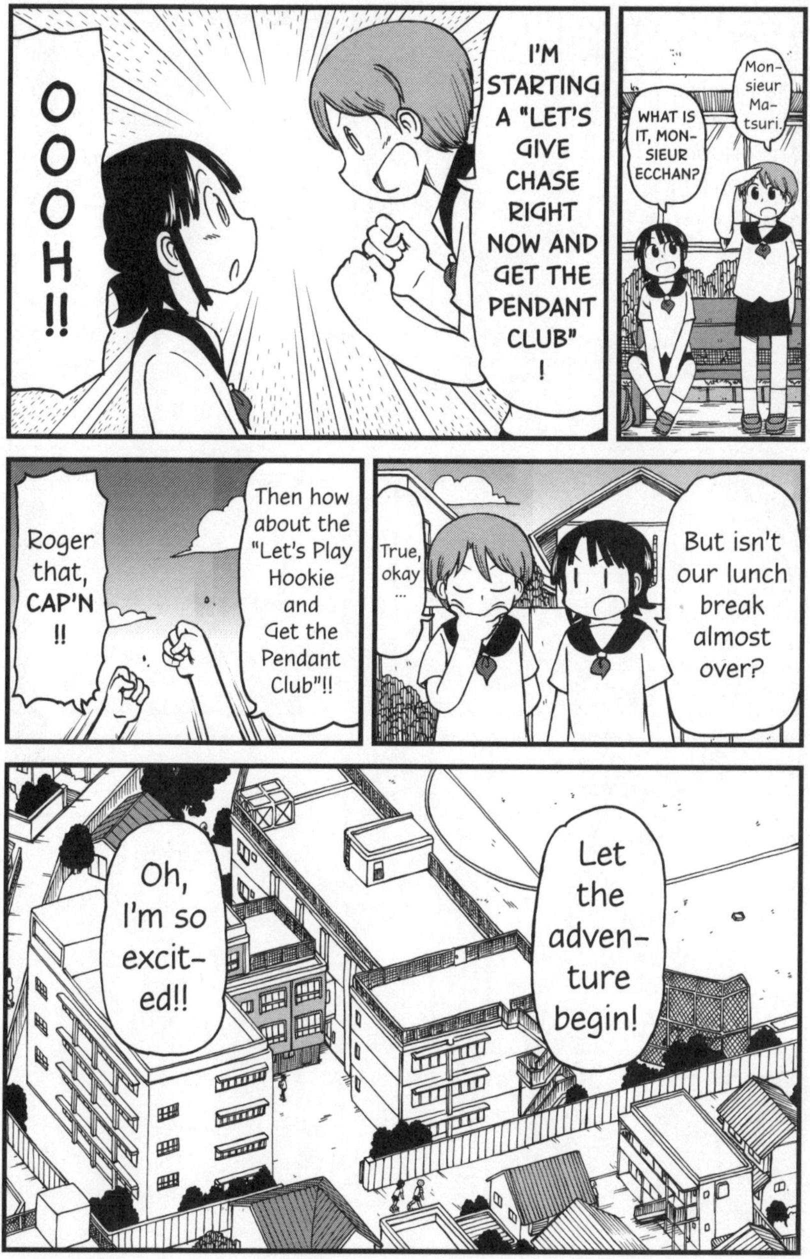
Monsieur Matsuri.
WHAT IS IT, MONSIEUR ECCHAN?
I'M STARTING A "LET'S GIVE CHASE RIGHT NOW AND GET THE PENDANT CLUB"!
OOOOH!!
But isn't our lunch break almost over?
True, okay...
Then how about the "Let's Play Hookie and Get the Pendant Club"!!
Roger that, CAP'N!!
Let the adventure begin!
Oh, I'm so excited!!

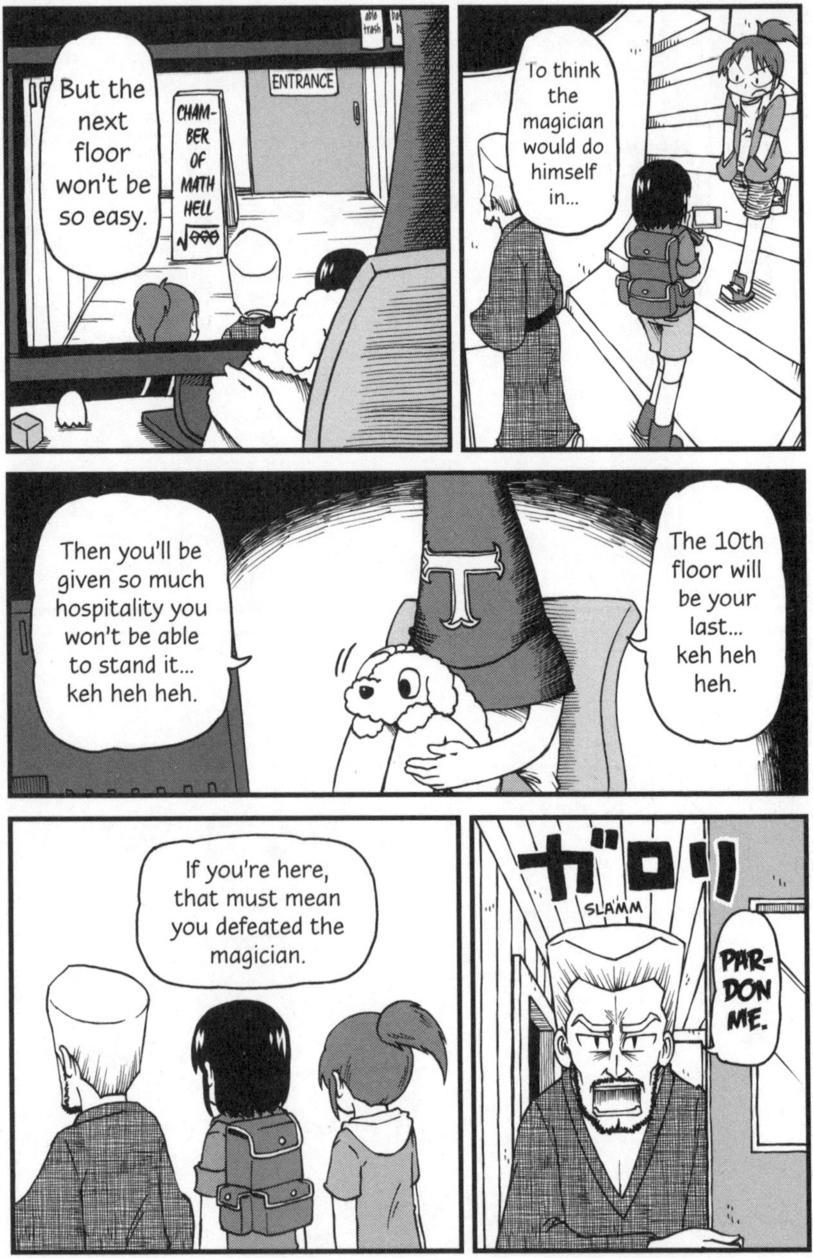

To think the magician would do himself in...
But the next floor won't be so easy.
ENTRANCE
CHAMBER OF MATH HELL
The 10th floor will be your last... keh heh heh.
Then you'll be given so much hospitality you won't be able to stand it... keh heh heh.
ガロリ
SLAMM
PARDON ME.
If you're here, that must mean you defeated the magician.

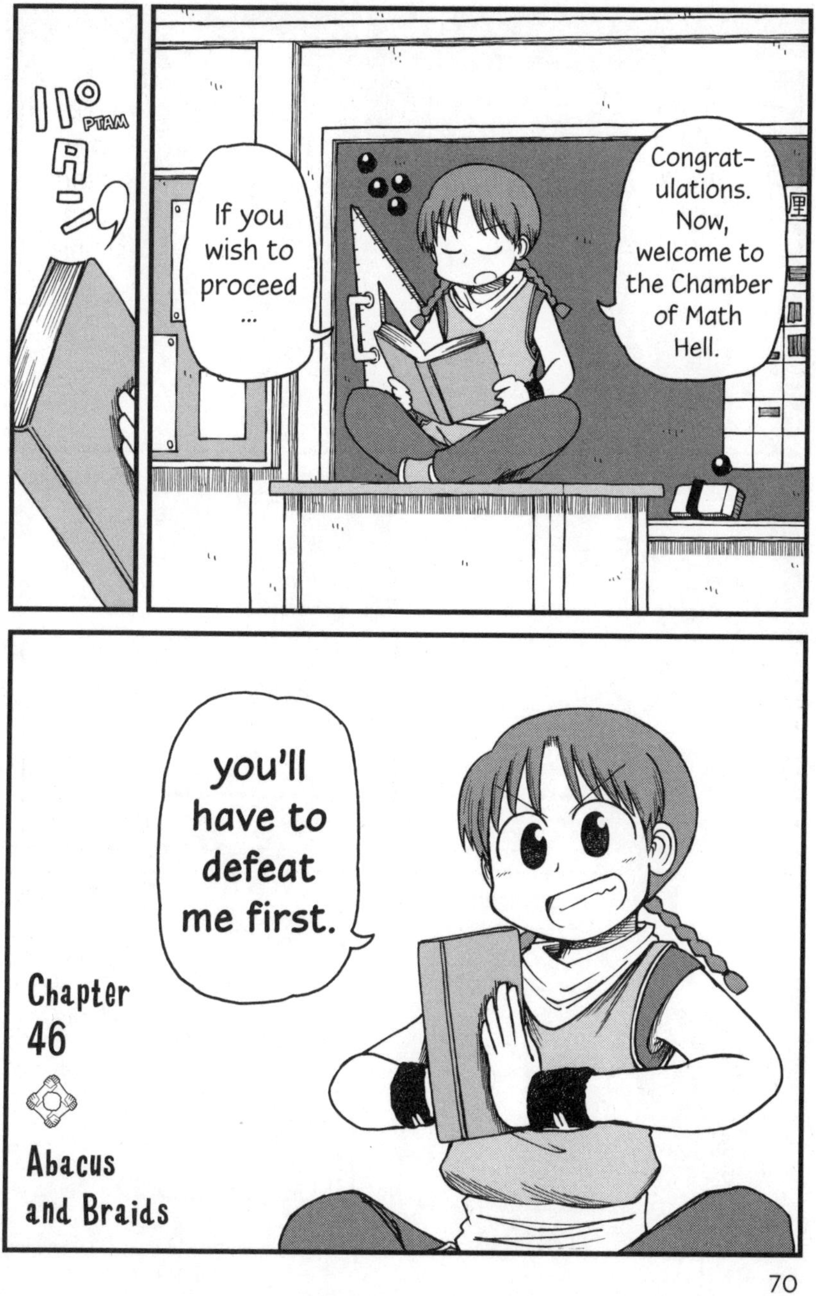
Congrat-ulations. Now, welcome to the Chamber of Math Hell.
If you wish to proceed ...
パターン
PTAM
you'll have to defeat me first.
Chapter 46
Abacus and Braids

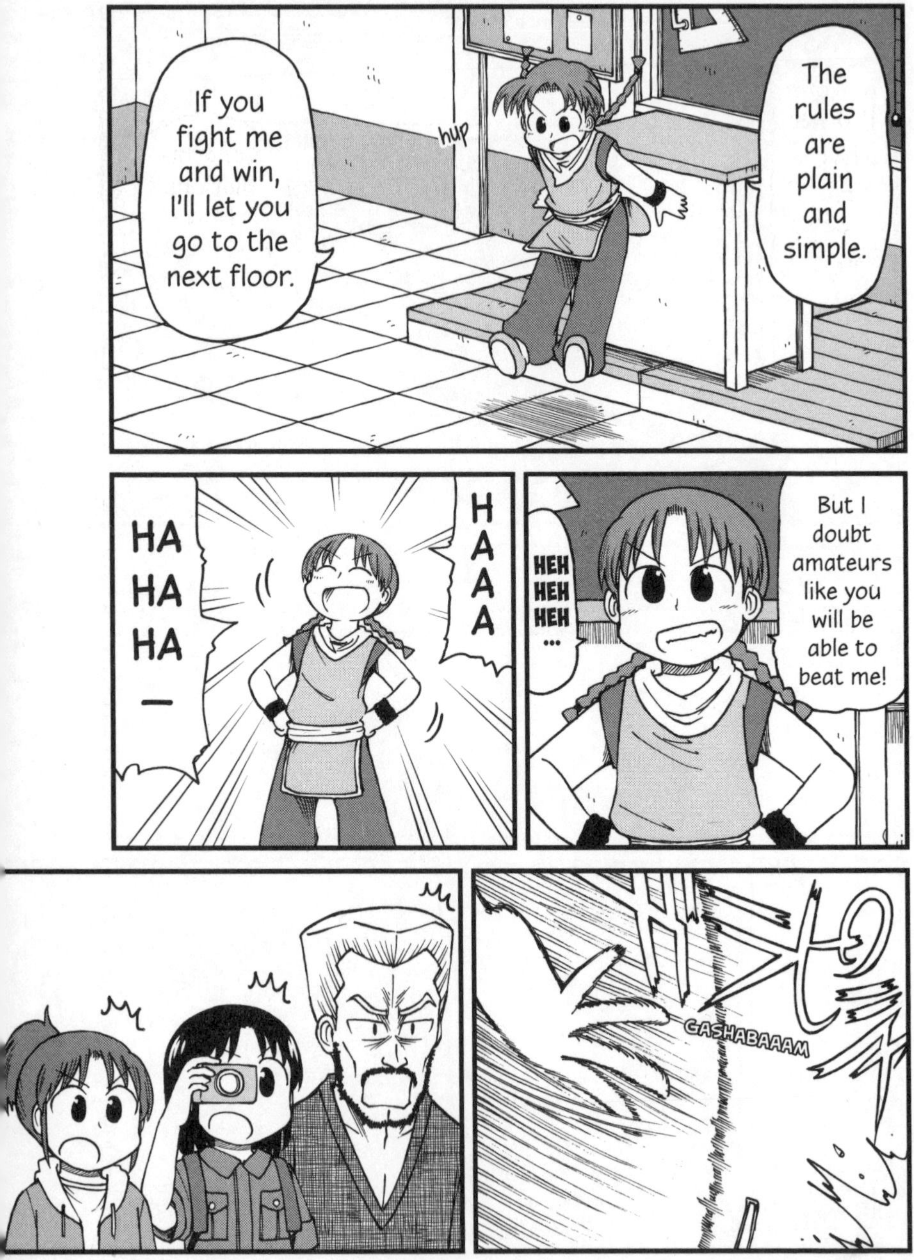
The rules are plain and simple.
hup
If you fight me and win, I'll let you go to the next floor.
But I doubt amateurs like you will be able to beat me!
HEH HEH HEH ...
HAAA
HA HA HA —
GASHABAAAM

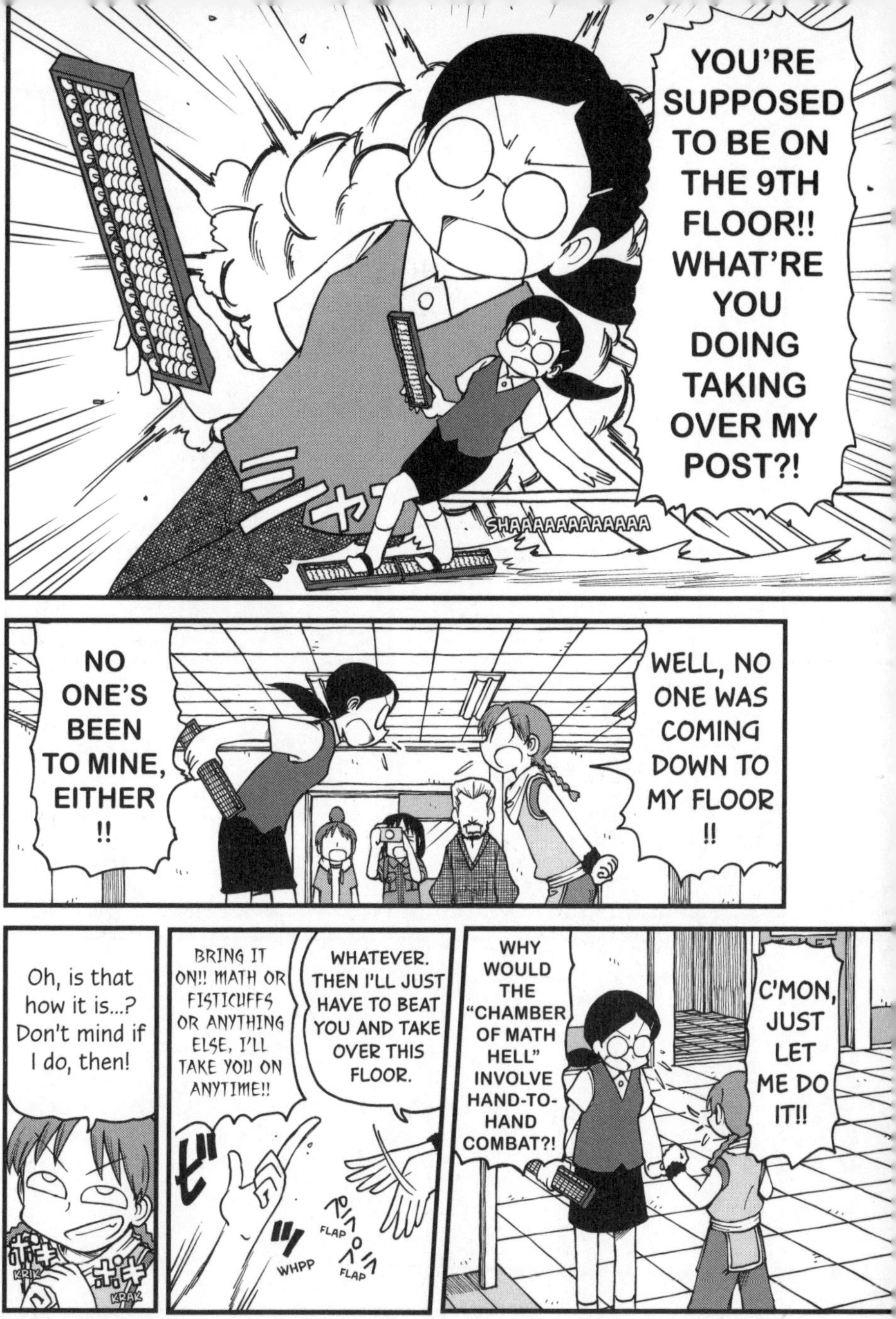
YOU'RE SUPPOSED TO BE ON THE 9TH FLOOR!! WHAT'RE YOU DOING TAKING OVER MY POST?!
SHAAAAAAAAAAAAA
WELL, NO ONE WAS COMING DOWN TO MY FLOOR!!
NO ONE'S BEEN TO MINE, EITHER!!
C'MON, JUST LET ME DO IT!!
WHY WOULD THE "CHAMBER OF MATH HELL" INVOLVE HAND-TO-HAND COMBAT?!
WHATEVER. THEN I'LL JUST HAVE TO BEAT YOU AND TAKE OVER THIS FLOOR.
BRING IT ON!! MATH OR FISTICUFFS OR ANYTHING ELSE, I'LL TAKE YOU ON ANYTIME!!
FLAP
FLAP
WHPP
Oh, is that how it is...? Don't mind if I do, then!
KRIK
KRAK

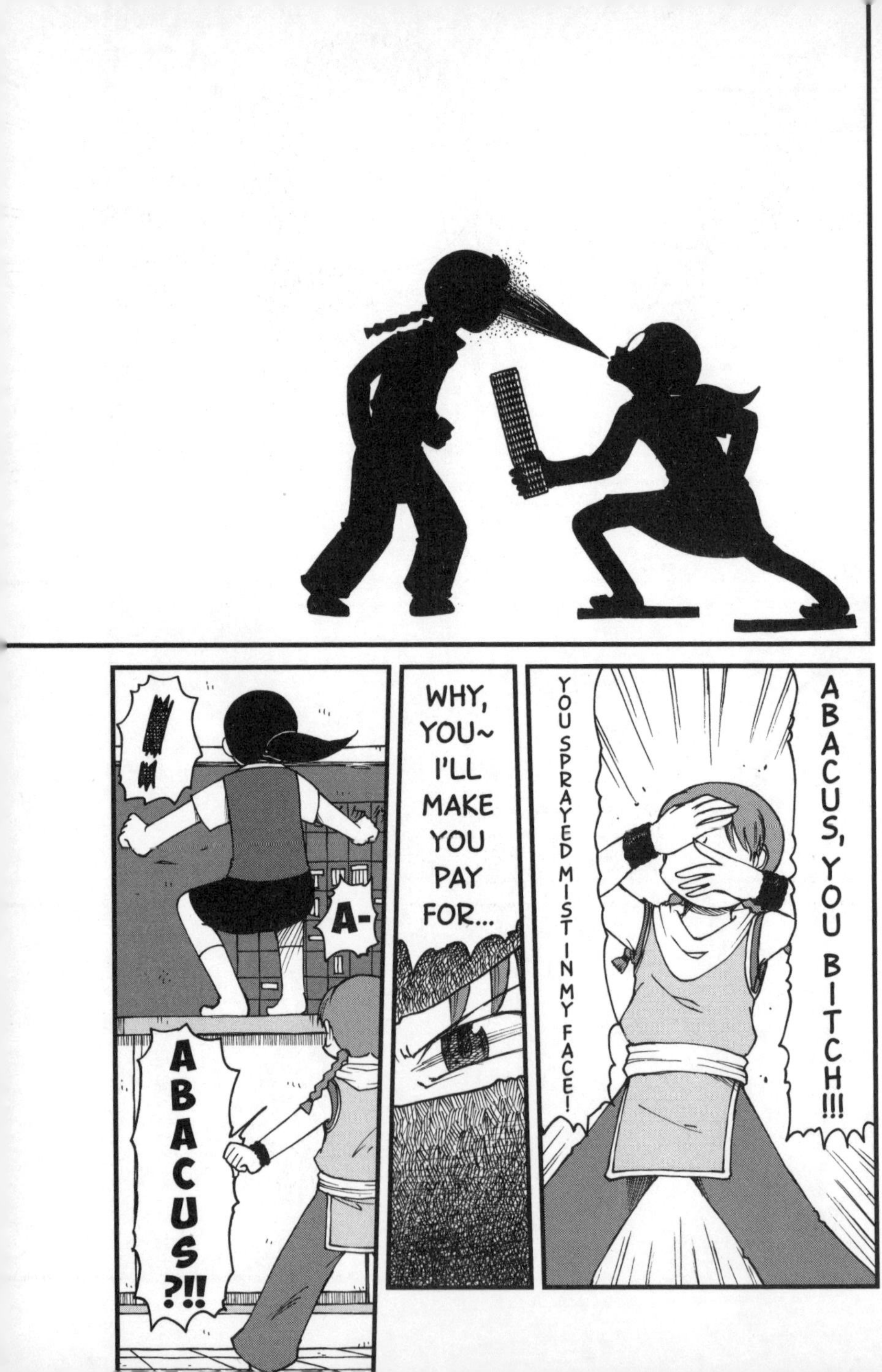
ABACUS, YOU BITCH!!!
YOU SPRAYED MIST IN MY FACE!
WHY, YOU~ I'LL MAKE YOU PAY FOR...
A-
ABACUS?!!

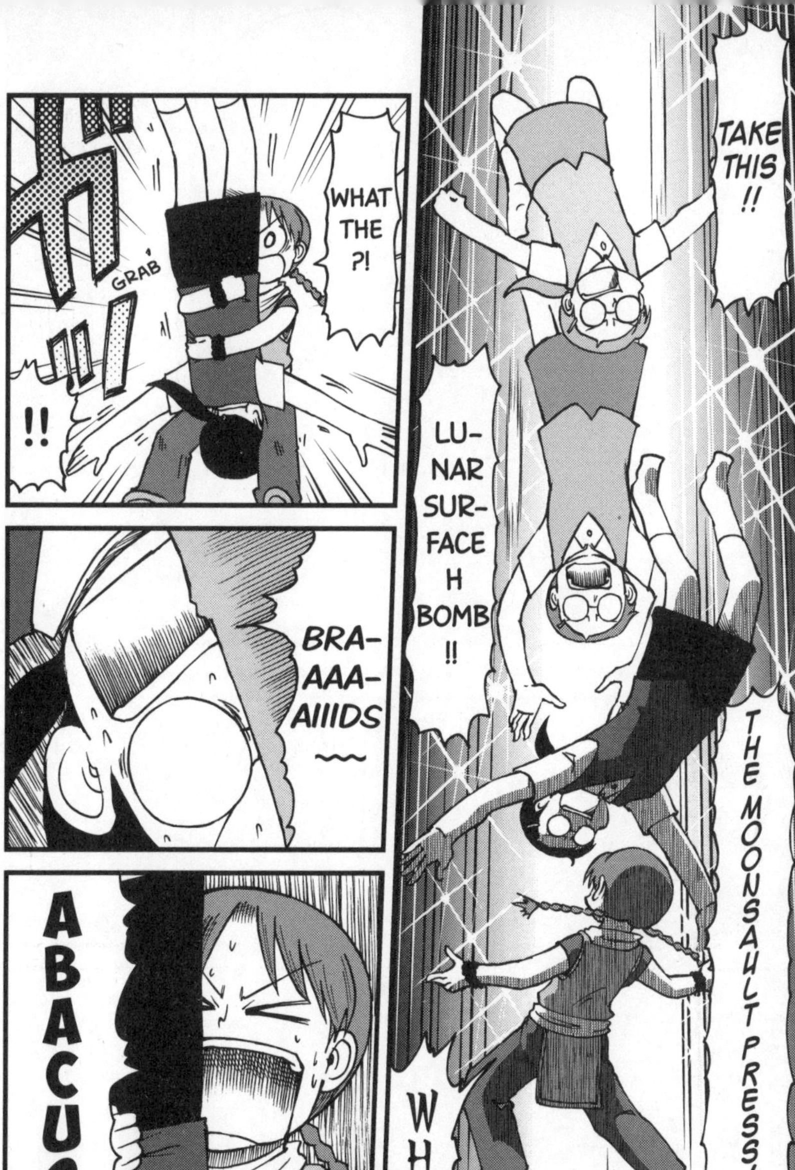
TAKE THIS!!
LU-NAR SUR-FACE H BOMB!!
THE MOONSAULT PRESS!
WHA!
WHAT THE ?!
GRAB
!!
BRA-AAA-AIIIDS ~~~
ABACUS!!!!

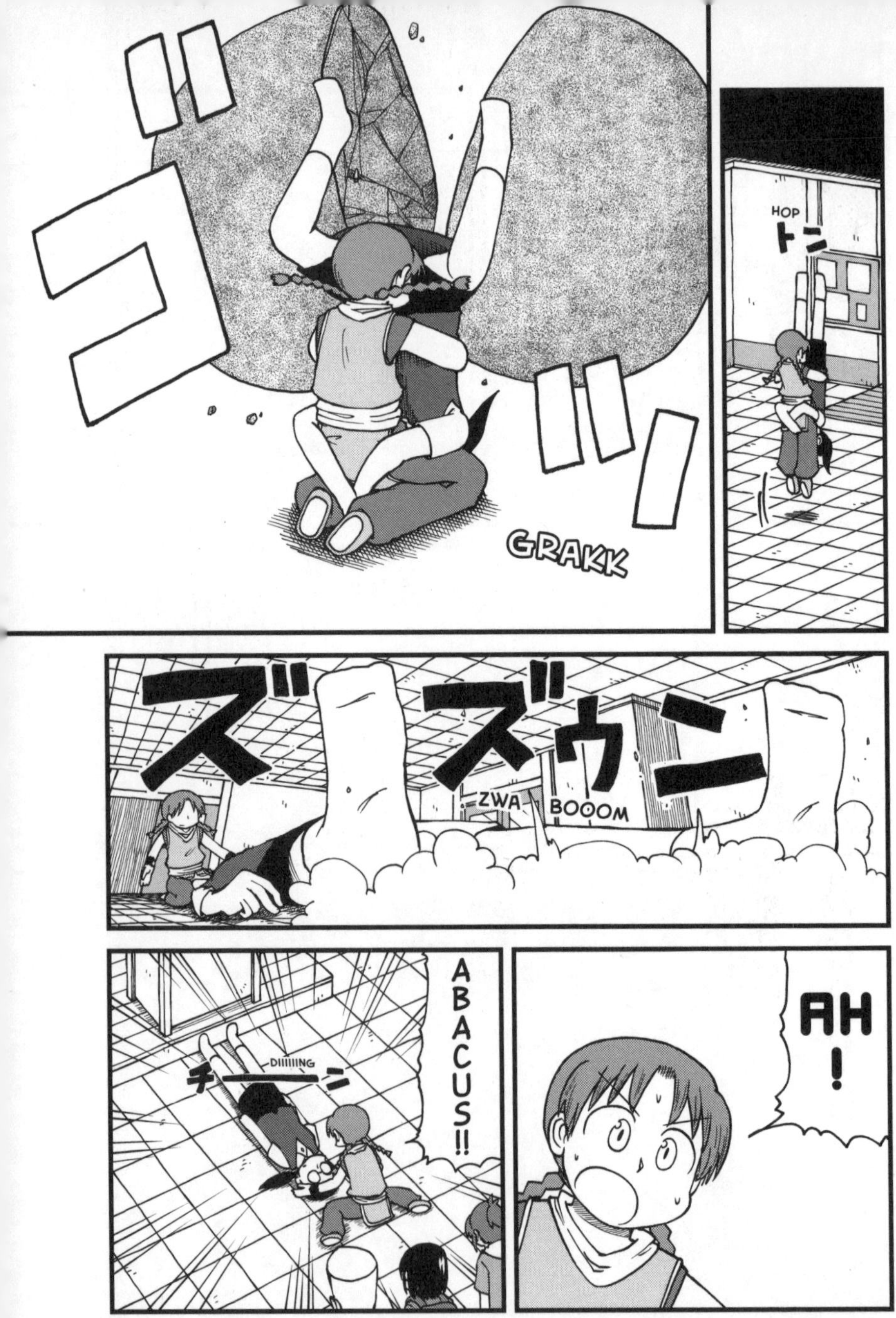
HOP
トン
ゴッ
GRAKK
ズズウーン
ZWA BOOOM
AH!
ABACUS!!
チーン
DIIIIING

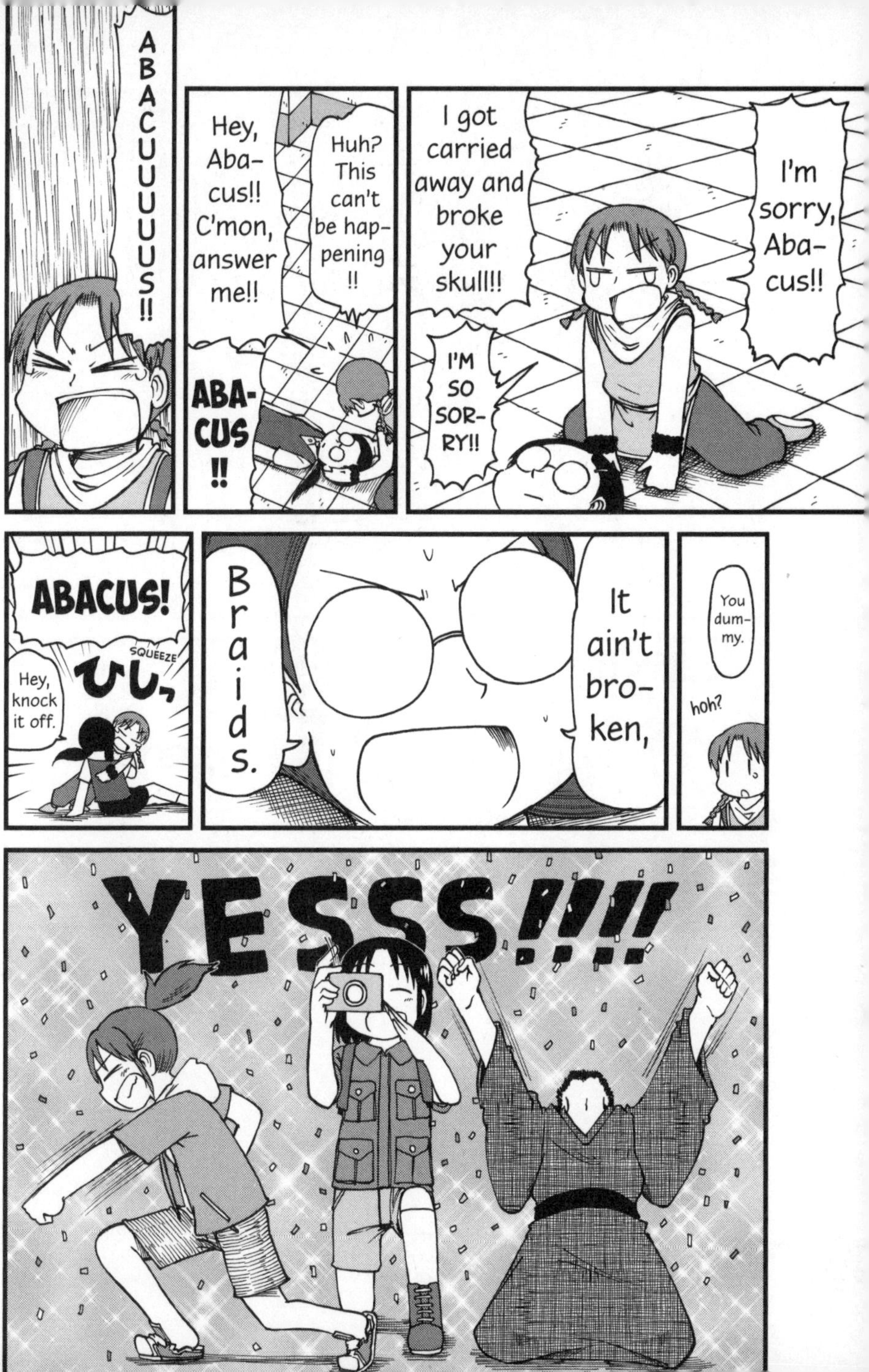
I'm sorry, Abacus!!
I got carried away and broke your skull!!!
I'M SO SORRY!!
Huh? This can't be happening!!
Hey, Abacus!! C'mon, answer me!!
ABACUS!!
ABACUUUUUUS!!
You dummy.
hoh?
It ain't broken,
Braids.
ABACUS!
SQUEEZE
ひし、
Hey, knock it off.
YESSS!!!!

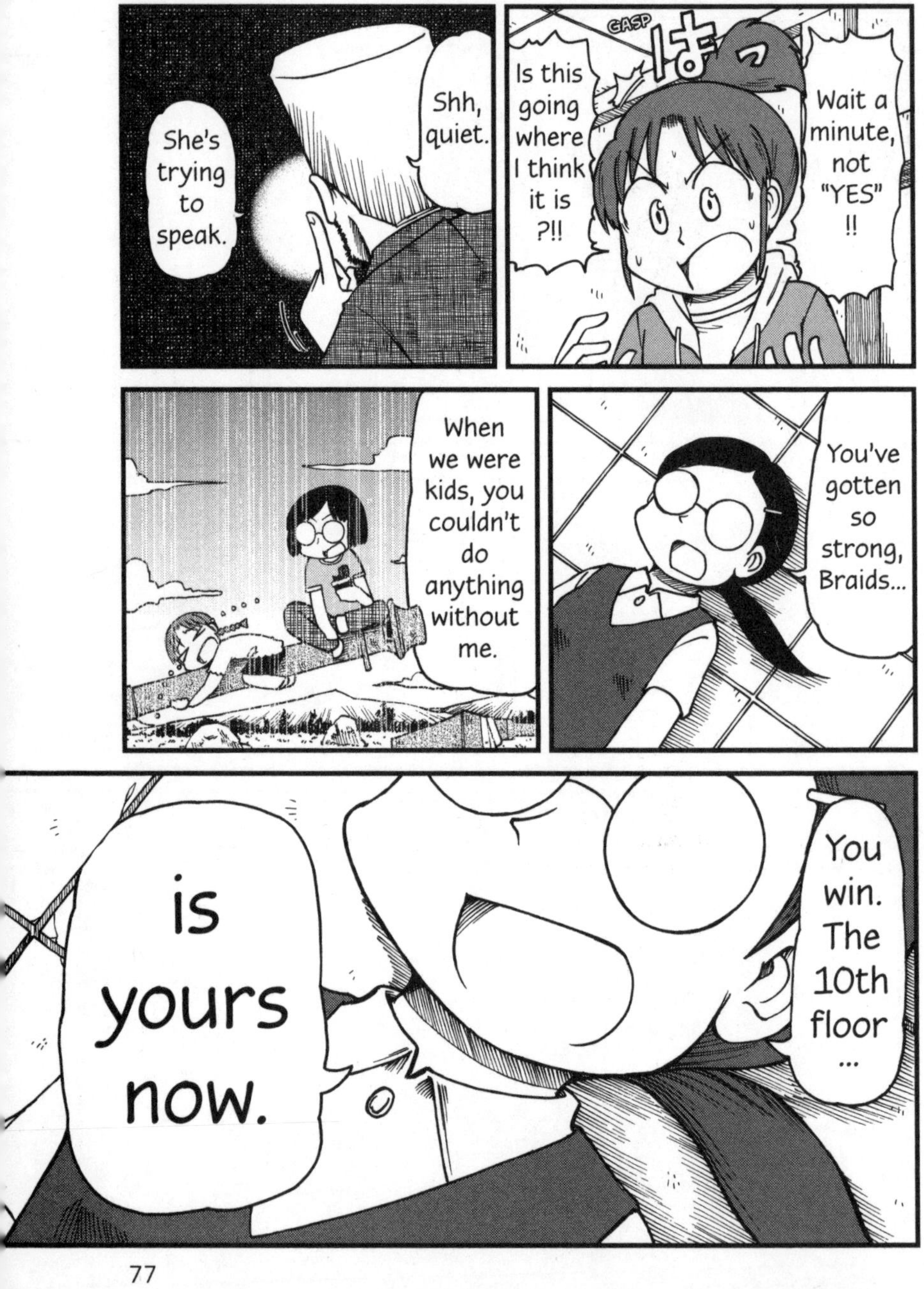

Wait a minute, not "YES" !!
GASP
はっ
Is this going where I think it is ?!!
Shh, quiet.
She's trying to speak.
You've gotten so strong, Braids...
When we were kids, you couldn't do anything without me.
You win. The 10th floor ...
is yours now.

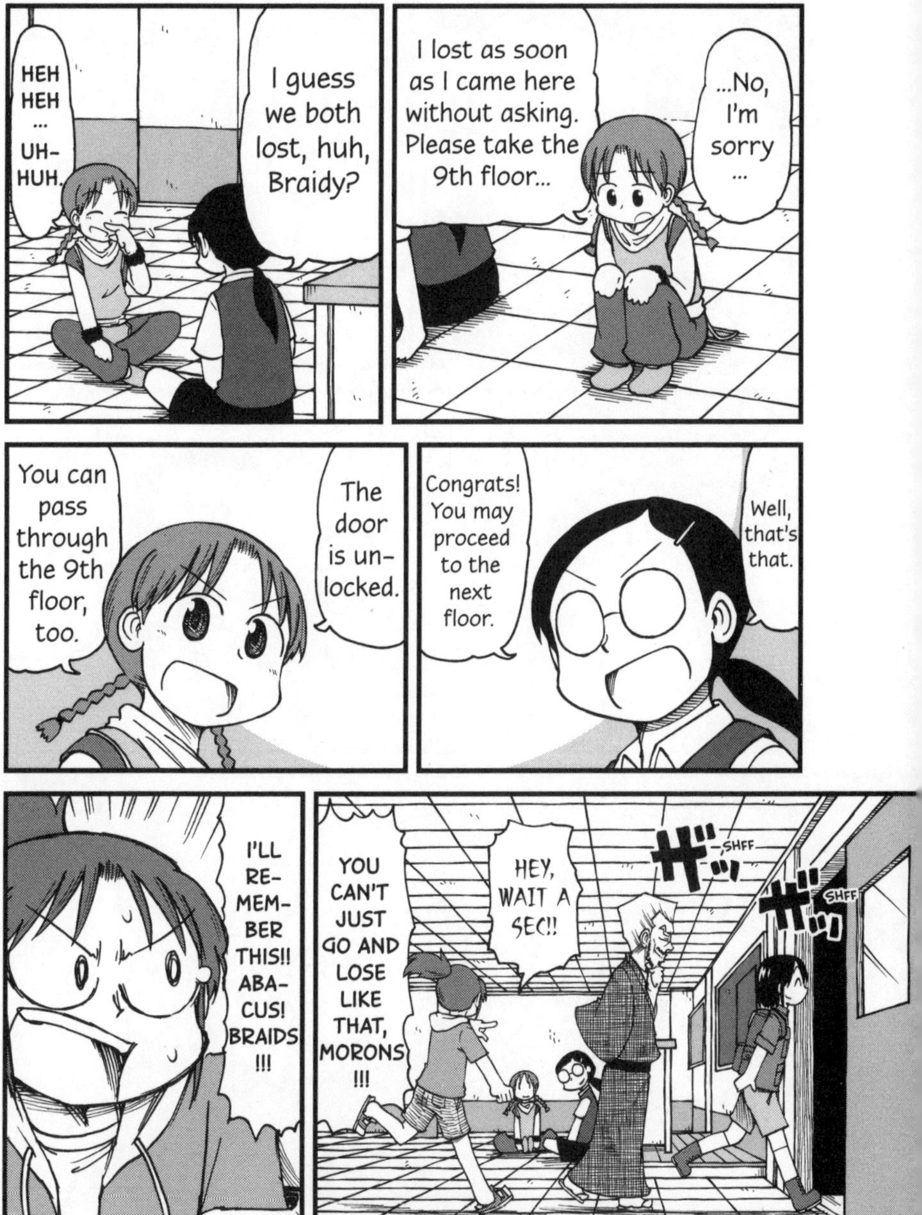
...No, I'm sorry ...
I lost as soon as I came here without asking. Please take the 9th floor...
I guess we both lost, huh, Braidy?
HEH HEH ... UH-HUH.
Well, that's that.
Congrats! You may proceed to the next floor.
The door is un-locked.
You can pass through the 9th floor, too.
ザッ SHFF
ザッ SHFF
HEY, WAIT A SEC!!
YOU CAN'T JUST GO AND LOSE LIKE THAT, MORONS!!!
I'LL RE-MEM-BER THIS!! ABA-CUS! BRAIDS!!!

Bonus Check
ACCOUNTING

Bonus Check
CLEANING

CITY

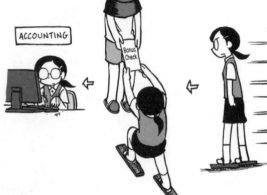

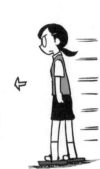

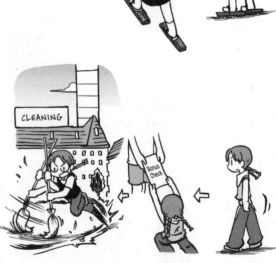

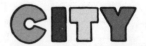

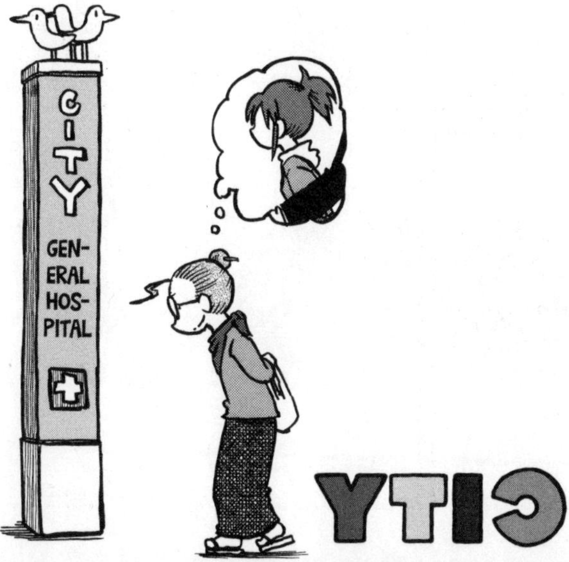
CITY
GEN-
ERAL
HOS-
PITAL

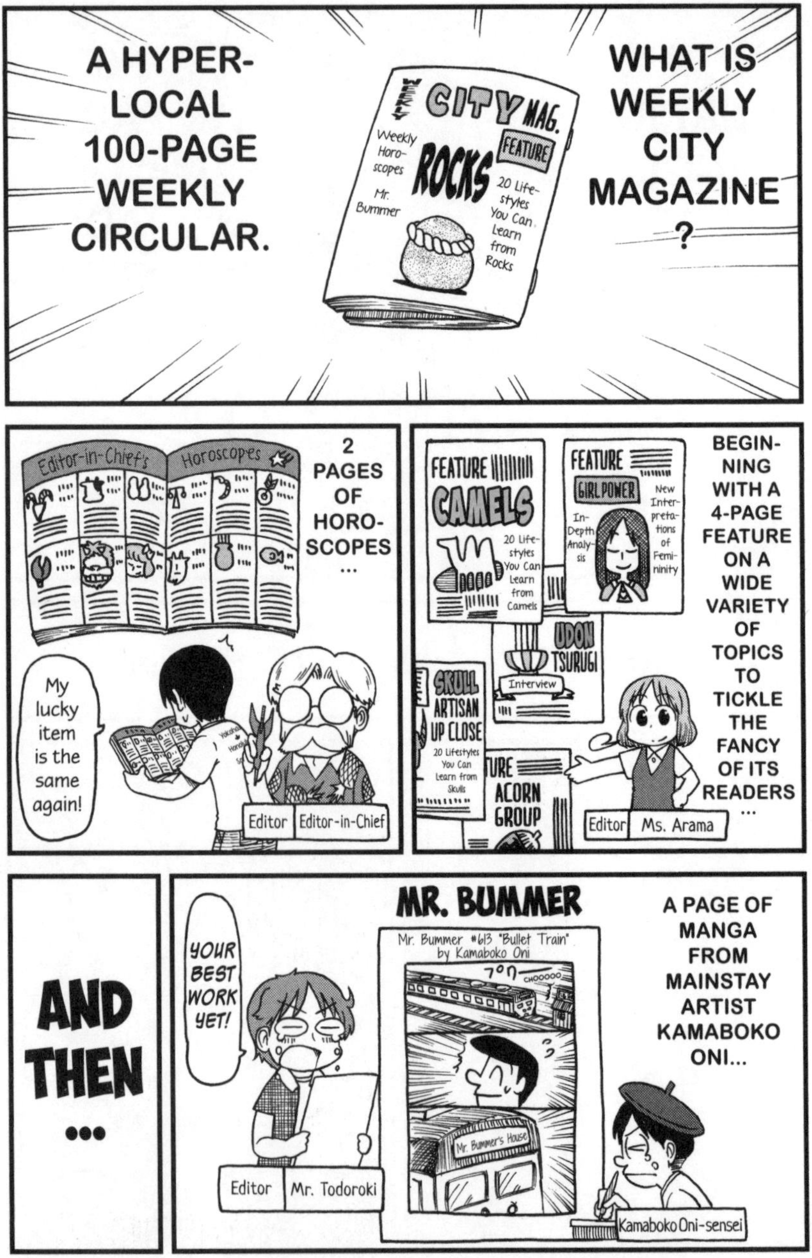

WHAT IS WEEKLY CITY MAGAZINE?
WEEKLY
CITY MAG.
FEATURE
ROCKS
Weekly Horoscopes
Mr. Bummer
20 Lifestyles You Can Learn from Rocks
A HYPER-LOCAL 100-PAGE WEEKLY CIRCULAR.
BEGINNING WITH A 4-PAGE FEATURE ON A WIDE VARIETY OF TOPICS TO TICKLE THE FANCY OF ITS READERS...
FEATURE
GIRL POWER
New Interpretations of Femininity
In-Depth Analysis
FEATURE
CAMELS
20 Lifestyles You Can Learn from Camels
UDON TSURUGI
Interview
SKULL ARTISAN UP CLOSE
20 Lifestyles You Can Learn from Skulls
ACORN GROUP
Ms. Arama
Editor
2 PAGES OF HOROSCOPES...
Editor-in-Chief's
Horoscopes
Editor-in-Chief
Editor
My lucky item is the same again!
A PAGE OF MANGA FROM MAINSTAY ARTIST KAMABOKO ONI...
MR. BUMMER
Mr. Bummer #613 "Bullet Train" by Kamaboko Oni
CHOOOOO
Mr. Bummer's House
Kamaboko Oni-sensei
YOUR BEST WORK YET!
Mr. Todoroki
Editor
AND THEN...

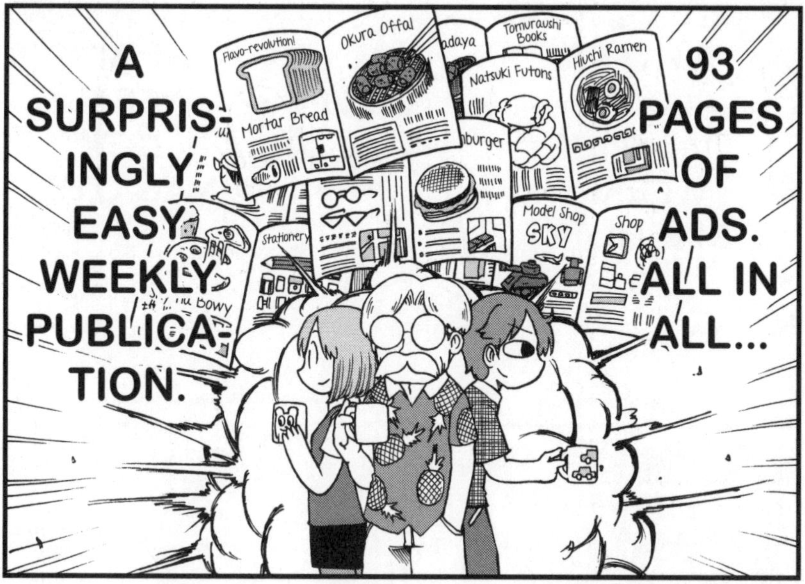
93 PAGES OF ADS. ALL IN ALL...
A SURPRISINGLY EASY WEEKLY PUBLICATION.
Flavo-revolution!
Mortar Bread
Okura Offal
Tomuraushi Books
Natsuki Futons
Hiuchi Ramen
Stationery
Model Shop SKY
Shop

Chapter 47 Weekly CITY Magazine

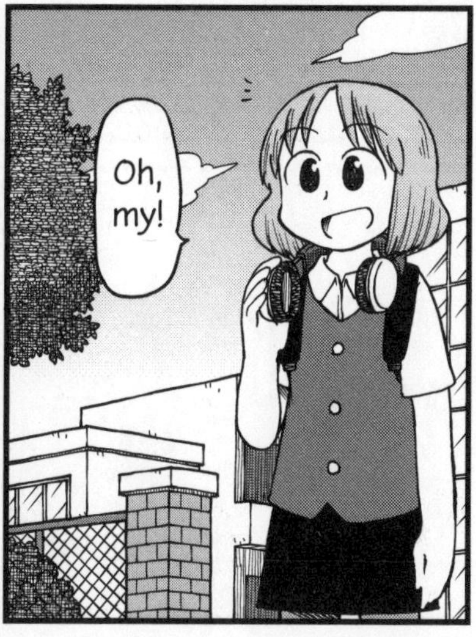
Oh, my!

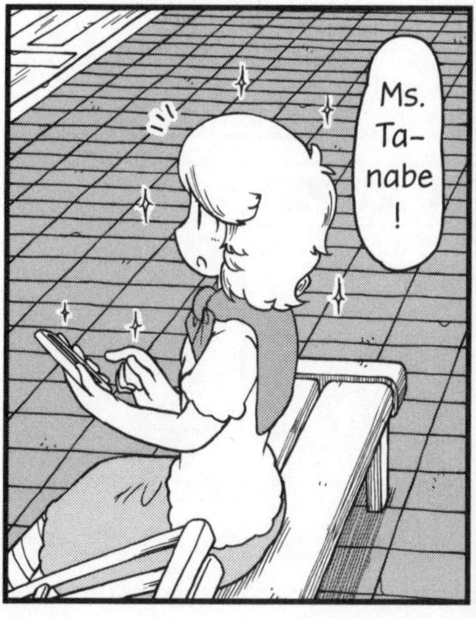
Ms. Tanabe!

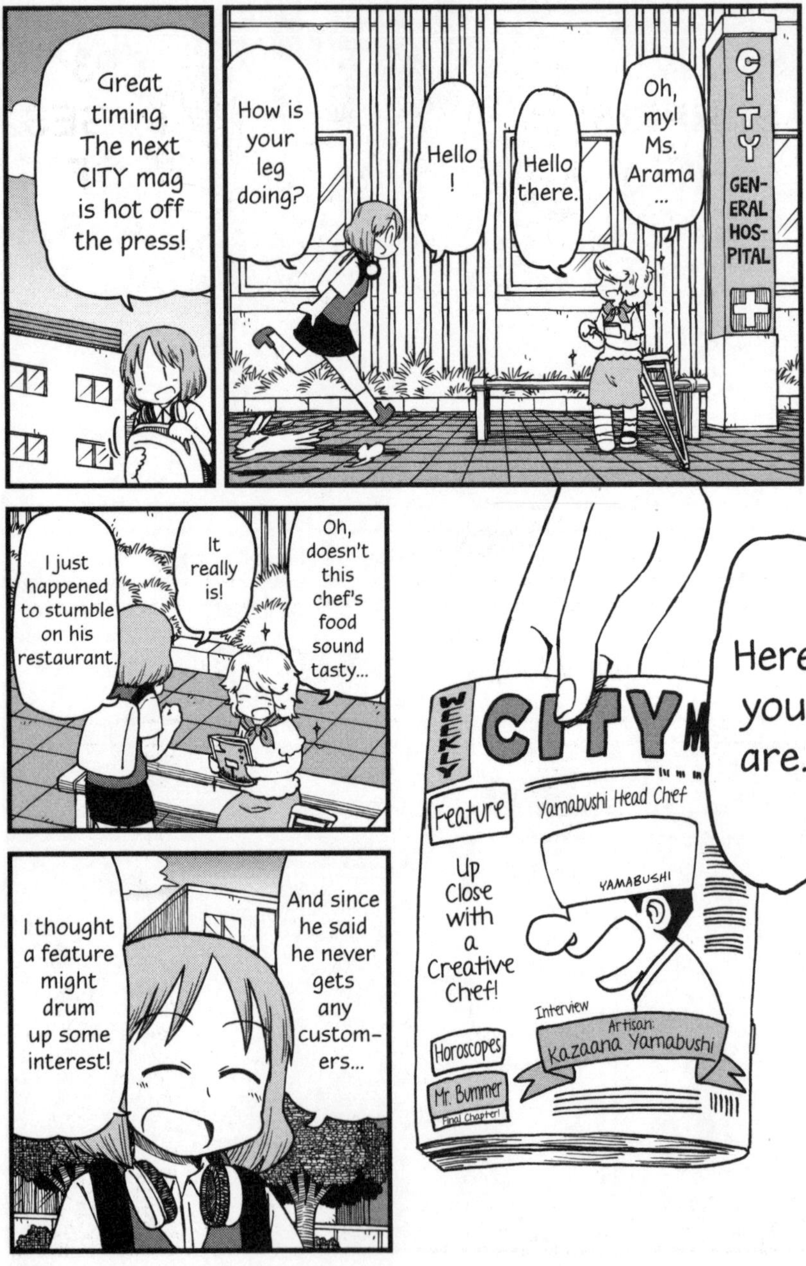
CITY GEN-ERAL HOS-PITAL
Oh, my! Ms. Arama ...
Hello there.
Hello!
How is your leg doing?
Great timing. The next CITY mag is hot off the press!
Here you are.
WEEKLY CITY M
Feature
Yamabushi Head Chef
Up Close with a Creative Chef!
YAMABUSHI
Interview
Artisan: Kazaana Yamabushi
Horoscopes
Mr. Bummer
Final Chapter!
Oh, doesn't this chef's food sound tasty...
It really is!
I just happened to stumble on his restaurant.
And since he said he never gets any customers...
I thought a feature might drum up some interest!

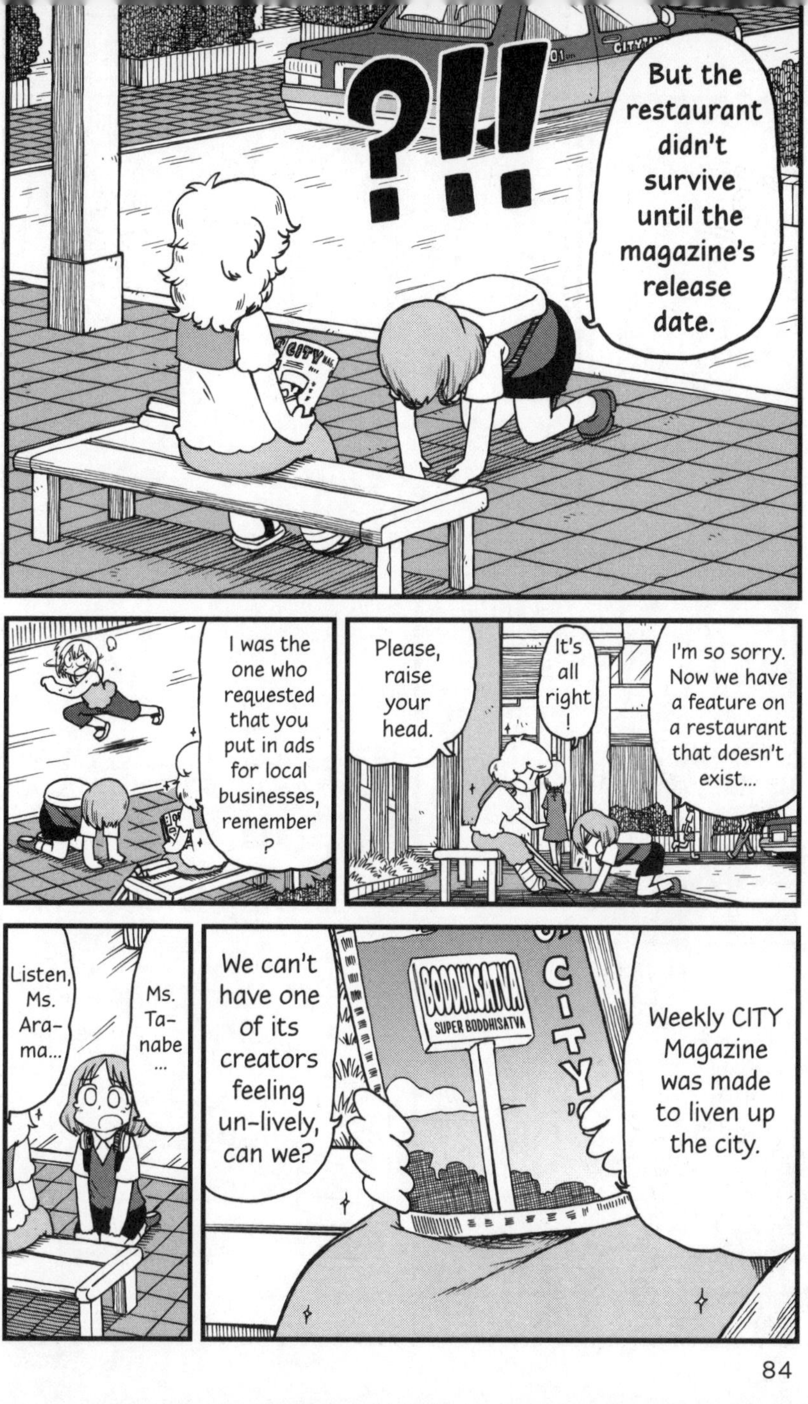

?!!
But the restaurant didn't survive until the magazine's release date.
I'm so sorry. Now we have a feature on a restaurant that doesn't exist...
It's all right!
Please, raise your head.
I was the one who requested that you put in ads for local businesses, remember?
Weekly CITY Magazine was made to liven up the city.
CITY
BODDHISATVA
SUPER BODDHISATVA
We can't have one of its creators feeling un-lively, can we?
Ms. Tanabe...
Listen, Ms. Arama...

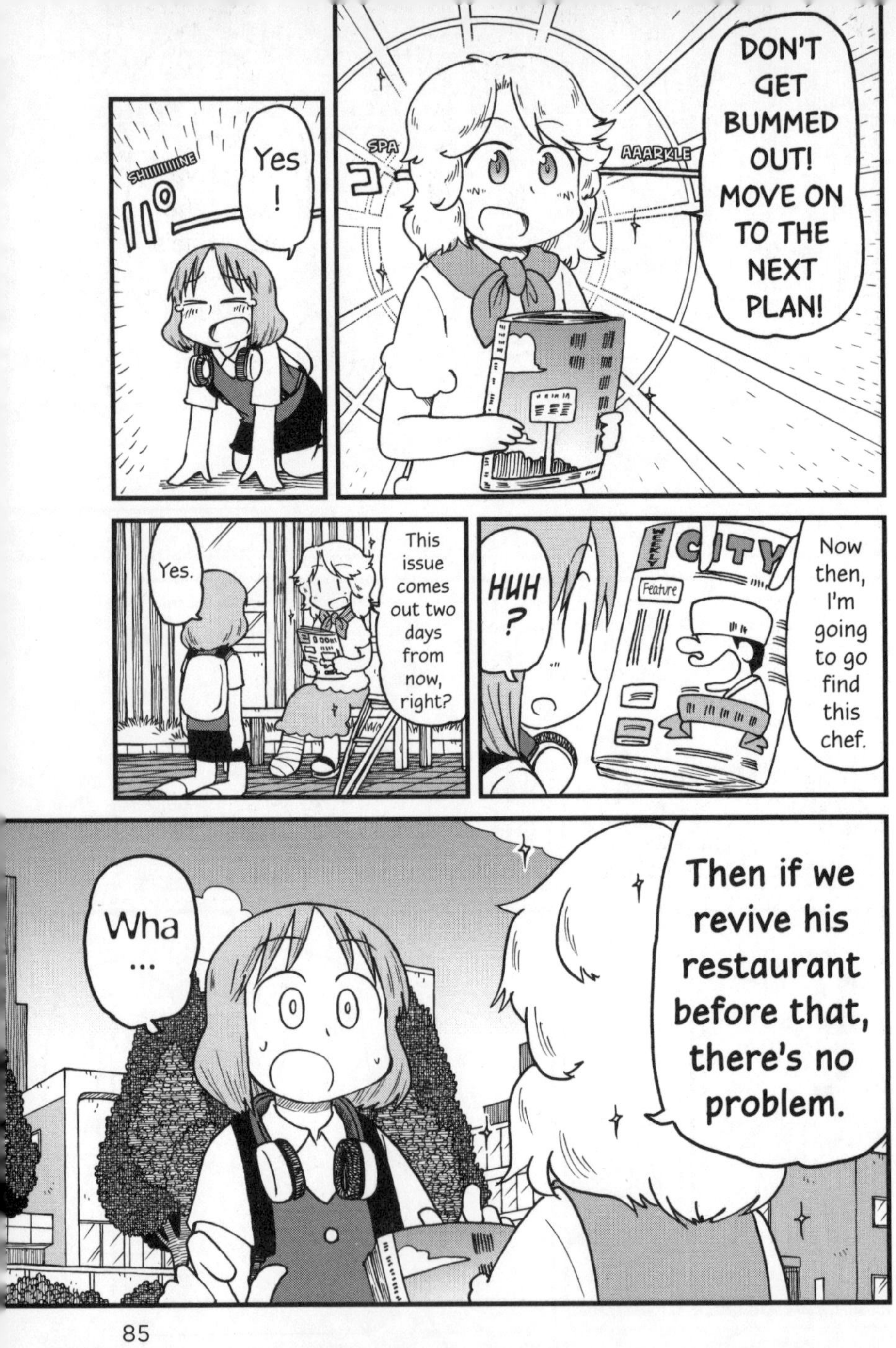
DON'T GET BUMMED OUT! MOVE ON TO THE NEXT PLAN!
SPA
AAARKLE
Yes!
SHIIIIIIIINE
Now then, I'm going to go find this chef.
WEEKLY CITY
Feature
HUH?
This issue comes out two days from now, right?
Yes.
Then if we revive his restaurant before that, there's no problem.
Wha...

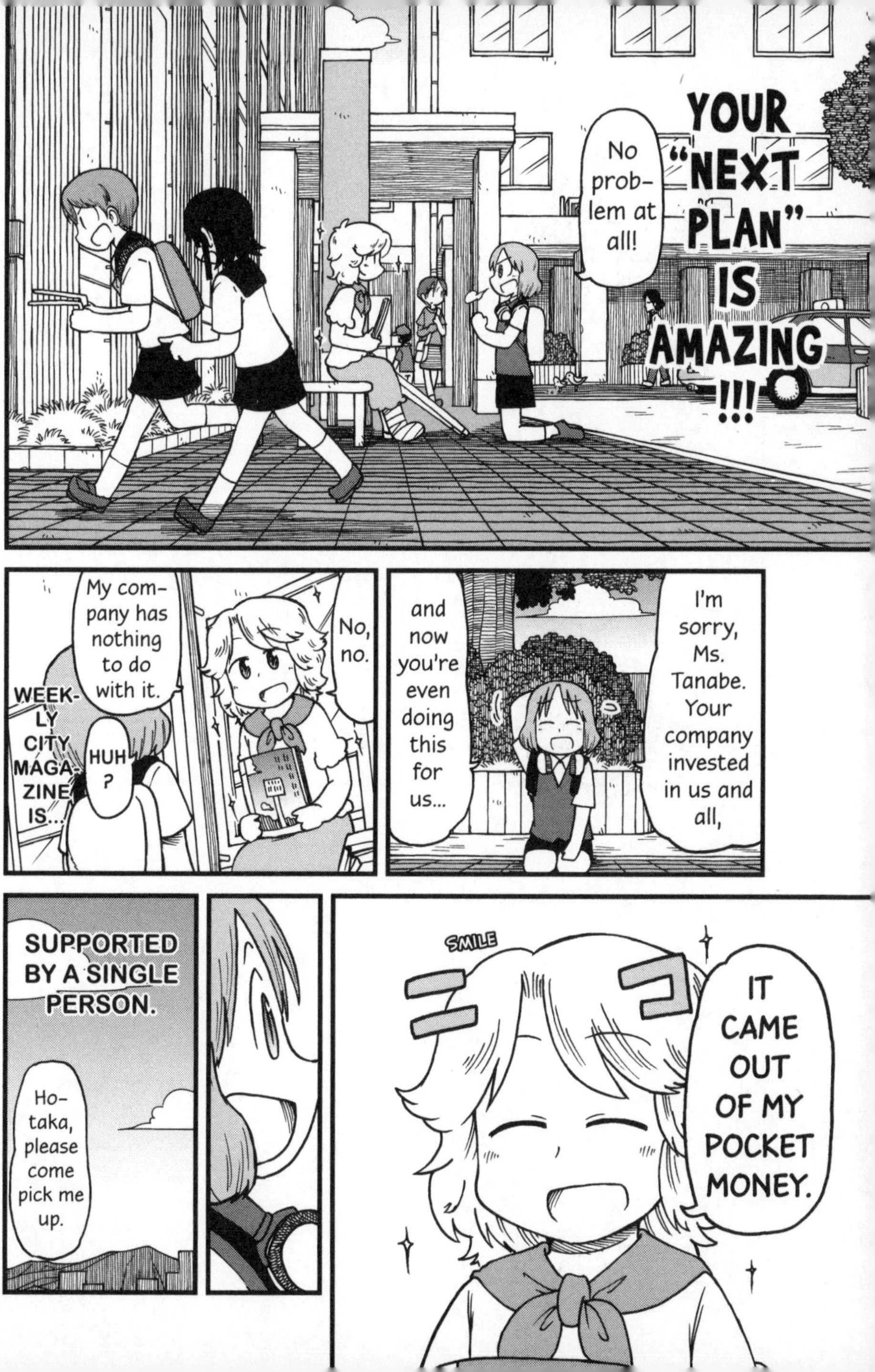
YOUR "NEXT PLAN" IS AMAZING!!!
No prob-lem at all!
I'm sorry, Ms. Tanabe. Your company invested in us and all,
and now you're even doing this for us...
No, no.
My com-pany has nothing to do with it.
HUH?
WEEK-LY CITY MAGA-ZINE IS...
SMILE
IT CAME OUT OF MY POCKET MONEY.
SUPPORTED BY A SINGLE PERSON.
Ho-taka, please come pick me up.

CITY

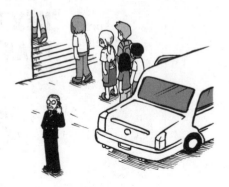

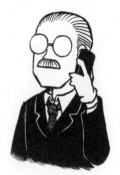

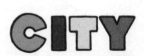

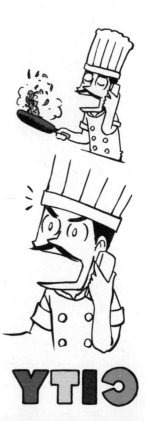

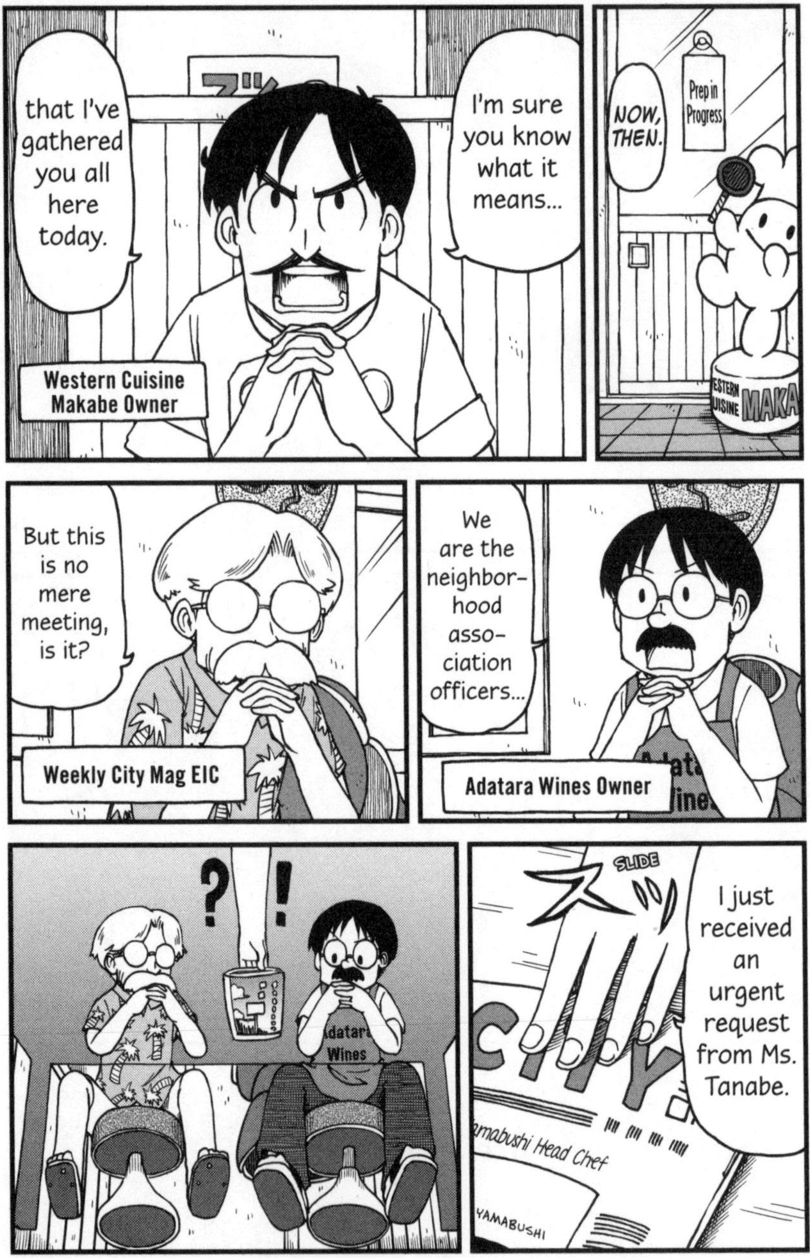
NOW, THEN.
Prep in Progress
WESTERN CUISINE MAKA
I'm sure you know what it means...
that I've gathered you all here today.
Western Cuisine Makabe Owner
We are the neighbor-hood asso-ciation officers...
Adatara Wines Owner
But this is no mere meeting, is it?
Weekly City Mag EIC
SLIDE
I just received an urgent request from Ms. Tanabe.
amabushi Head Chef
YAMABUSHI
?
!
Adatara Wines

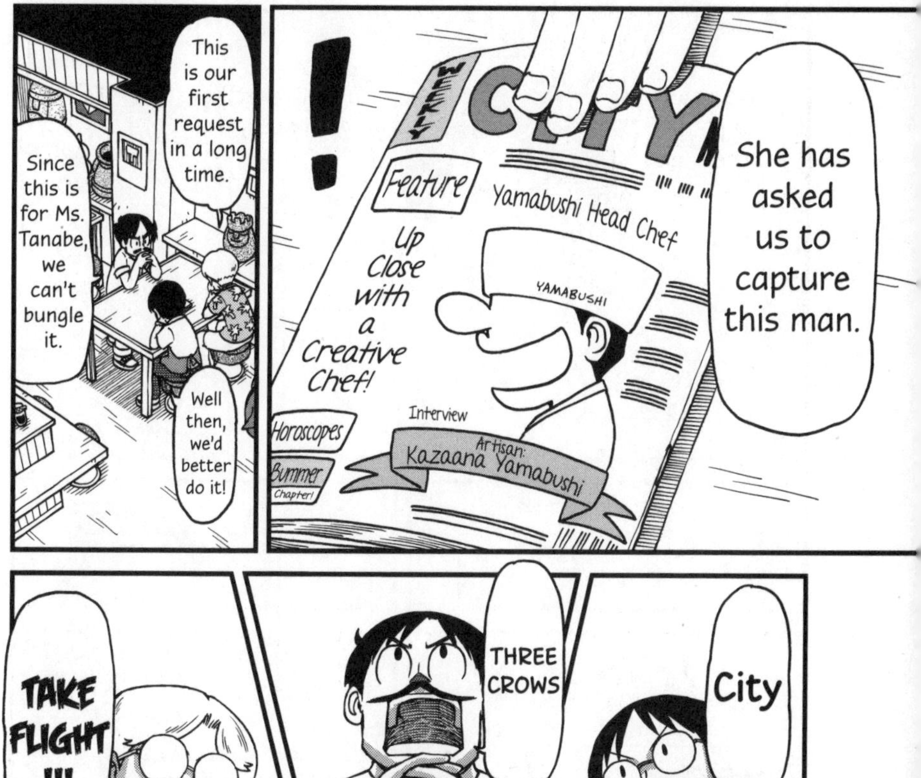

She has asked us to capture this man.
!
WEEKLY
CITY
Feature
Yamabushi Head Chef
Up Close with a Creative Chef!
YAMABUSHI
Interview
Artisan: Kazaana Yamabushi
Horoscopes
Bummer Chapter!
This is our first request in a long time.
Since this is for Ms. Tanabe, we can't bungle it.
Well then, we'd better do it!
City
Adatara Wines
THREE CROWS
TAKE FLIGHT!!!

Chapter 48 ◇ CITY Three Crows

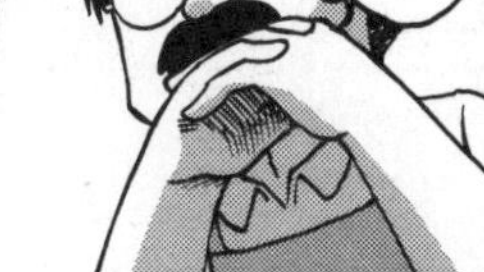

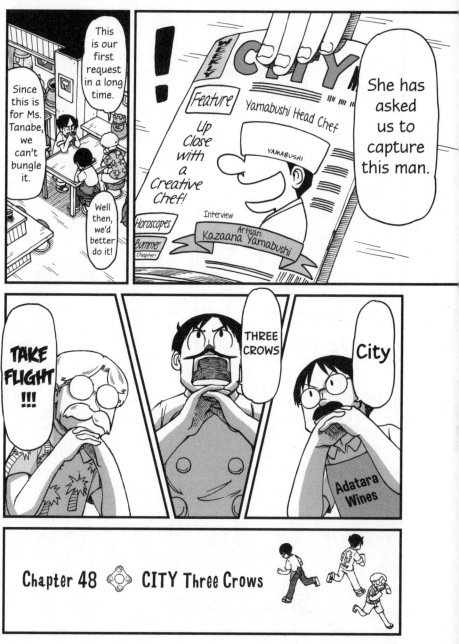

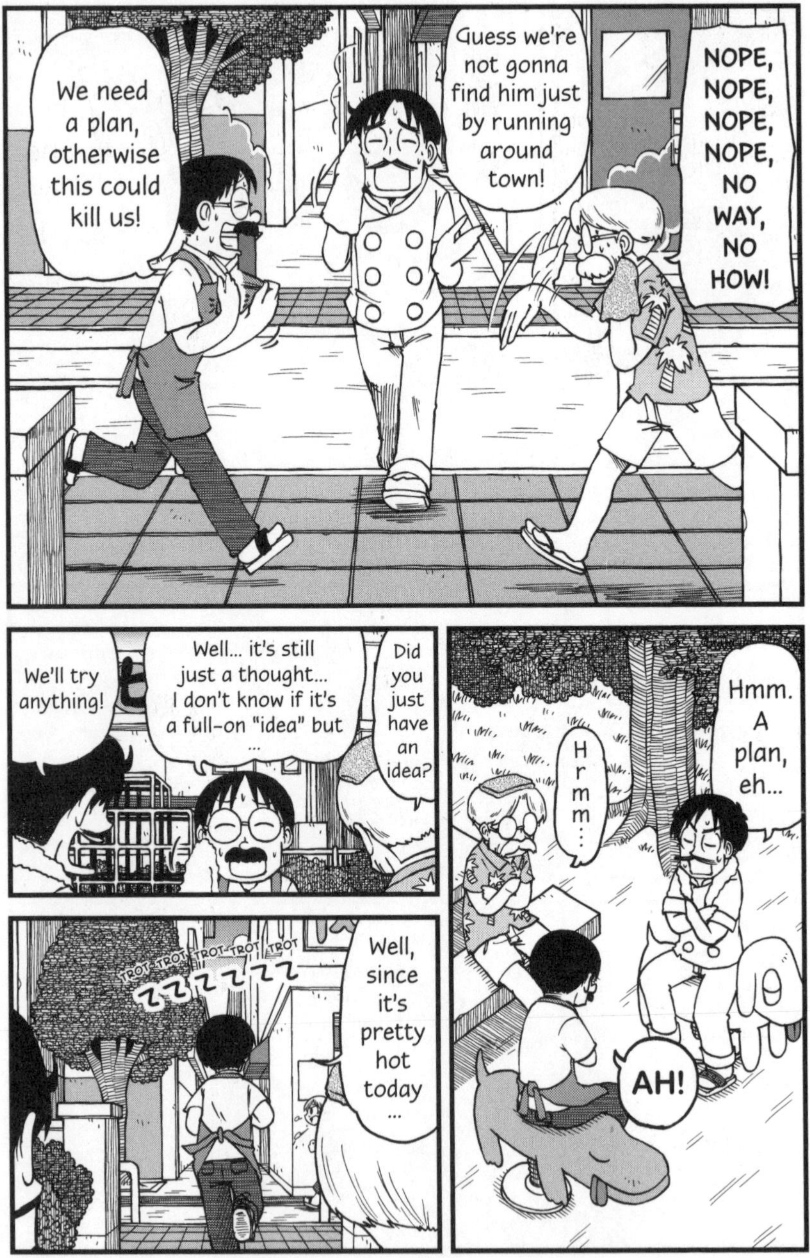
NOPE, NOPE, NOPE, NOPE, NO WAY, NO HOW!
Guess we're not gonna find him just by running around town!
We need a plan, otherwise this could kill us!
Hmm. A plan, eh...
Hrmm...
AH!
Did you just have an idea?
Well... it's still just a thought... I don't know if it's a full-on "idea" but ...
We'll try anything!
Well, since it's pretty hot today ...
TROT TROT TROT TROT TROT
ZZZZZZZ

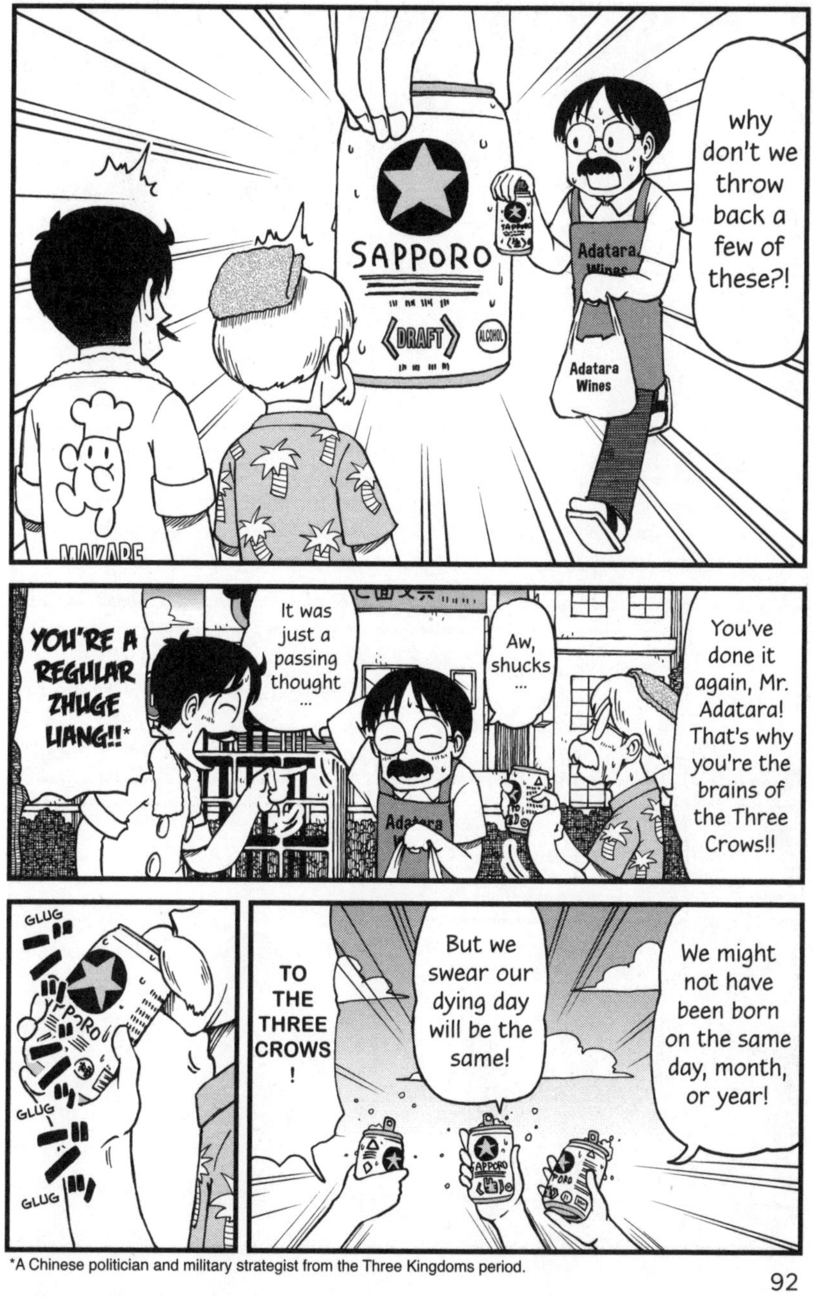
why don't we throw back a few of these?!
SAPPORO
DRAFT
ALCOHOL
Adatara Wines
Adatara Wines
You've done it again, Mr. Adatara! That's why you're the brains of the Three Crows!!
Aw, shucks...
It was just a passing thought...
YOU'RE A REGULAR ZHUGE LIANG!!*
We might not have been born on the same day, month, or year!
But we swear our dying day will be the same!
TO THE THREE CROWS!
GLUG
GLUG
GLUG

*A Chinese politician and military strategist from the Three Kingdoms period.

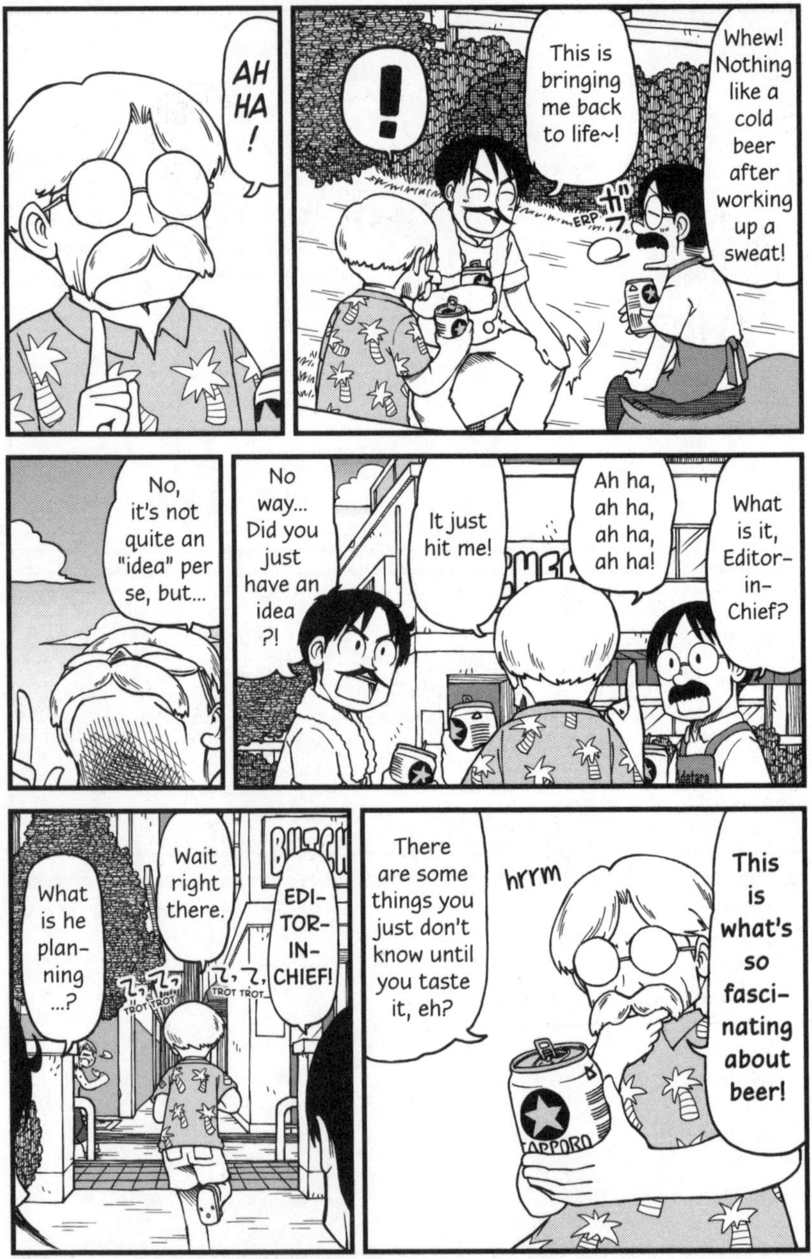
Whew! Nothing like a cold beer after working up a sweat!
ERP
This is bringing me back to life~!
!
AH HA!
What is it, Editor-in-Chief?
Ah ha, ah ha, ah ha, ah ha!
It just hit me!
No way... Did you just have an idea?!
No, it's not quite an "idea" per se, but...
This is what's so fascinating about beer!
hrrm
There are some things you just don't know until you taste it, eh?
SAPPORO
EDITOR-IN-CHIEF!
Wait right there.
BUTCH
TROT TROT
TROT TROT
What is he planning...?

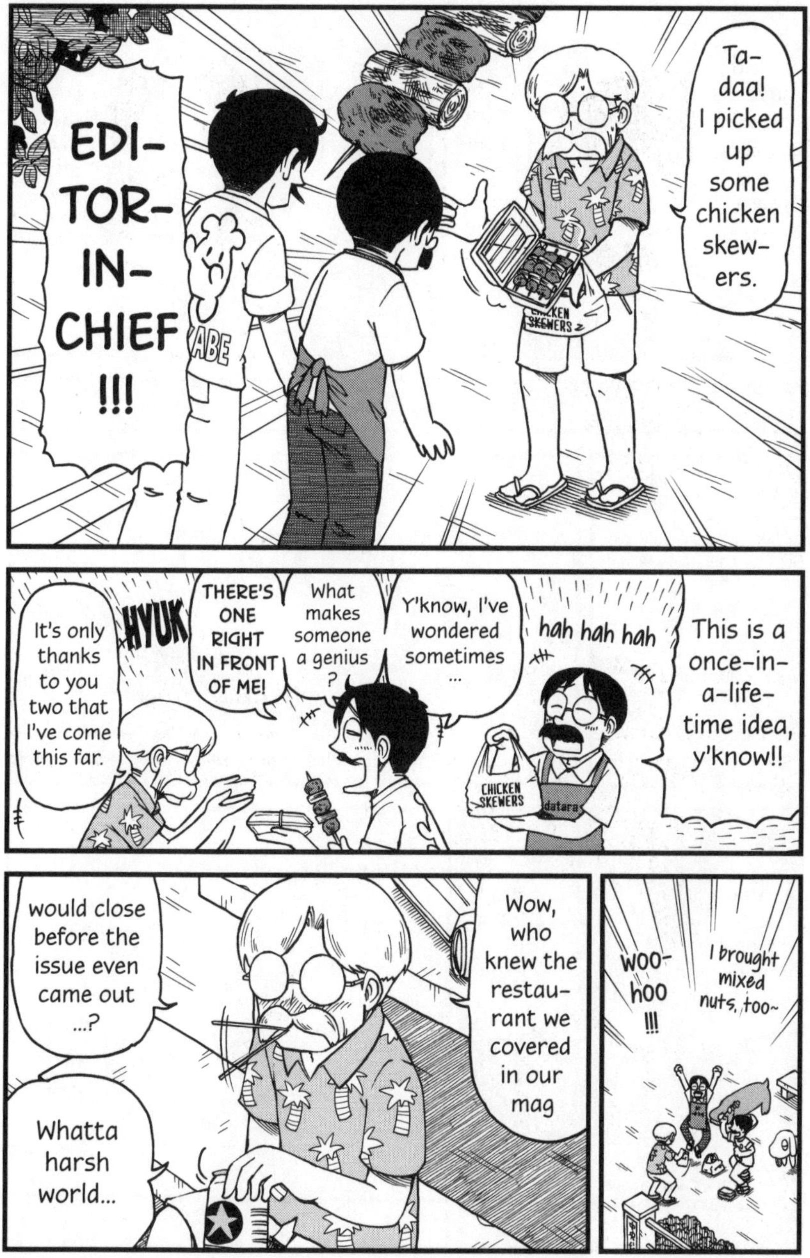
Ta-daa! I picked up some chicken skewers.
EDI-TOR-IN-CHIEF!!!
CHICKEN SKEWERS
ABE
This is a once-in-a-life-time idea, y'know!!
hah hah hah
Y'know, I've wondered sometimes ...
What makes someone a genius ?
THERE'S ONE RIGHT IN FRONT OF ME!
HYUK
It's only thanks to you two that I've come this far.
CHICKEN SKEWERS
datara
I brought mixed nuts, too~
WOO-hOO!!!
Wow, who knew the restaurant we covered in our mag
would close before the issue even came out ...?
Whatta harsh world...

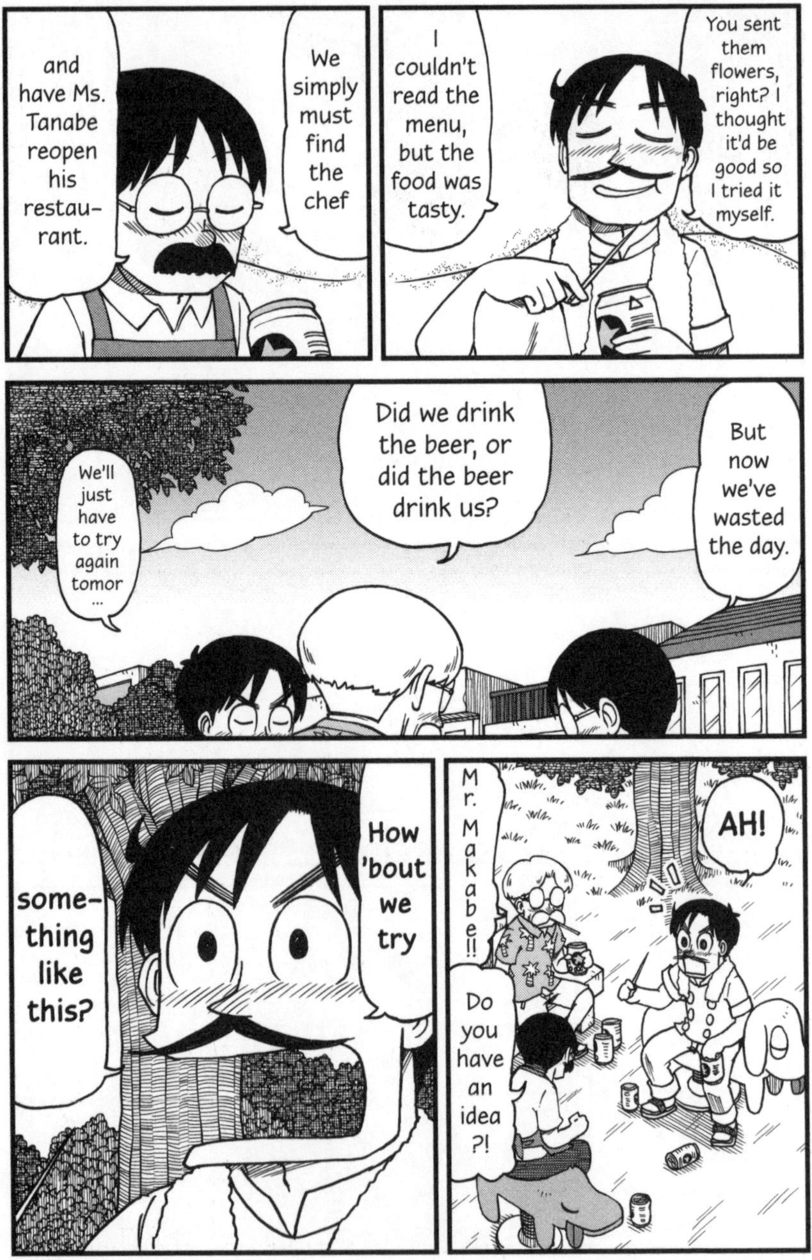
You sent them flowers, right? I thought it'd be good so I tried it myself.
I couldn't read the menu, but the food was tasty.
We simply must find the chef
and have Ms. Tanabe reopen his restaurant.
But now we've wasted the day.
Did we drink the beer, or did the beer drink us?
We'll just have to try again tomor...
AH!
Mr. Makabe!!
Do you have an idea?!
How 'bout we try
something like this?

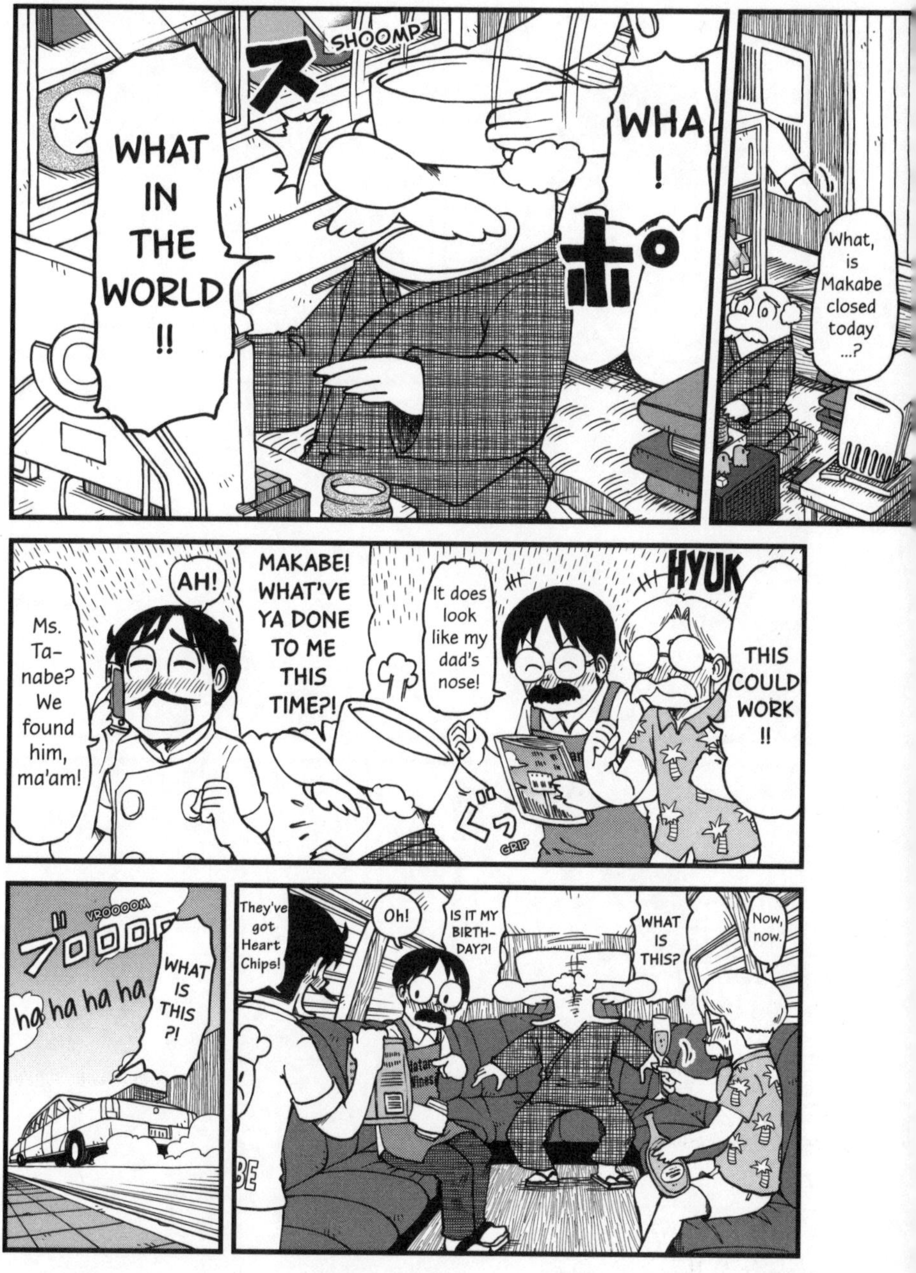
What, is Makabe closed today ...?
WHA!
SHOOMP
WHAT IN THE WORLD!!
HYUK
THIS COULD WORK!!
It does look like my dad's nose!
MAKABE! WHAT'VE YA DONE TO ME THIS TIME?!
AH!
Ms. Ta-nabe? We found him, ma'am!
GRIP
Now, now.
WHAT IS THIS?
IS IT MY BIRTH-DAY?!
Oh!
They've got Heart Chips!
VROOOOM
WHAT IS THIS?!
ha ha ha ha

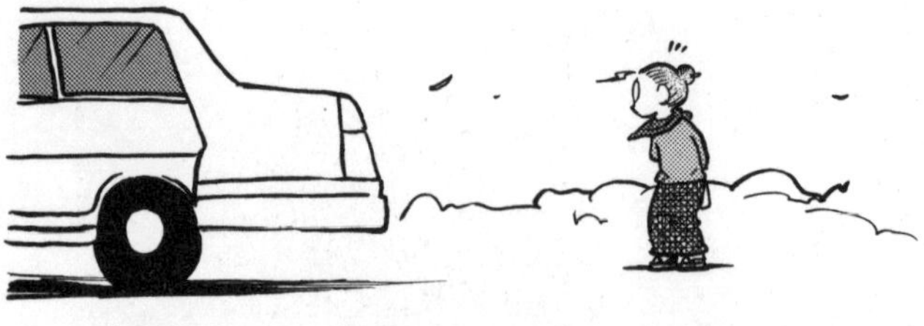

CITY

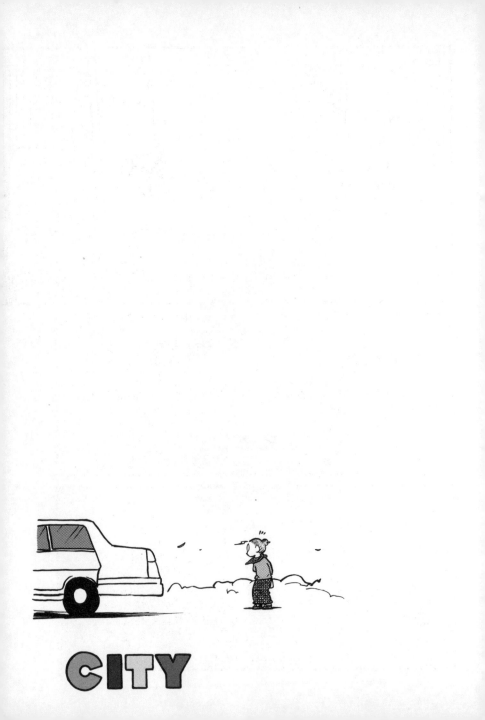

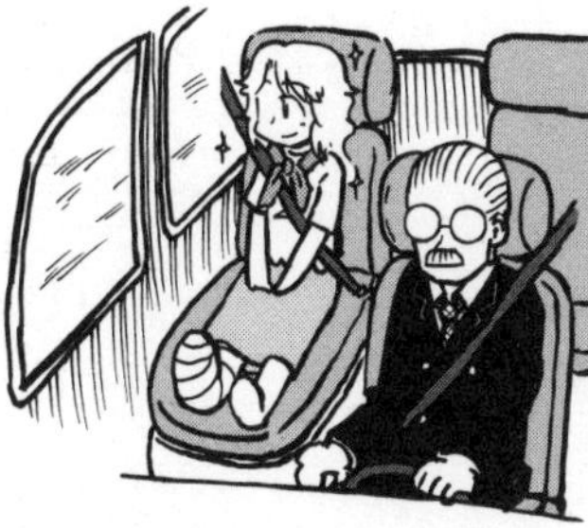

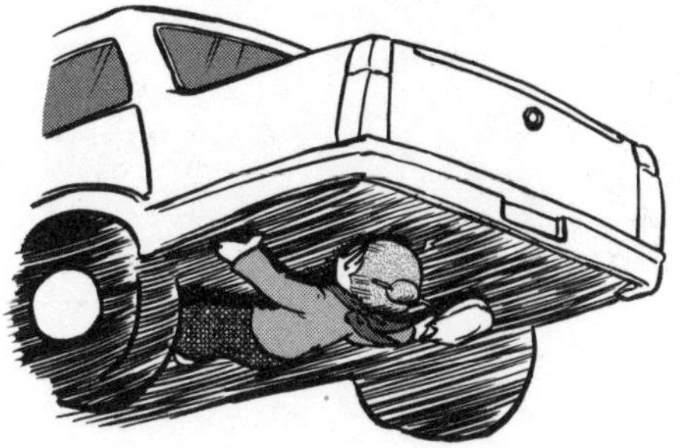

CITY

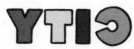

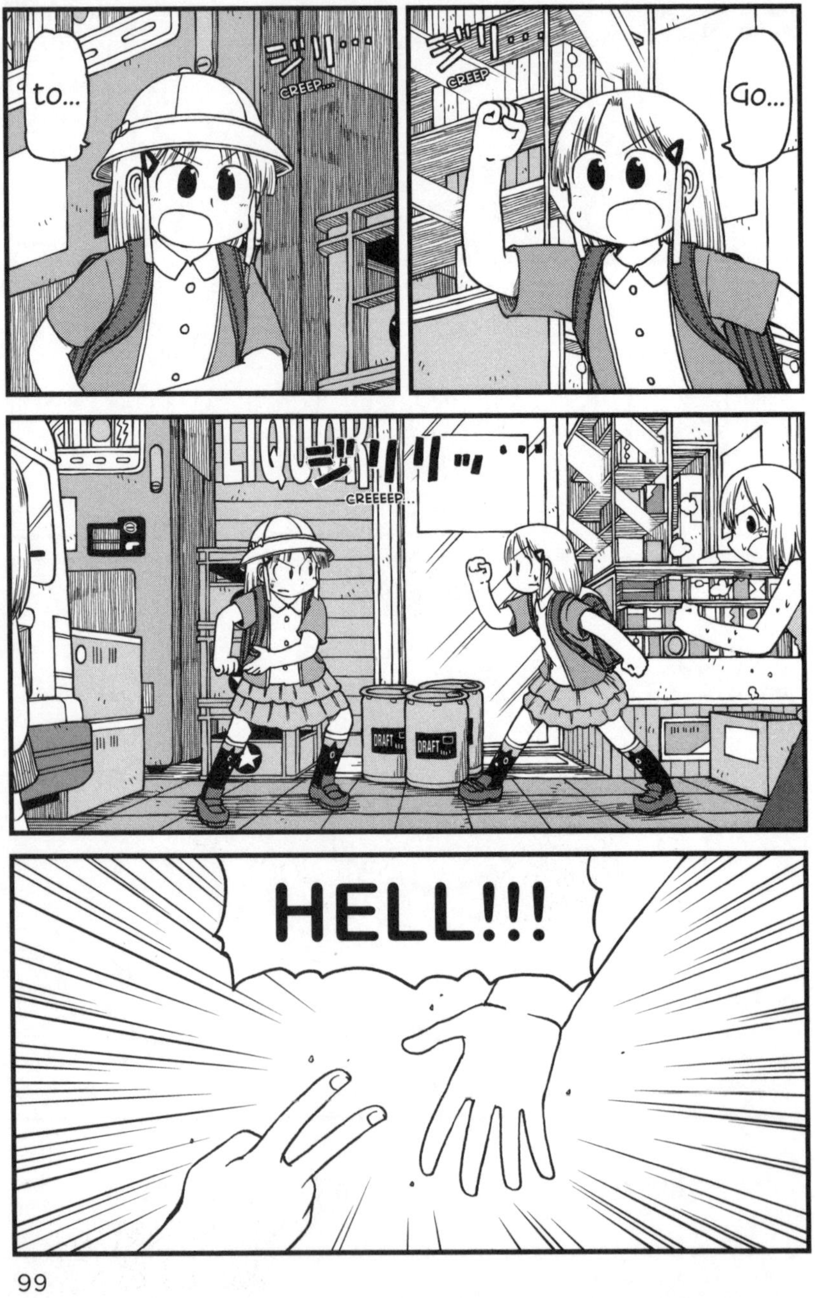
Go...
CREEP
to...
CREEP...
CREEEEP...
HELL!!!

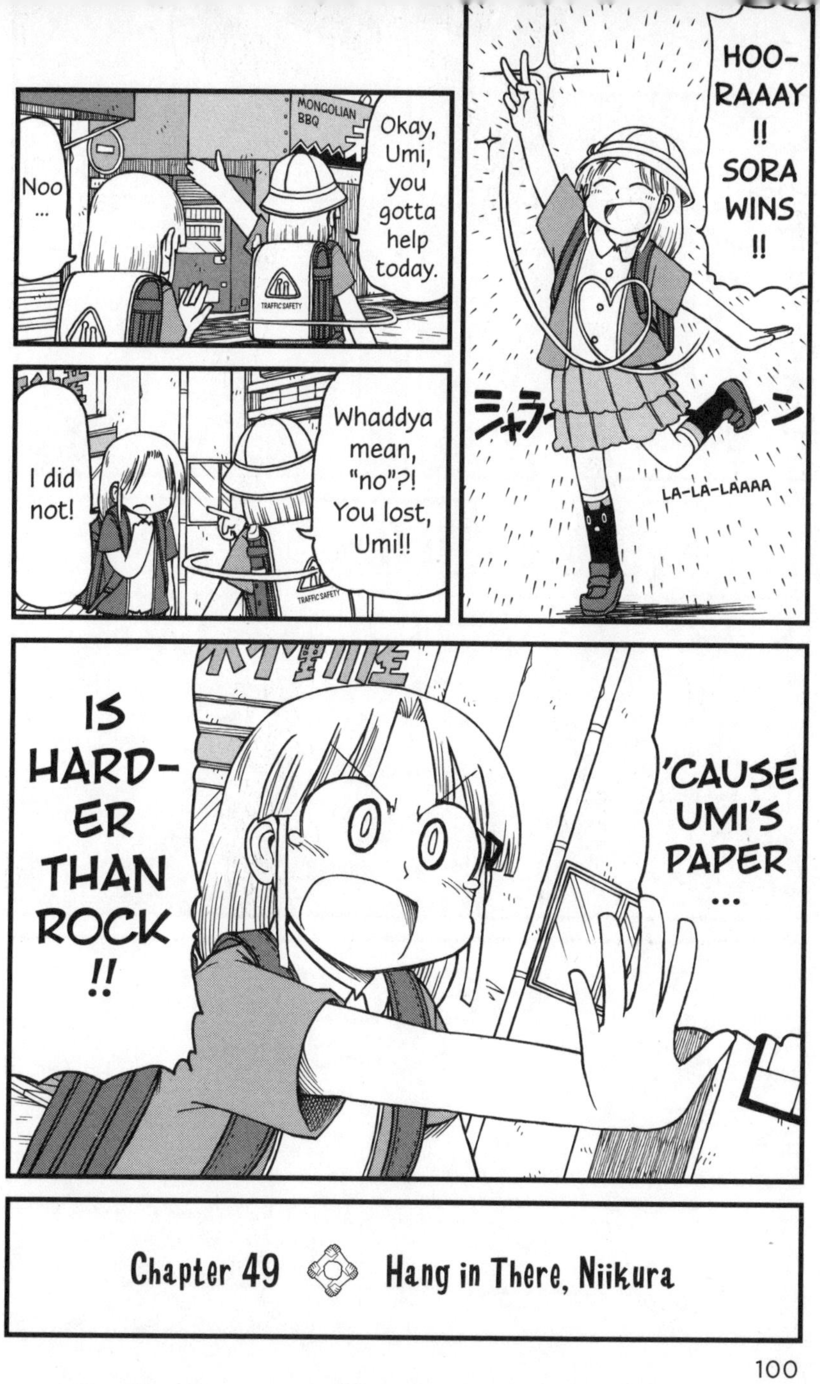
HOO-RAAAY!! SORA WINS!!
LA-LA-LAAAA
MONGOLIAN BBQ
Okay, Umi, you gotta help today.
Noo ...
TRAFFIC SAFETY
Whaddya mean, "no"?! You lost, Umi!!
I did not!
TRAFFIC SAFETY
'CAUSE UMI'S PAPER ...
IS HARDER-ER THAN ROCK!!

Chapter 49 ◇ Hang in There, Niikura

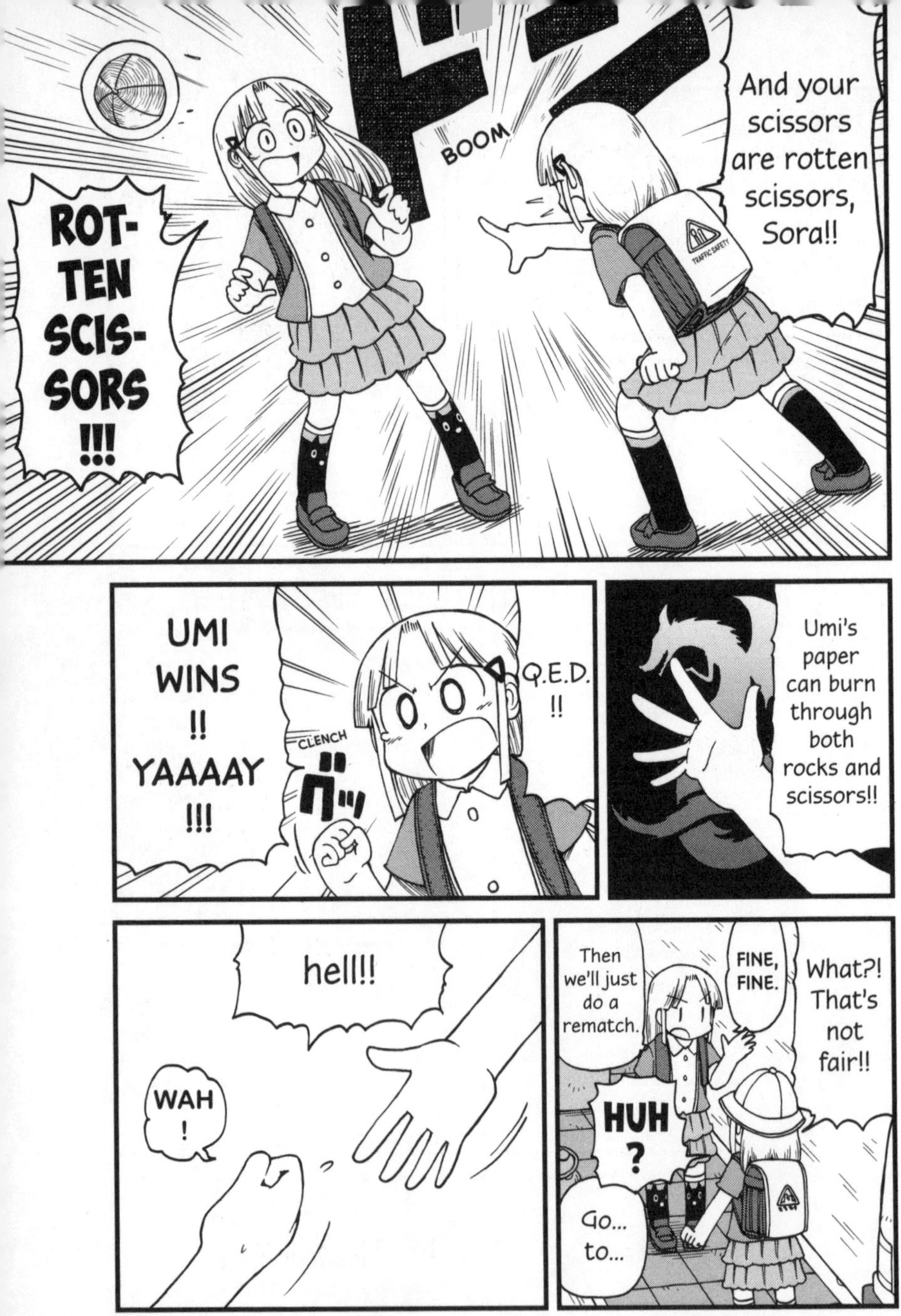
And your scissors are rotten scissors, Sora!!
BOOM
ROT-TEN SCIS-SORS!!!
Umi's paper can burn through both rocks and scissors!!
Q.E.D. !!
UMI WINS!! YAAAAY!!!
CLENCH
What?! That's not fair!!
FINE, FINE.
Then we'll just do a rematch.
HUH?
Go... to...
hell!!
WAH!

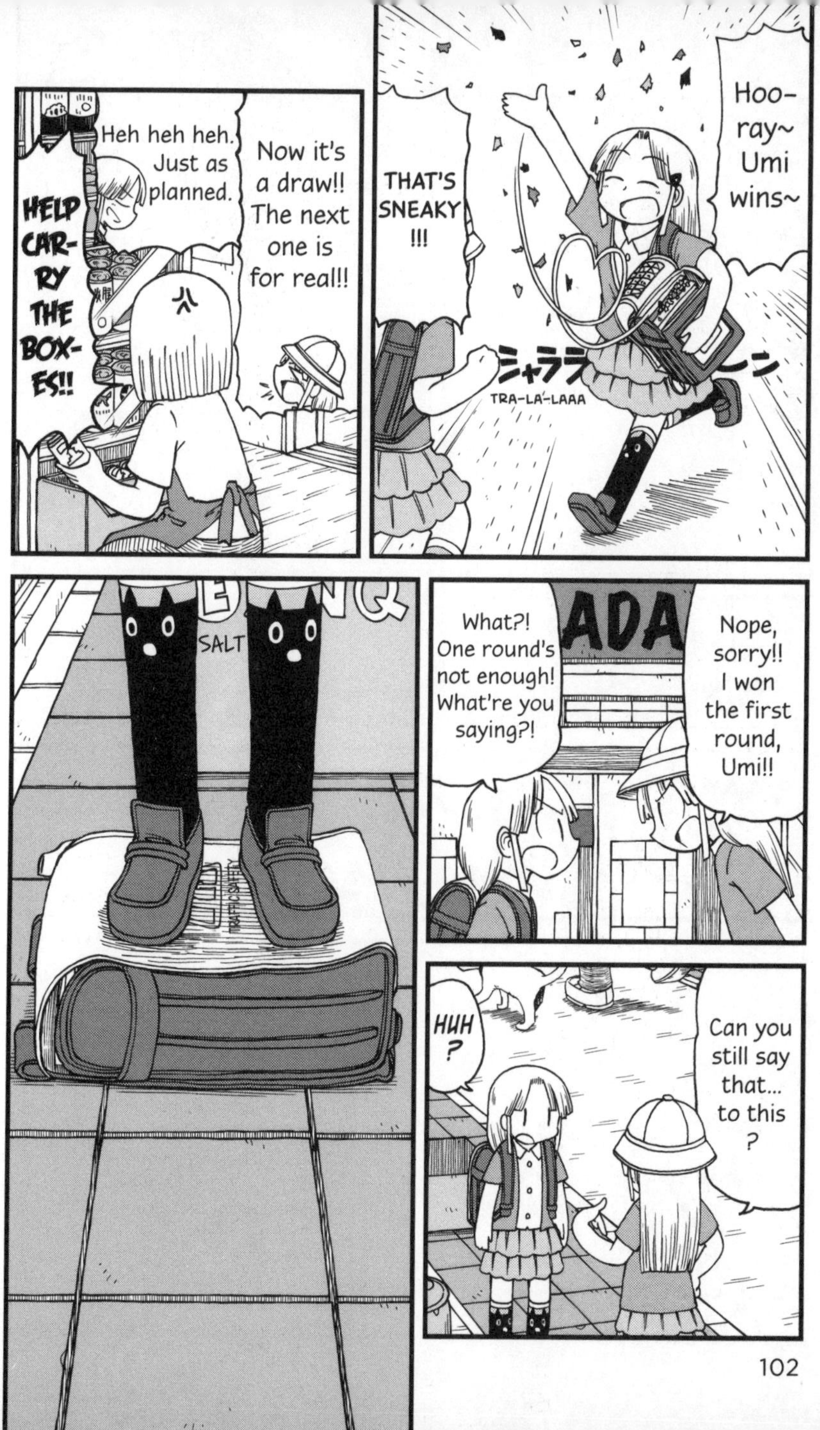

Hoo-ray~ Umi wins~
THAT'S SNEAKY!!!
シャララーン
TRA-LA-LAAA
Now it's a draw!! The next one is for real!!
Heh heh heh. Just as planned.
HELP CARRY THE BOXES!!
ADA
Nope, sorry!! I won the first round, Umi!!
What?! One round's not enough! What're you saying?!
Can you still say that... to this?
HUH?
SALT
TRAFFIC SAFETY

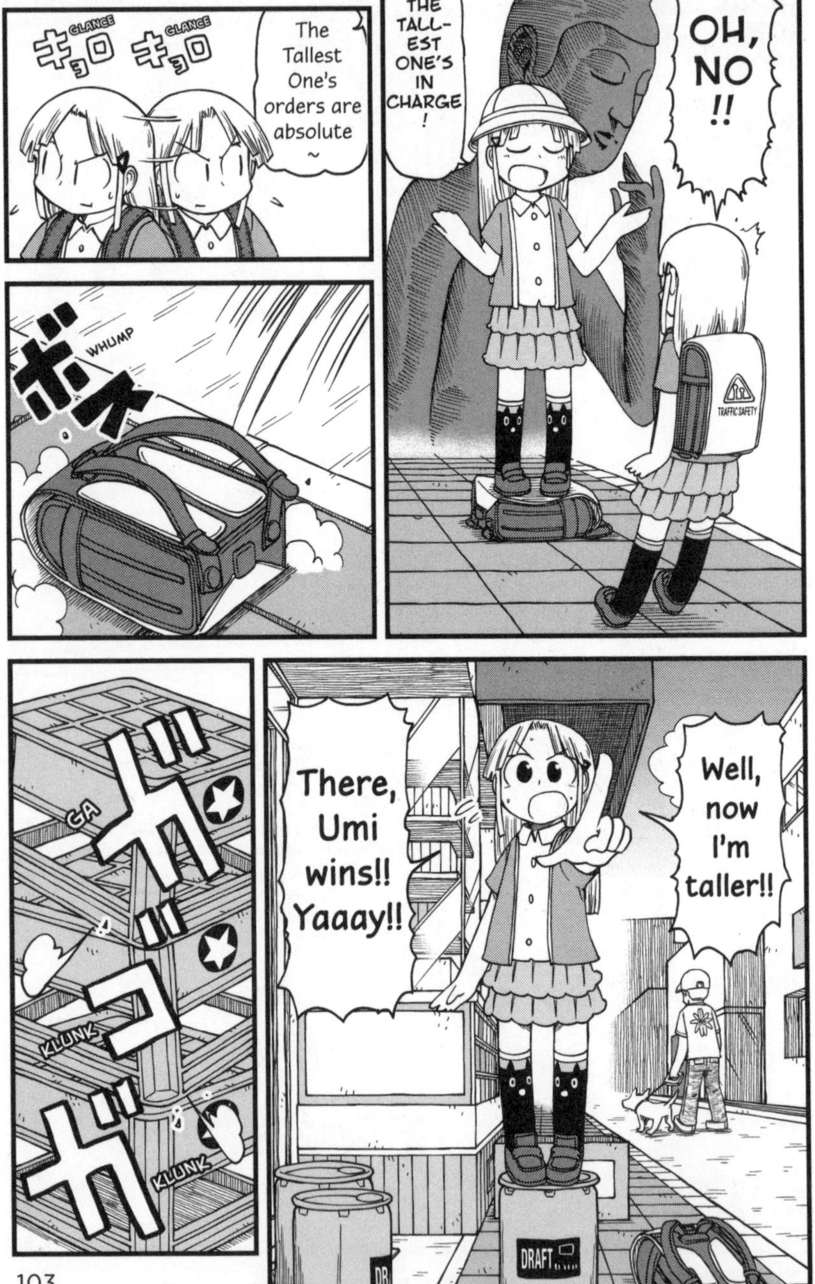
OH, NO!!
THE TALLEST ONE'S IN CHARGE!
TRAFFIC SAFETY
キョロ GLANCE キョロ GLANCE
The Tallest One's orders are absolute ~
ボス WHUMP
Well, now I'm taller!!
There, Umi wins!! Yaaay!!
DRAFT
GA
KLUNK
KLUNK

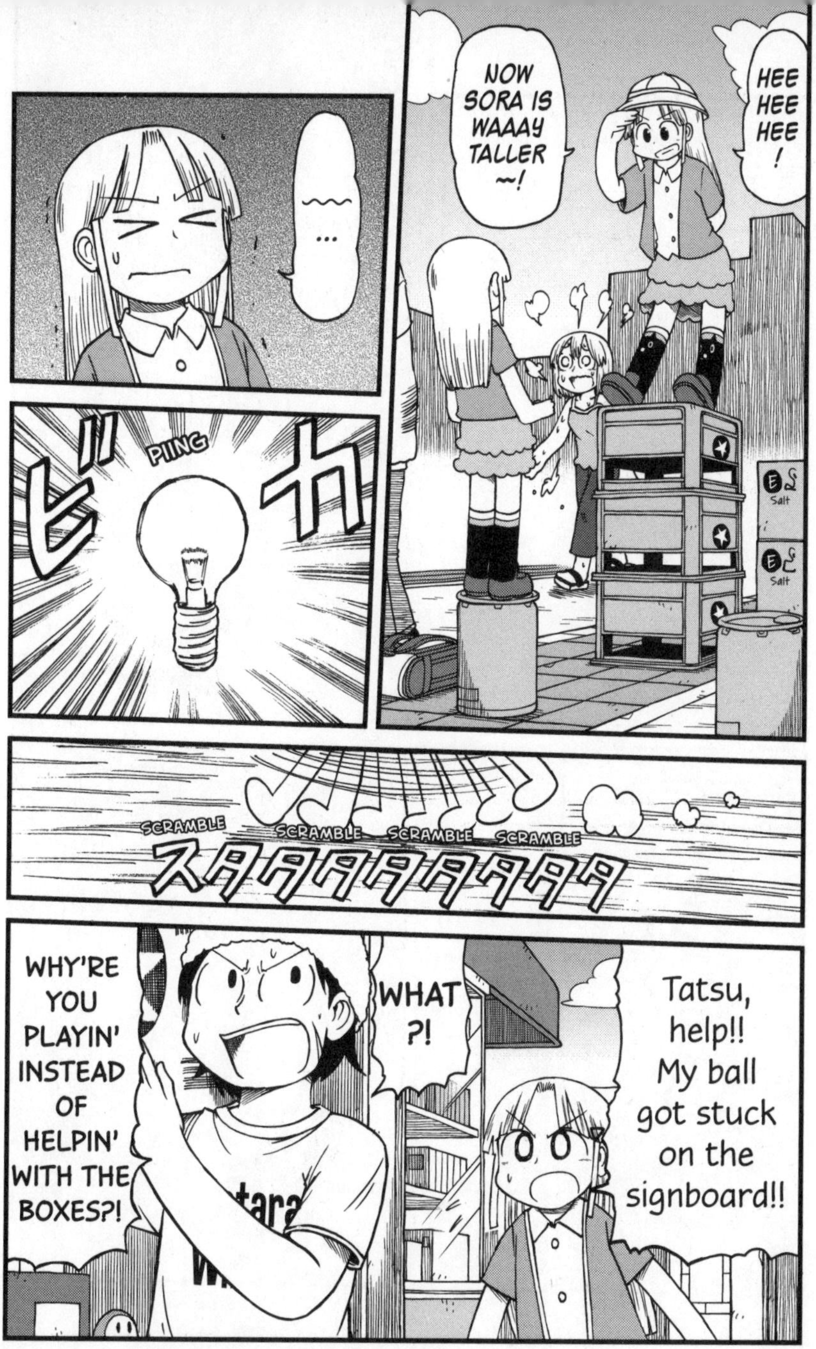
HEE HEE HEE!
NOW SORA IS WAAAY TALLER ~!
Salt
Salt
~~~ ...
ビカ
PIING
スタタタタタタタタタ
SCRAMBLE
SCRAMBLE
SCRAMBLE
SCRAMBLE
Tatsu, help!! My ball got stuck on the signboard!!
WHAT?!
WHY'RE YOU PLAYIN' INSTEAD OF HELPIN' WITH THE BOXES?!
~~~

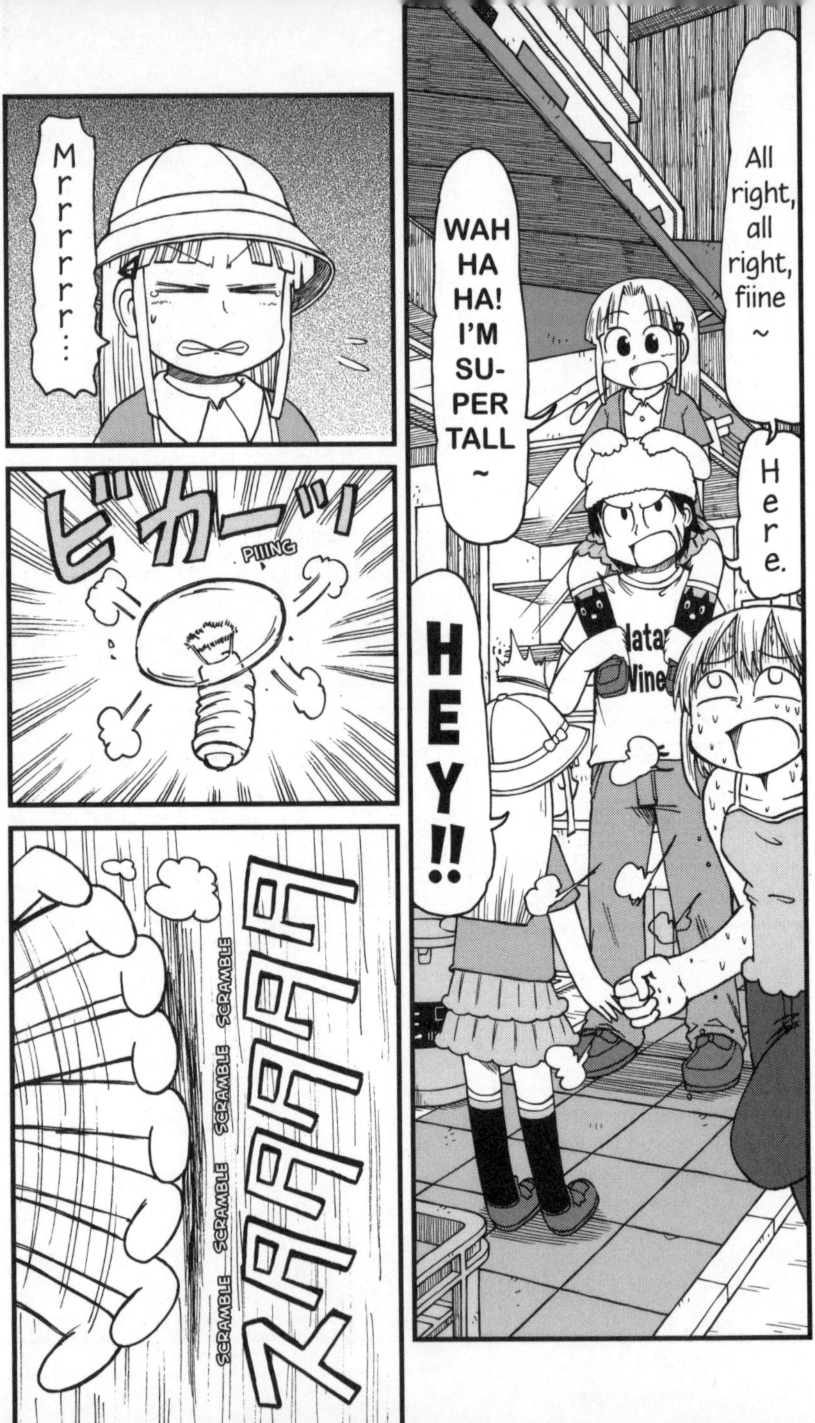
All right, all right, fiine ~
WAH HA HA! I'M SU-PER TALL ~
Here.
HEY!!
Mrrrrrr…
PIIING
SCRAMBLE SCRAMBLE SCRAMBLE SCRAMBLE SCRAMBLE

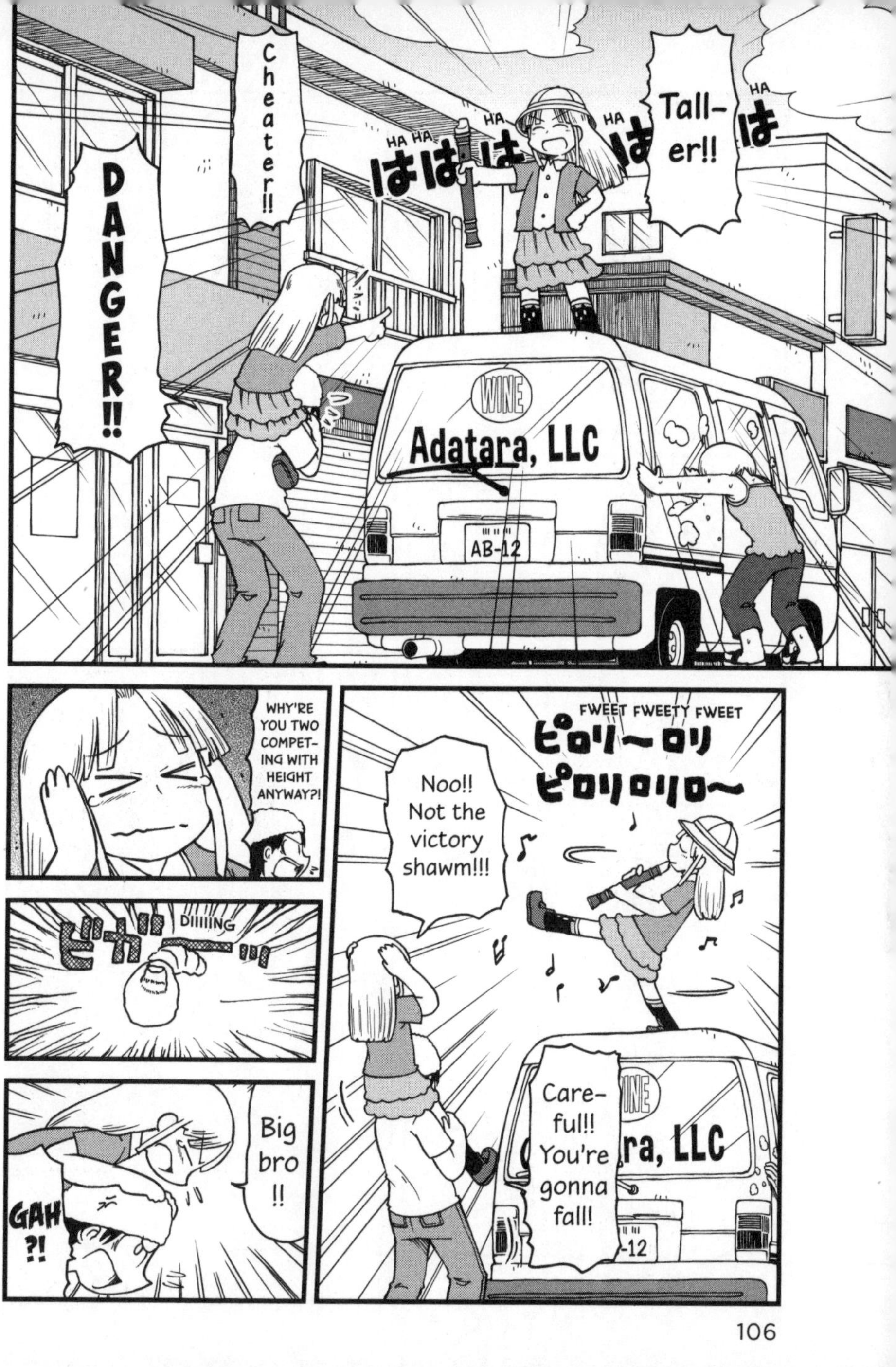
HA
は
Tall—
er!!
HA
は
HA
は
HA HA
はは
Cheater!!
DANGER!!
WINE
Adatara, LLC
AB-12
FWEET FWEETY FWEET
ピロリ～ロリ
ピロリロリロ～
Noo!! Not the victory shawm!!!
Care-ful!! You're gonna fall!
WINE
ra, LLC
-12
WHY'RE YOU TWO COMPET-ING WITH HEIGHT ANYWAY?!
DIIIIING
ピカーーッ
Big bro !!
GAH ?!

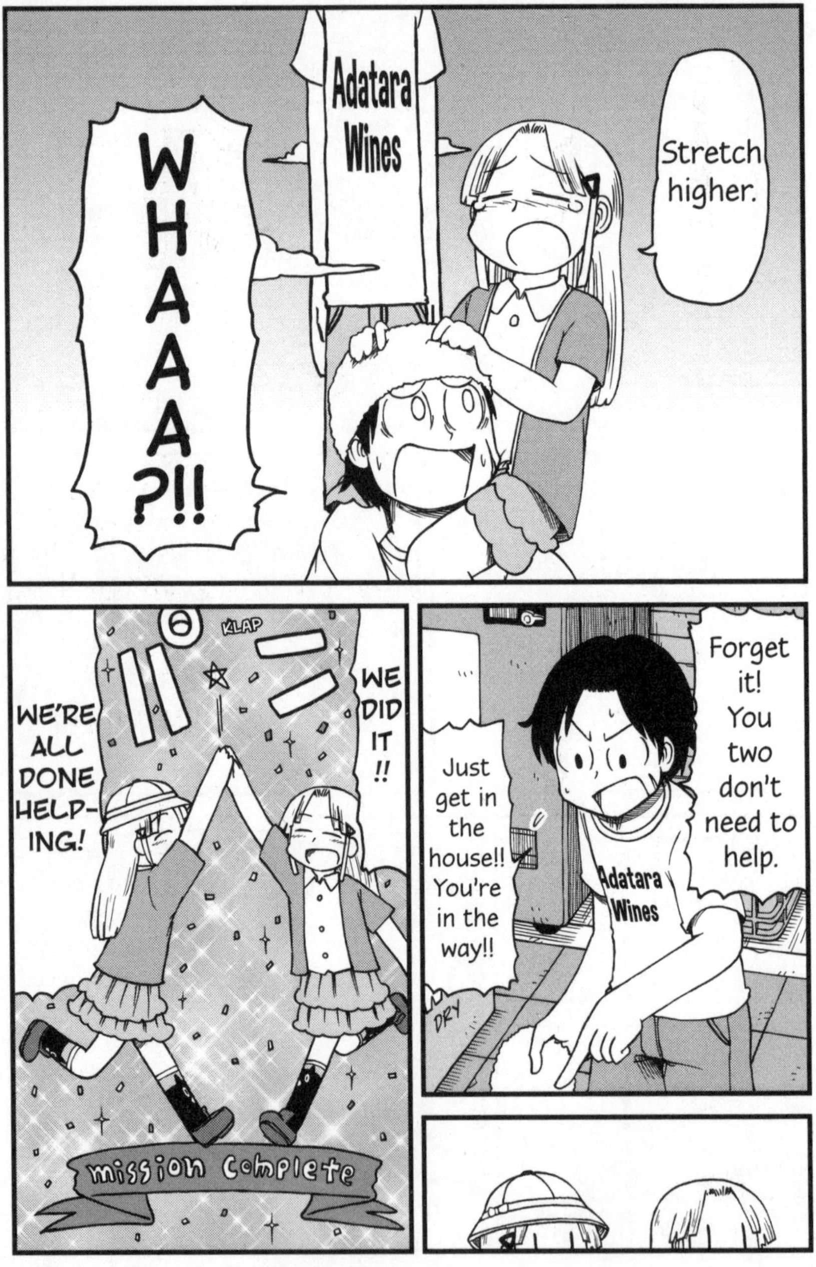
Stretch higher.
Adatara Wines
WHAAAA?!!
Forget it! You two don't need to help.
Just get in the house!! You're in the way!!
Adatara Wines
DRY
KLAP
WE DID IT!!
WE'RE ALL DONE HELPING!
mission complete

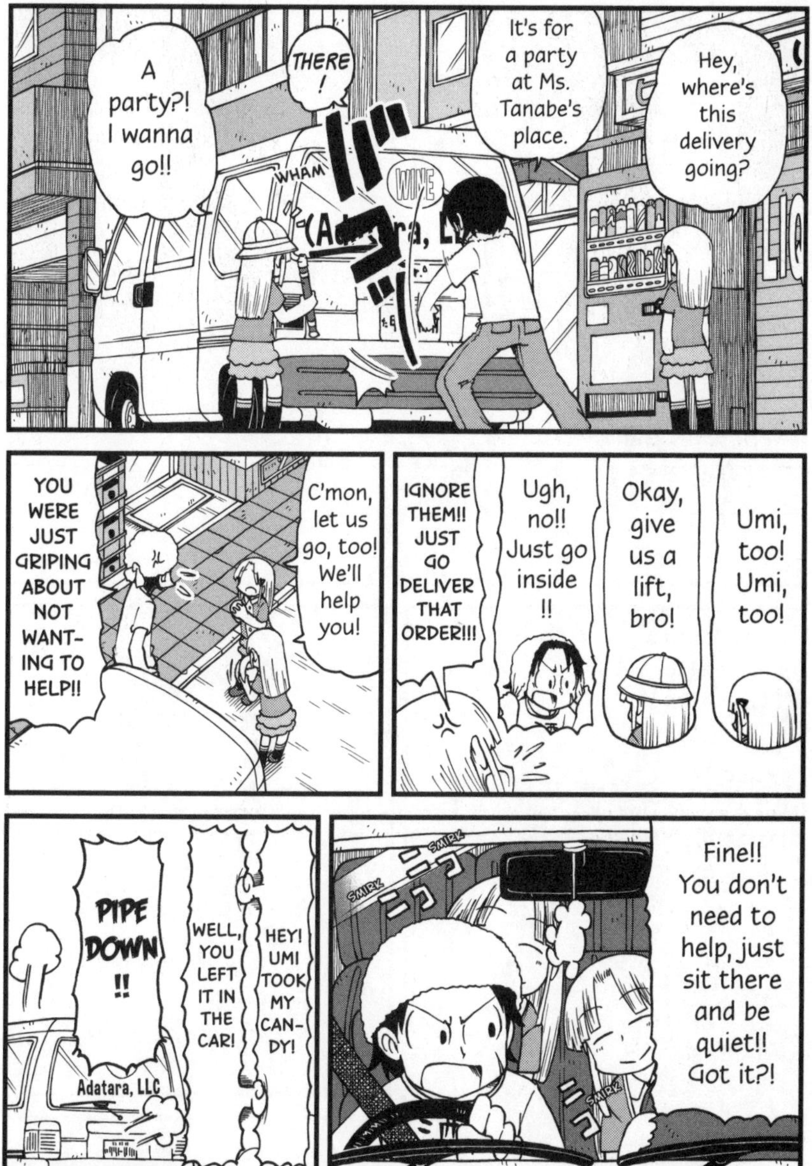
Hey, where's this delivery going?
It's for a party at Ms. Tanabe's place.
THERE!
A party?! I wanna go!!
WHAM
WINE
Umi, too! Umi, too!
Okay, give us a lift, bro!
Ugh, no!! Just go inside !!
IGNORE THEM!! JUST GO DELIVER THAT ORDER!!!
C'mon, let us go, too! We'll help you!
YOU WERE JUST GRIPING ABOUT NOT WANTING TO HELP!!
Fine!! You don't need to help, just sit there and be quiet!! Got it?!
SMIRK
SMIRK
SMIRK
HEY! UMI TOOK MY CANDY!
WELL, YOU LEFT IT IN THE CAR!
PIPE DOWN !!
Adatara, LLC
VROOOOOOM

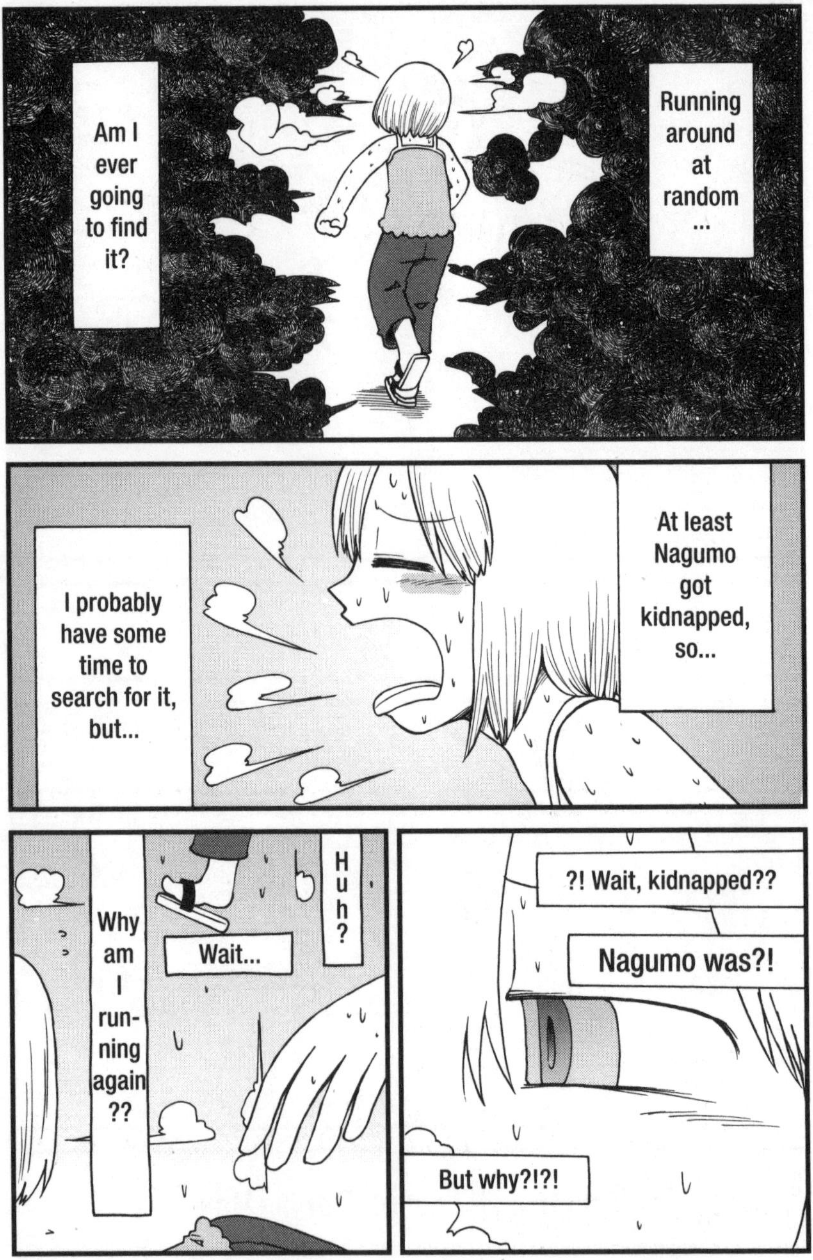
Running around at random ...
Am I ever going to find it?
At least Nagumo got kidnapped, so...
I probably have some time to search for it, but...
?! Wait, kidnapped??
Nagumo was?!
But why?!?!
Huh?
Wait...
Why am I run-ning again??

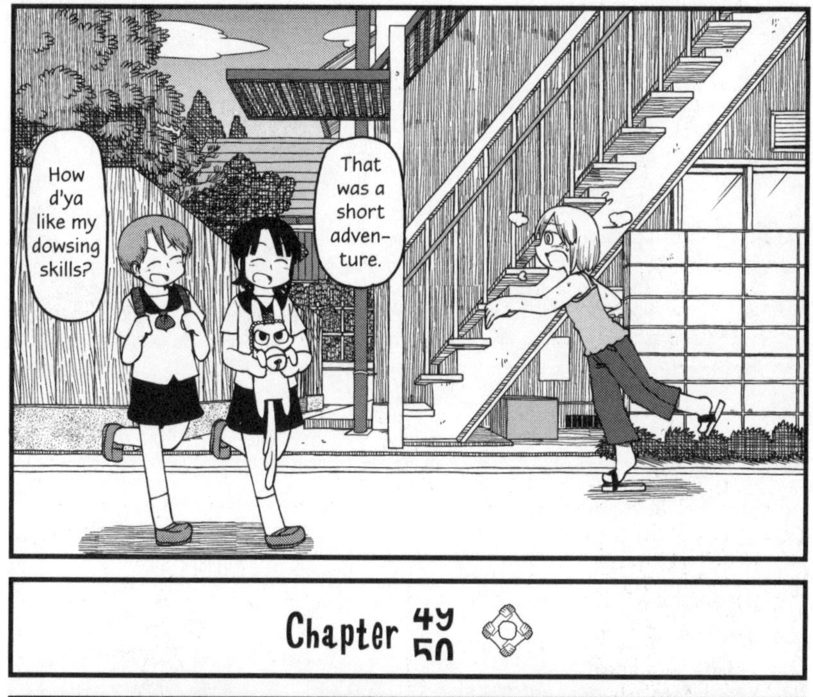
That was a short adven-ture.
How d'ya like my dowsing skills?

Chapter 49 50

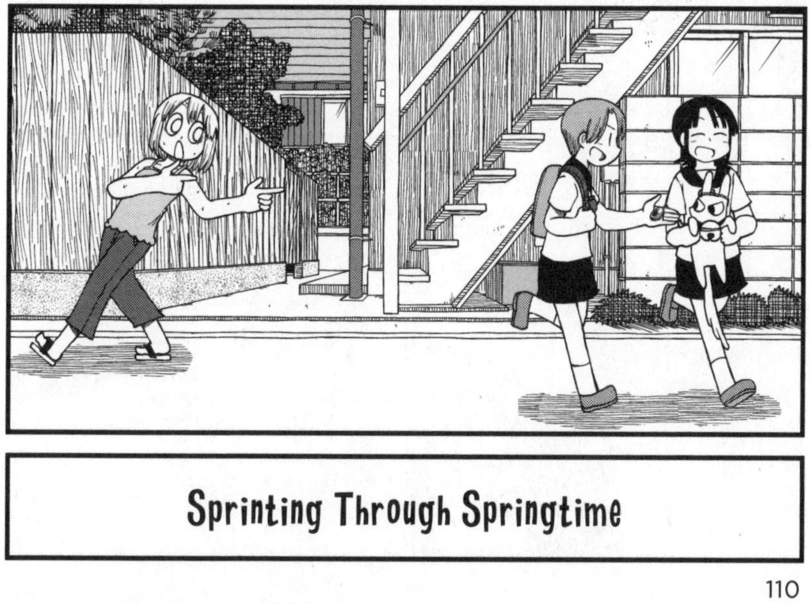

Sprinting Through Springtime

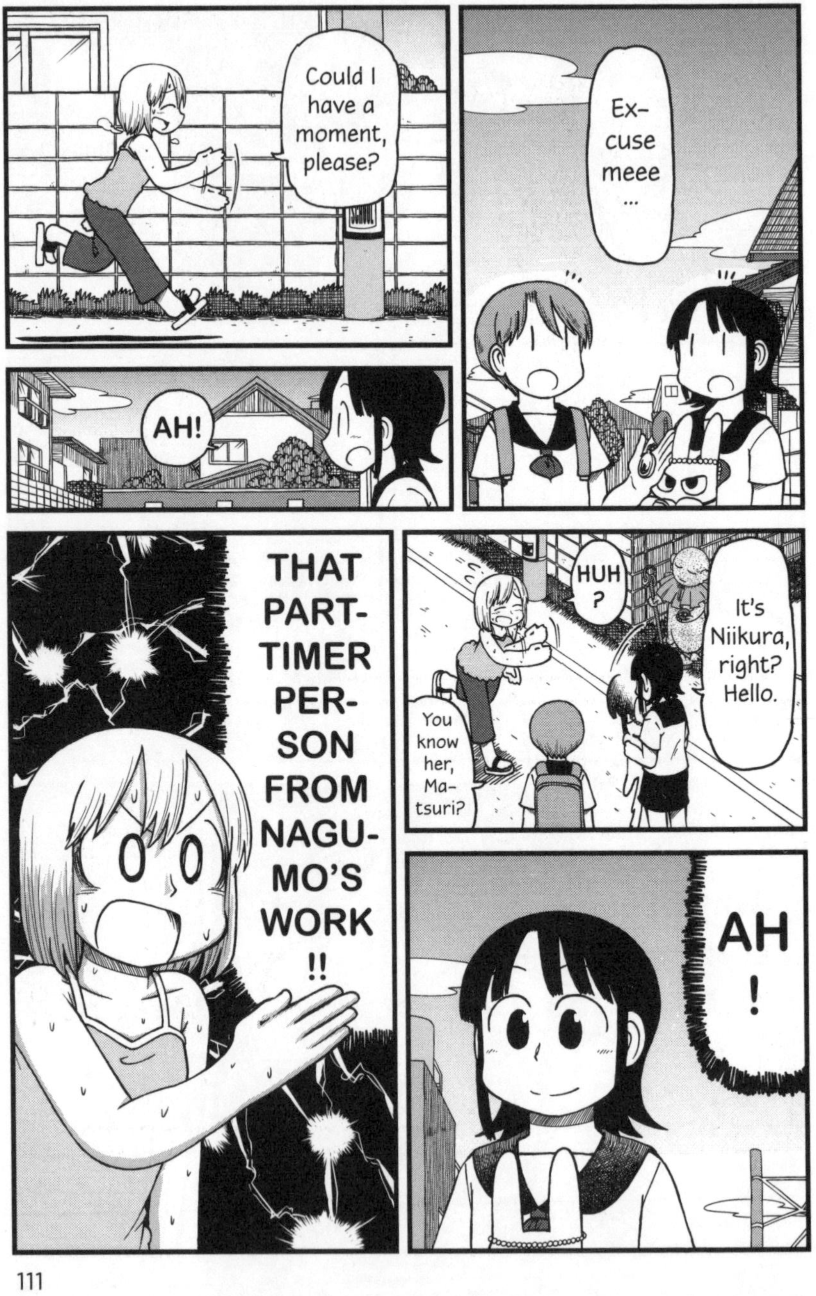
Ex–cuse meee ...
Could I have a moment, please?
AH!
It's Niikura, right? Hello.
HUH ?
You know her, Ma-tsuri?
AH !
THAT PART-TIMER PER-SON FROM NAGU-MO'S WORK !!

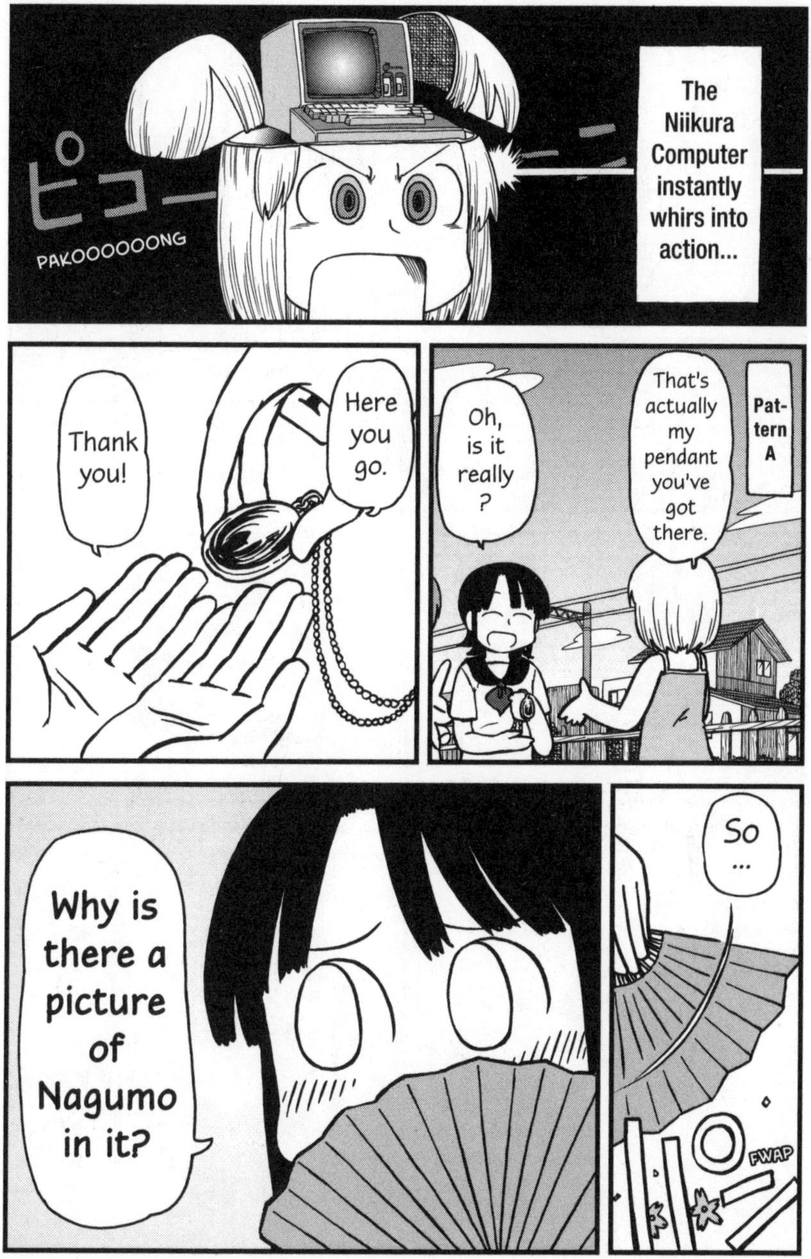

The Niikura Computer instantly whirs into action...
ピコー
PAKOOOOOONG
Pattern A
That's actually my pendant you've got there.
Oh, is it really?
Here you go.
Thank you!
So ...
FWAP
Why is there a picture of Nagumo in it?

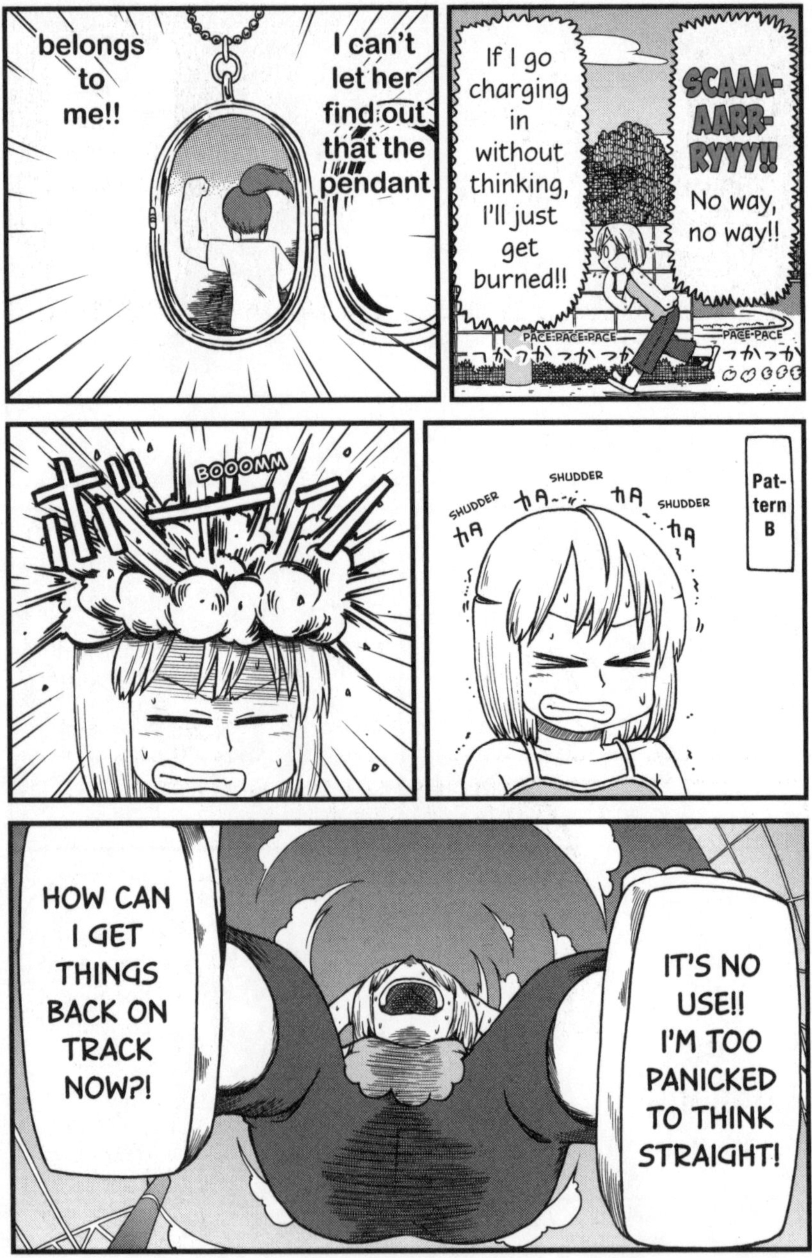
SCAAA-AARR-RYYY!!
No way, no way!!
If I go charging in without thinking, I'll just get burned!!
PACE PACE
PACE PACE PACE
I can't let her find out that the pendant
belongs to me!!
Pat-tern B
SHUDDER
SHUDDER
SHUDDER
BOOOMM
IT'S NO USE!! I'M TOO PANICKED TO THINK STRAIGHT!
HOW CAN I GET THINGS BACK ON TRACK NOW?!

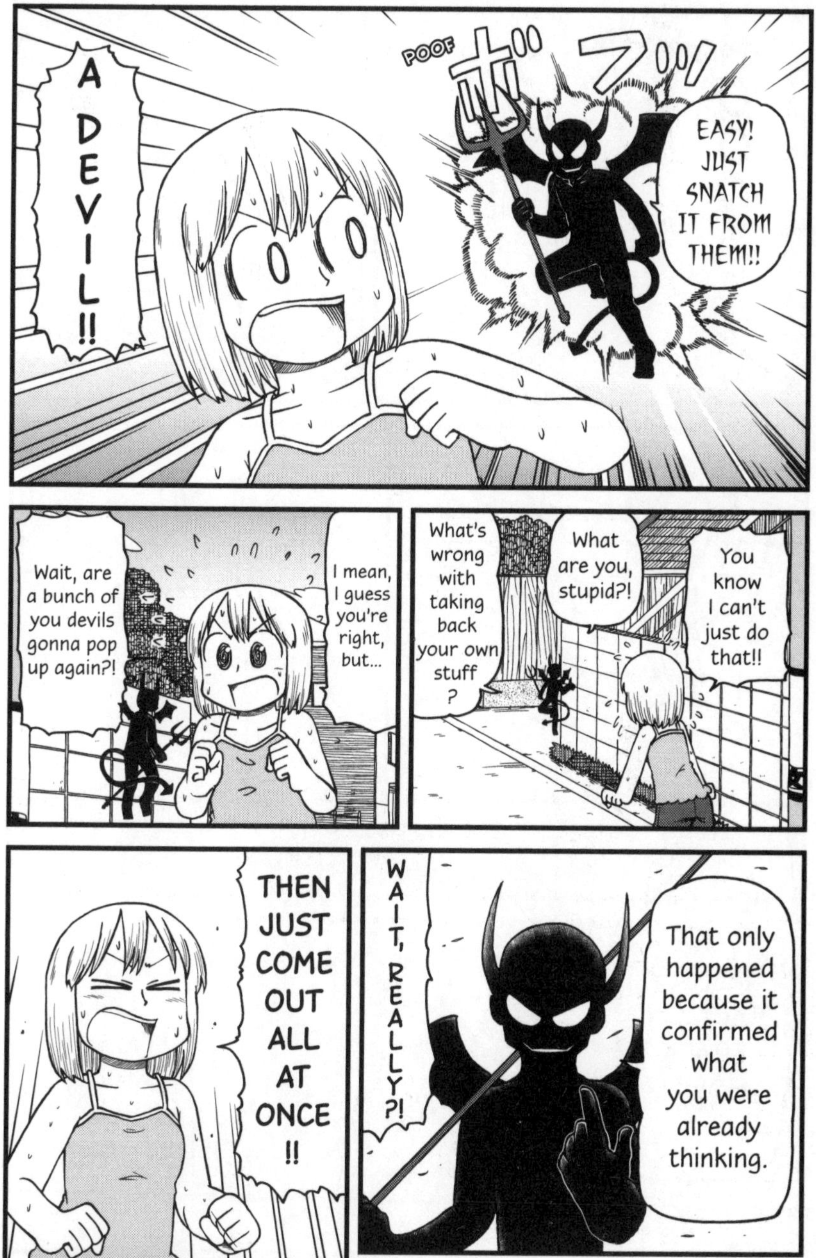
POOF
EASY! JUST SNATCH IT FROM THEM!!
A DEVIL!!
You know I can't just do that!!
What are you, stupid?!
What's wrong with taking back your own stuff?
I mean, I guess you're right, but...
Wait, are a bunch of you devils gonna pop up again?!
That only happened because it confirmed what you were already thinking.
WAIT, REALLY?!
THEN JUST COME OUT ALL AT ONCE!!

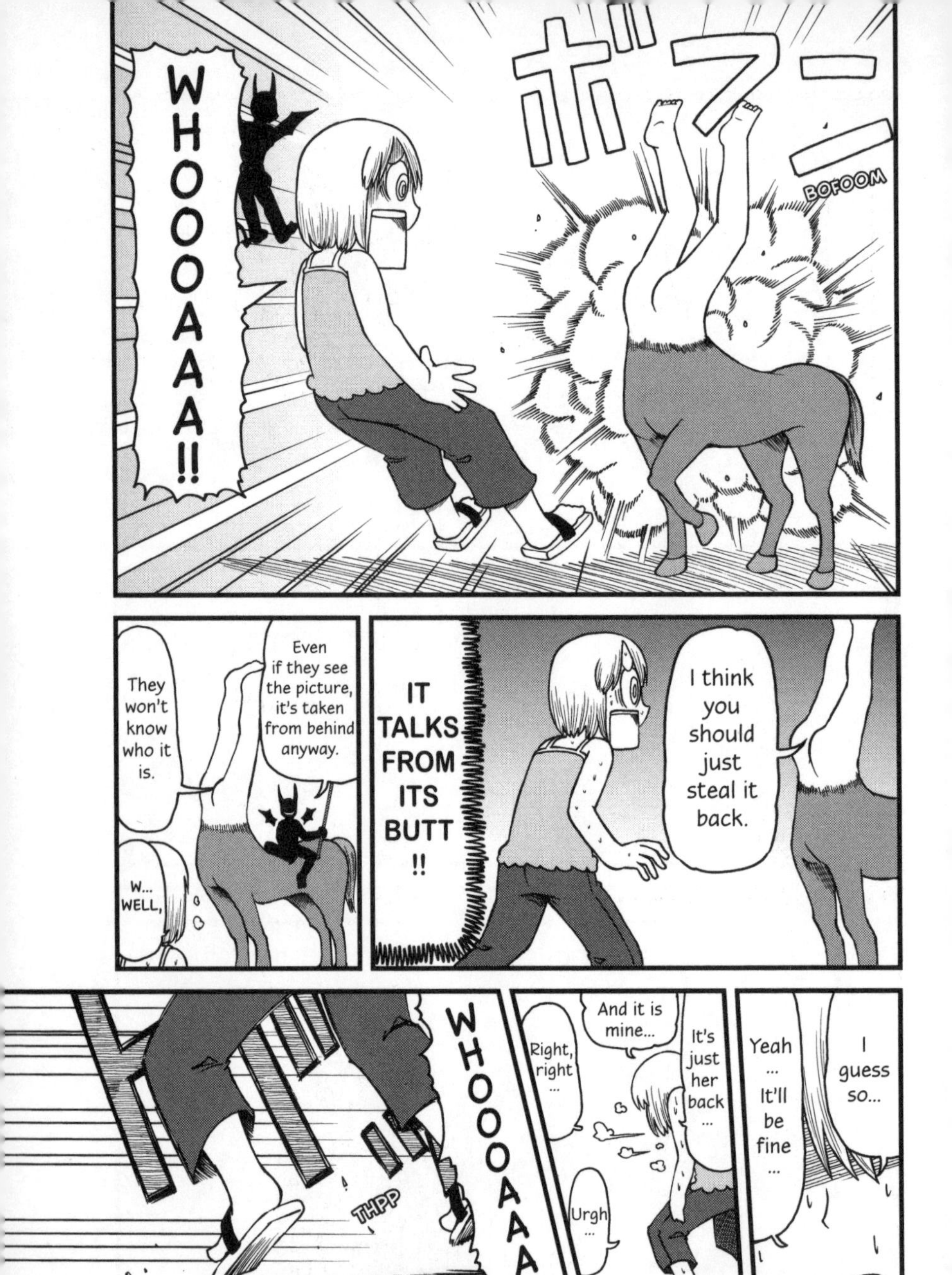

ボフーー
BOFOOM
WHOOOAAAA!!
I think you should just steal it back.
IT TALKS FROM ITS BUTT !!
Even if they see the picture, it's taken from behind anyway.
They won't know who it is.
W... WELL,
I guess so...
Yeah ... It'll be fine ...
It's just her back ...
And it is mine...
Right, right ...
Urgh ...
WHOOOAAA!
THPP

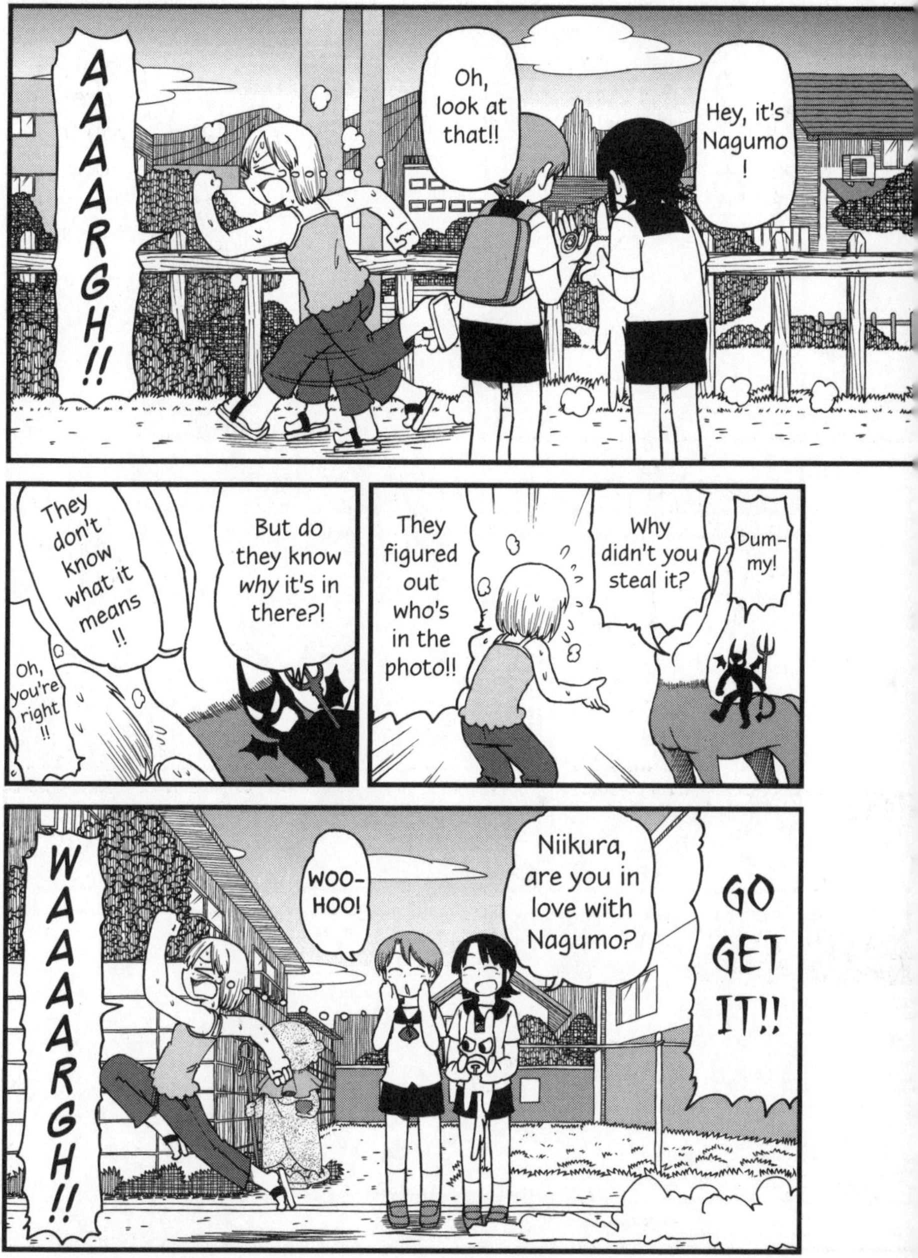
Hey, it's Nagumo!
Oh, look at that!!
AAAAARGH!!
Dum-my!
Why didn't you steal it?
They figured out who's in the photo!!
But do they know *why* it's in there?!
They don't know what it means!!
Oh, you're right!!
GO GET IT!!
Niikura, are you in love with Nagumo?
WOO-HOO!
WAAAAARGH!!

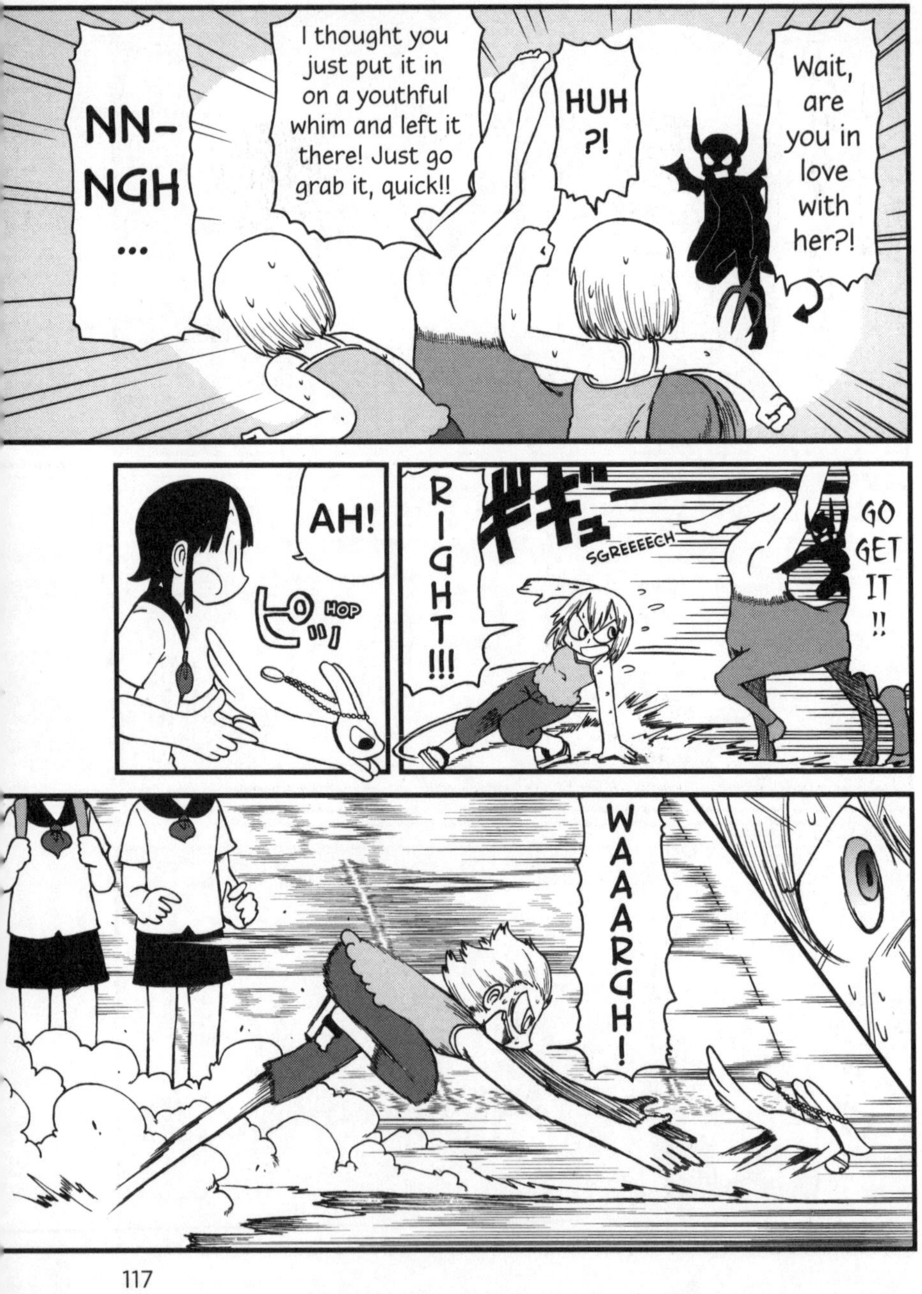
Wait, are you in love with her?!
HUH ?!
I thought you just put it in on a youthful whim and left it there! Just go grab it, quick!!
NN-NGH ...
GO GET IT !!
SGREEEECH
RIGHT!!!
AH!
HOP
WAAARGH!

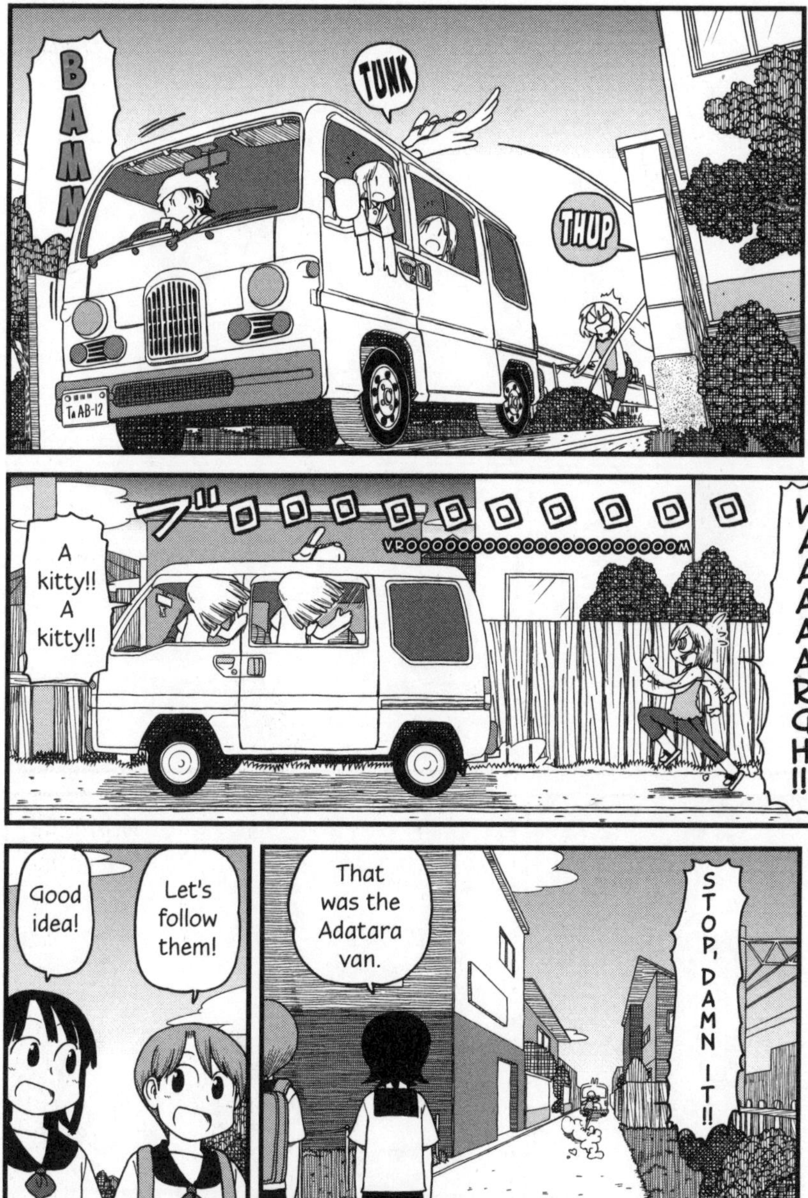
TUNK
BAMM
THUP
WAAAAARGH!!
ブロロロロロロロロロロ
VROOOOOOOOOOOOOOOOOOOOOM
A kitty!! A kitty!!
STOP, DAMN IT!!
That was the Adatara van.
Let's follow them!
Good idea!

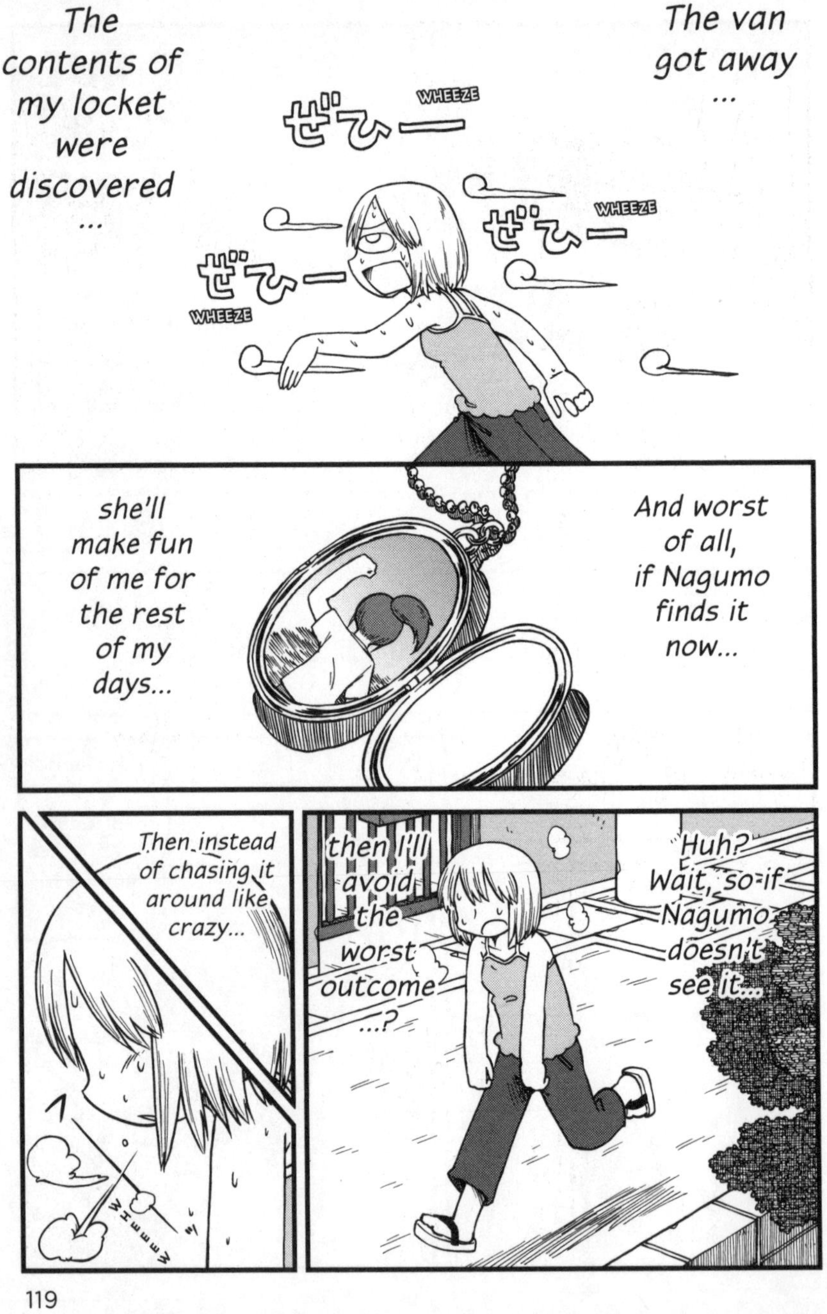
The van got away ...
The contents of my locket were discovered ...
ぜひー
WHEEZE
ぜひー
WHEEZE
ぜひー
WHEEZE
And worst of all, if Nagumo finds it now...
she'll make fun of me for the rest of my days...
Huh? Wait, so if Nagumo doesn't see it...
then I'll avoid the worst outcome ...?
Then instead of chasing it around like crazy...
WHEEEEW

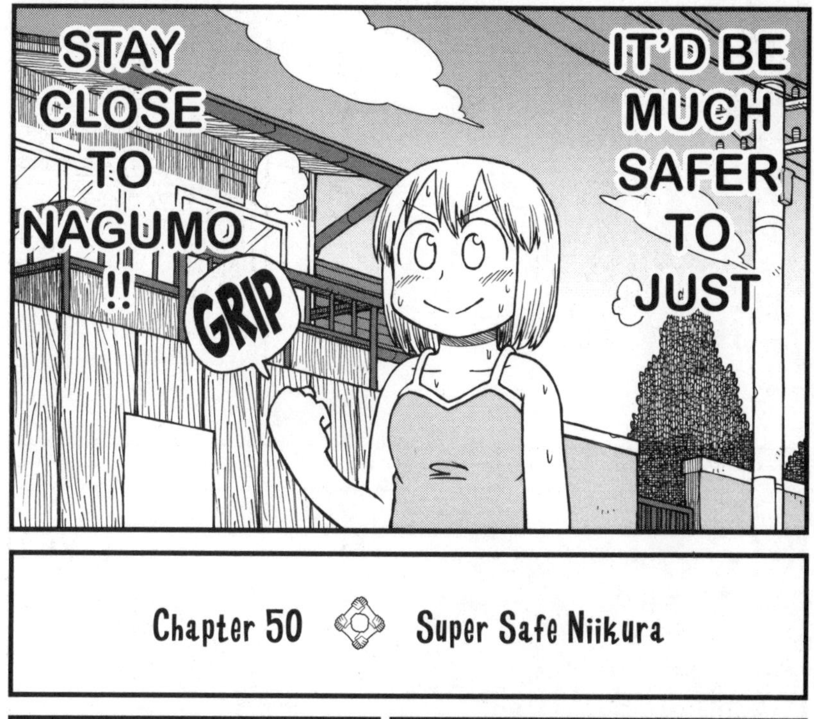
IT'D BE MUCH SAFER TO JUST
STAY CLOSE TO NAGUMO !!
GRIP

Chapter 50 Super Safe Niikura

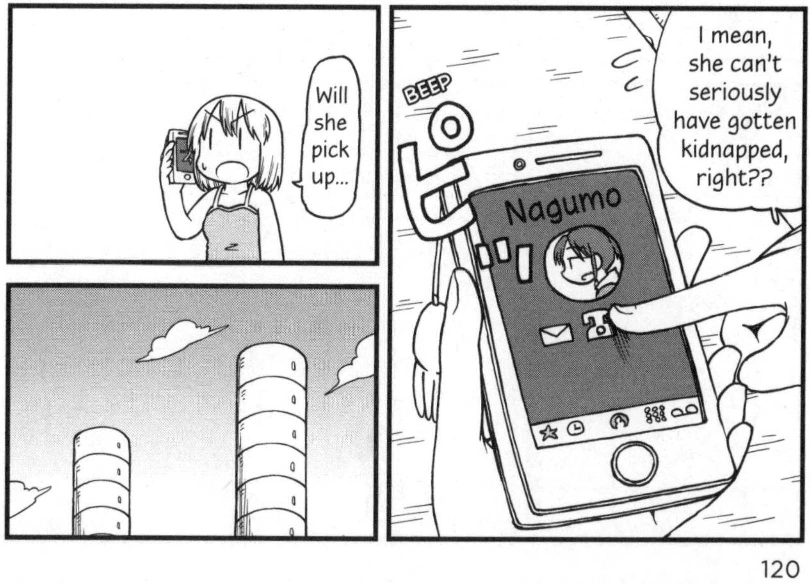
BEEP
I mean, she can't seriously have gotten kidnapped, right??
Nagumo
Will she pick up...

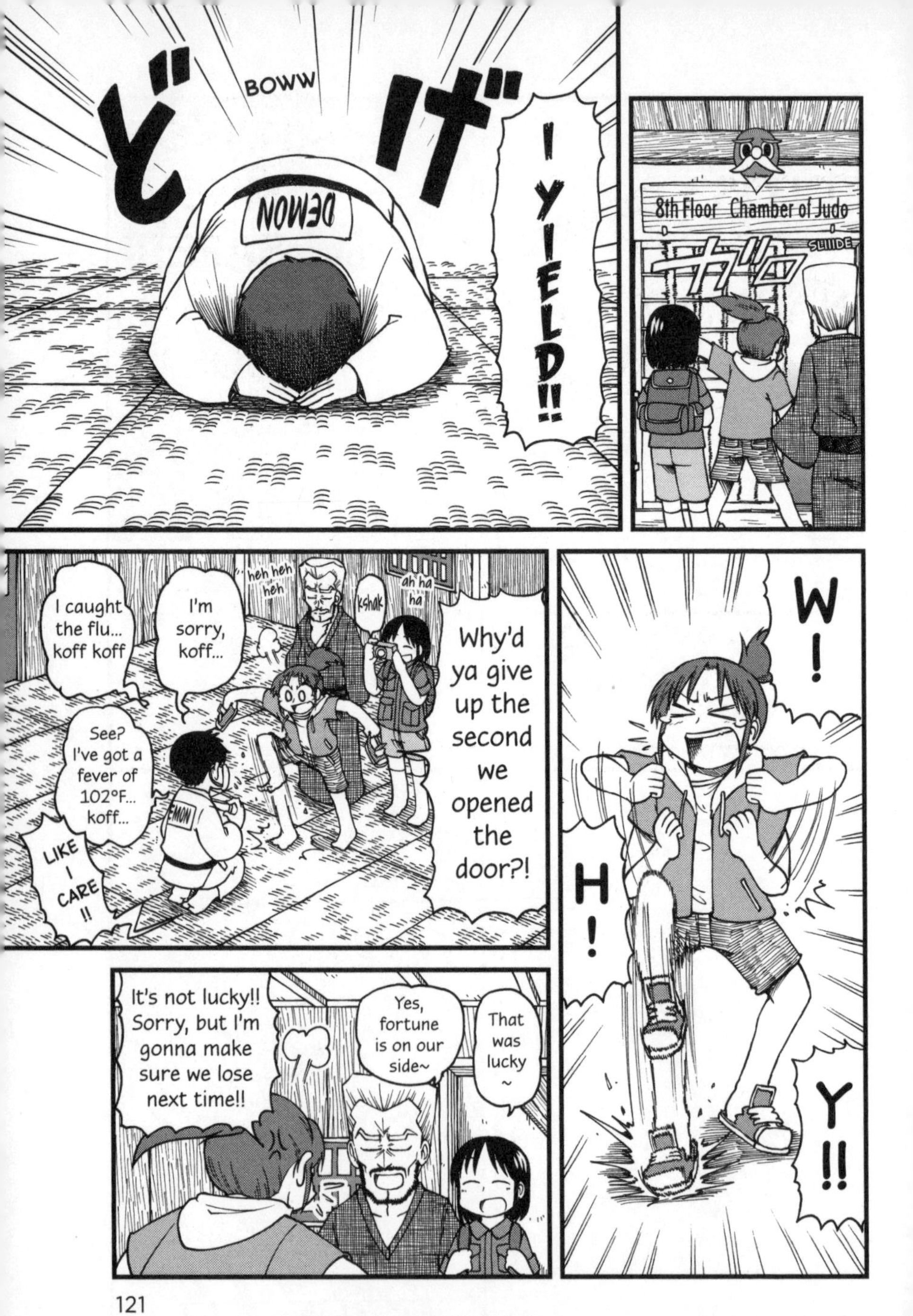
8th Floor Chamber of Judo
SLIIIDE
ど
BOWW
げ
DEMON
I YIELD!!
W! H! Y!!
Why'd ya give up the second we opened the door?!
ah ha ha
kshak
heh heh heh
I'm sorry, koff...
I caught the flu... koff koff
See? I've got a fever of 102°F... koff...
EMON
LIKE I CARE!!
That was lucky ~
Yes, fortune is on our side~
It's not lucky!! Sorry, but I'm gonna make sure we lose next time!!

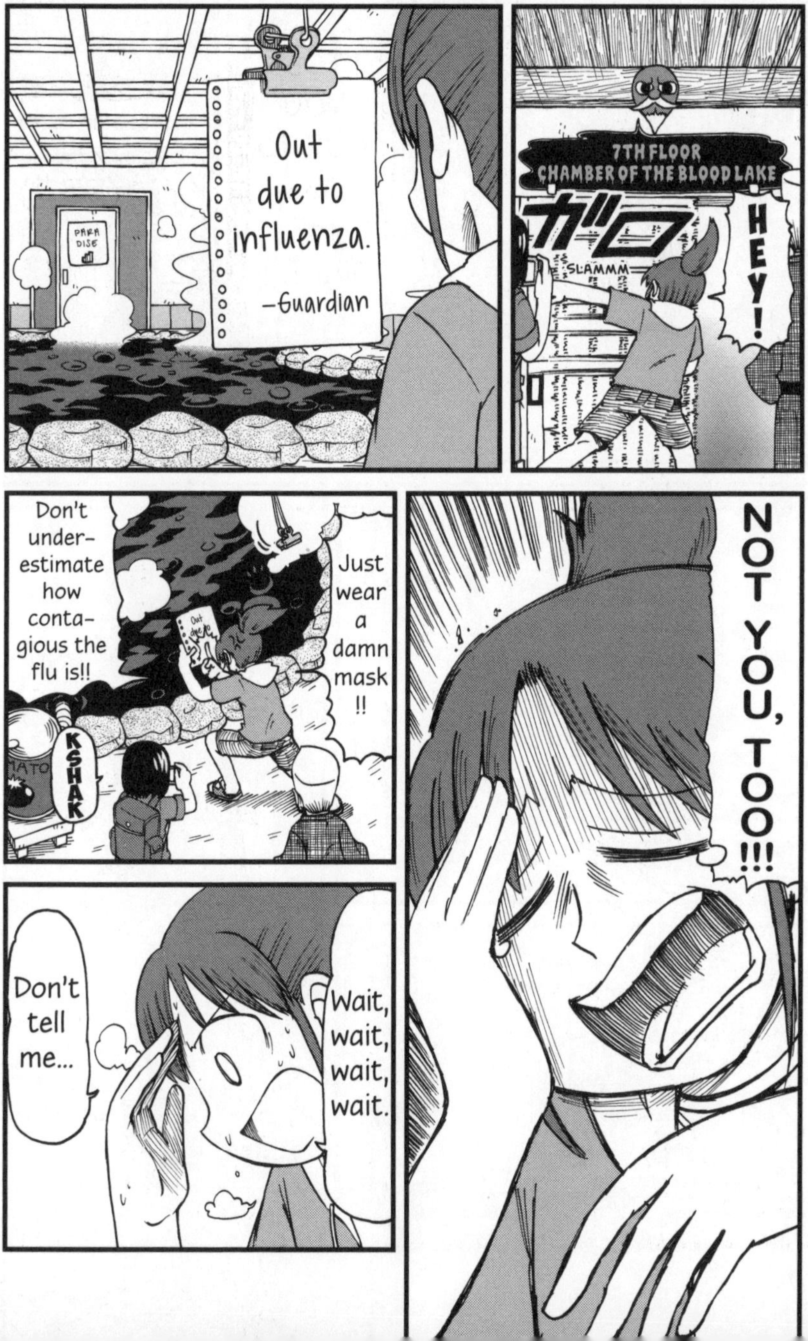
7TH FLOOR
CHAMBER OF THE BLOOD LAKE
ガロ
SLAMMM
HEY!
Out due to influenza.
–Guardian
PARA DISE
NOT YOU, TOO!!!
Just wear a damn mask!!
Don't underestimate how contagious the flu is!!
KSHAK
Wait, wait, wait, wait.
Don't tell me...

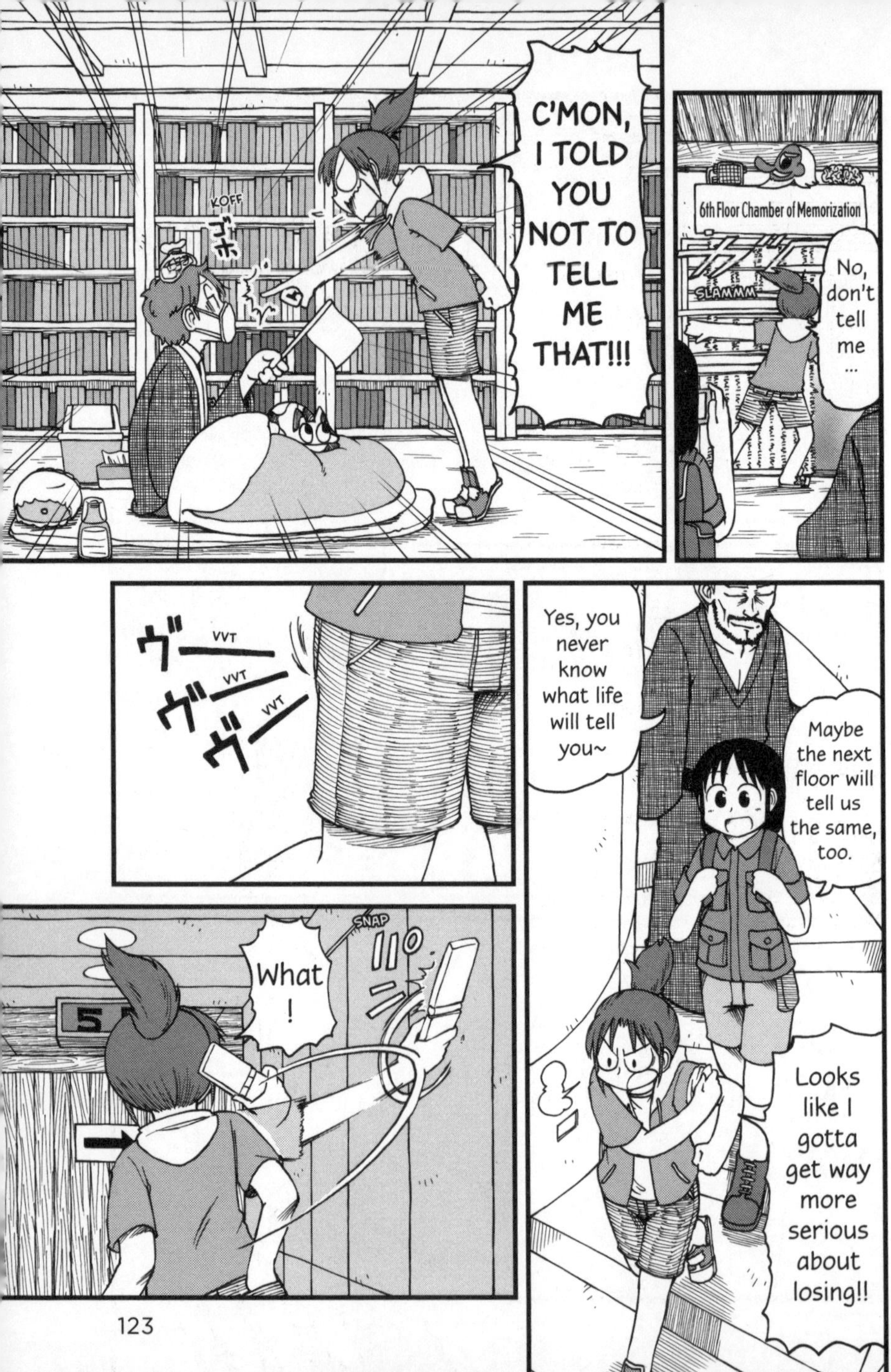
6th Floor Chamber of Memorization
SLAMMM
No, don't tell me ...
KOFF
ゴホ
C'MON, I TOLD YOU NOT TO TELL ME THAT!!!
Yes, you never know what life will tell you~
Maybe the next floor will tell us the same, too.
Looks like I gotta get way more serious about losing!!
ヴー VVT
ヴー VVT
ヴー VVT
SNAP
What !

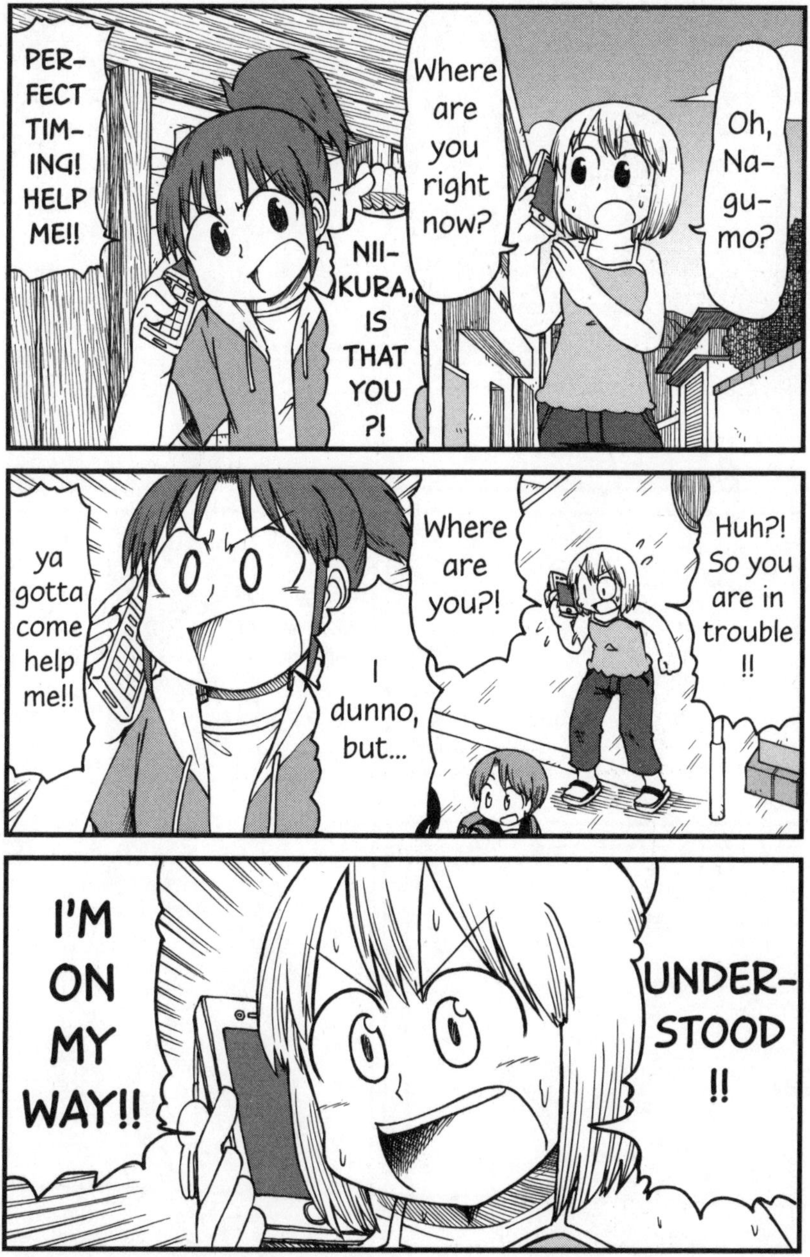
Oh, Na-gu-mo?
Where are you right now?
NII-KURA, IS THAT YOU?!
PER-FECT TIM-ING! HELP ME!!
Huh?! So you are in trouble!!
Where are you?!
I dunno, but...
ya gotta come help me!!
UNDER-STOOD!!
I'M ON MY WAY!!

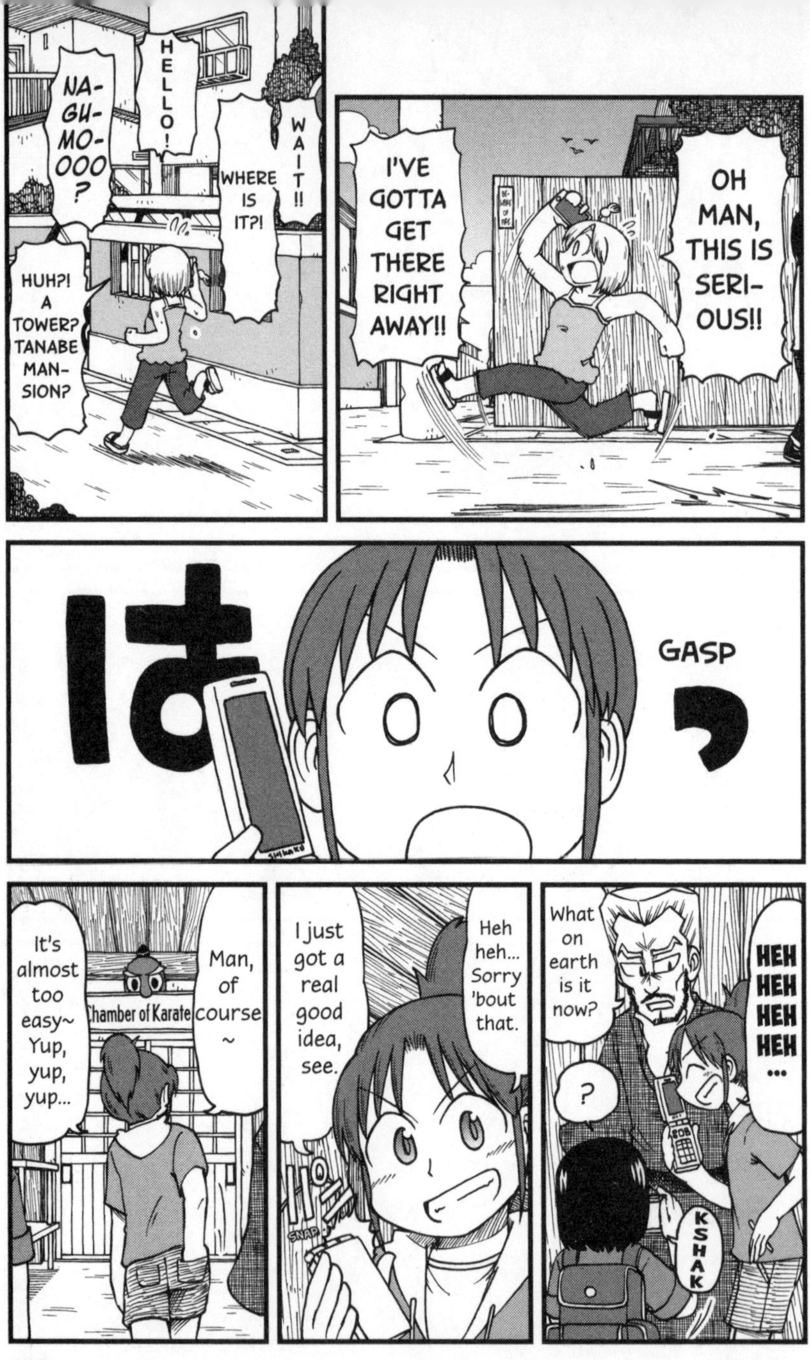
OH MAN, THIS IS SERI-OUS!!
I'VE GOTTA GET THERE RIGHT AWAY!!
WAIT!!
WHERE IS IT?!
HELLO!
NA-GU-MO-OOO?
HUH?! A TOWER? TANABE MAN-SION?
はっ
GASP
HEH HEH HEH HEH...
What on earth is it now?
?
KSHAK
Heh heh... Sorry 'bout that.
I just got a real good idea, see.
SNAP
Man, of course~
Chamber of Karate
It's almost too easy~ Yup, yup, yup...

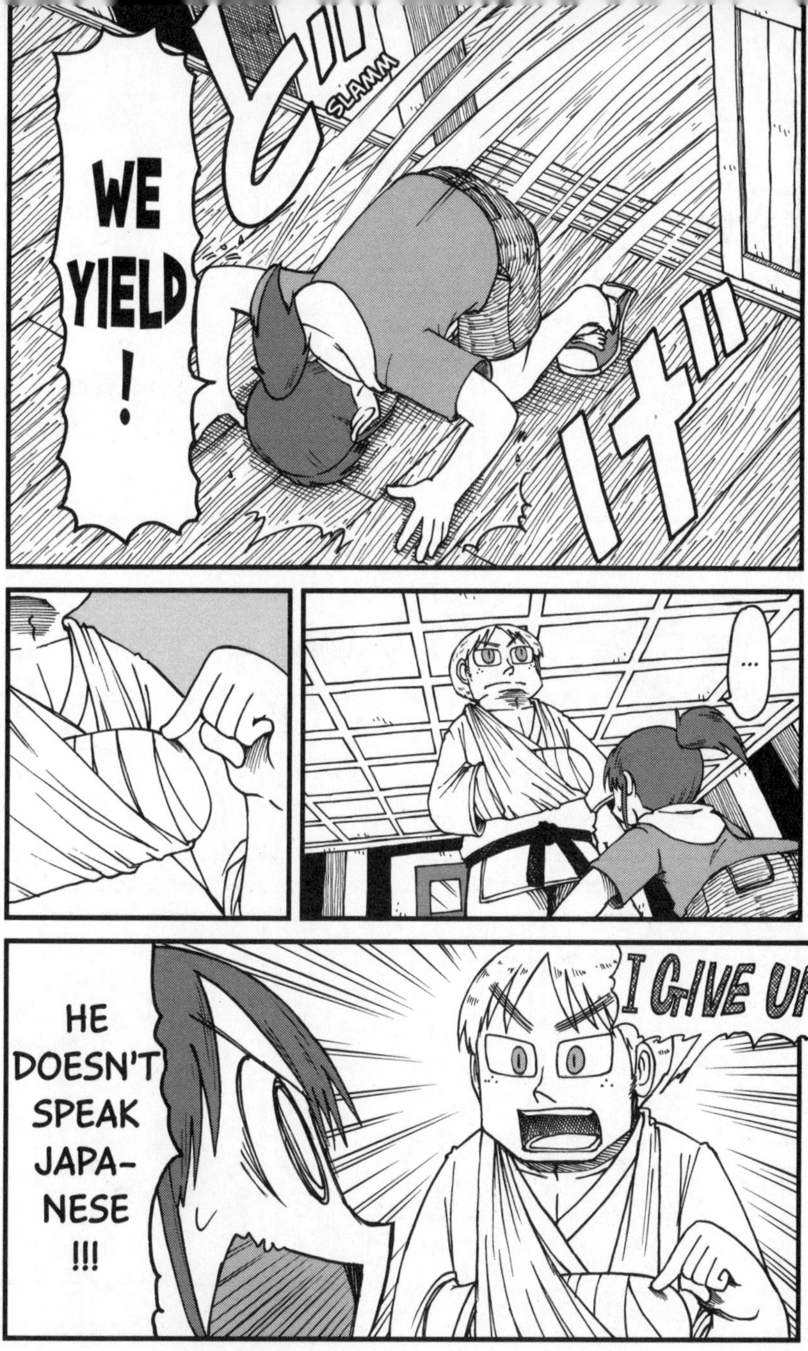
SLAMM
WE YIELD!
...
I GIVE UP!
HE DOESN'T SPEAK JAPA-NESE!!!

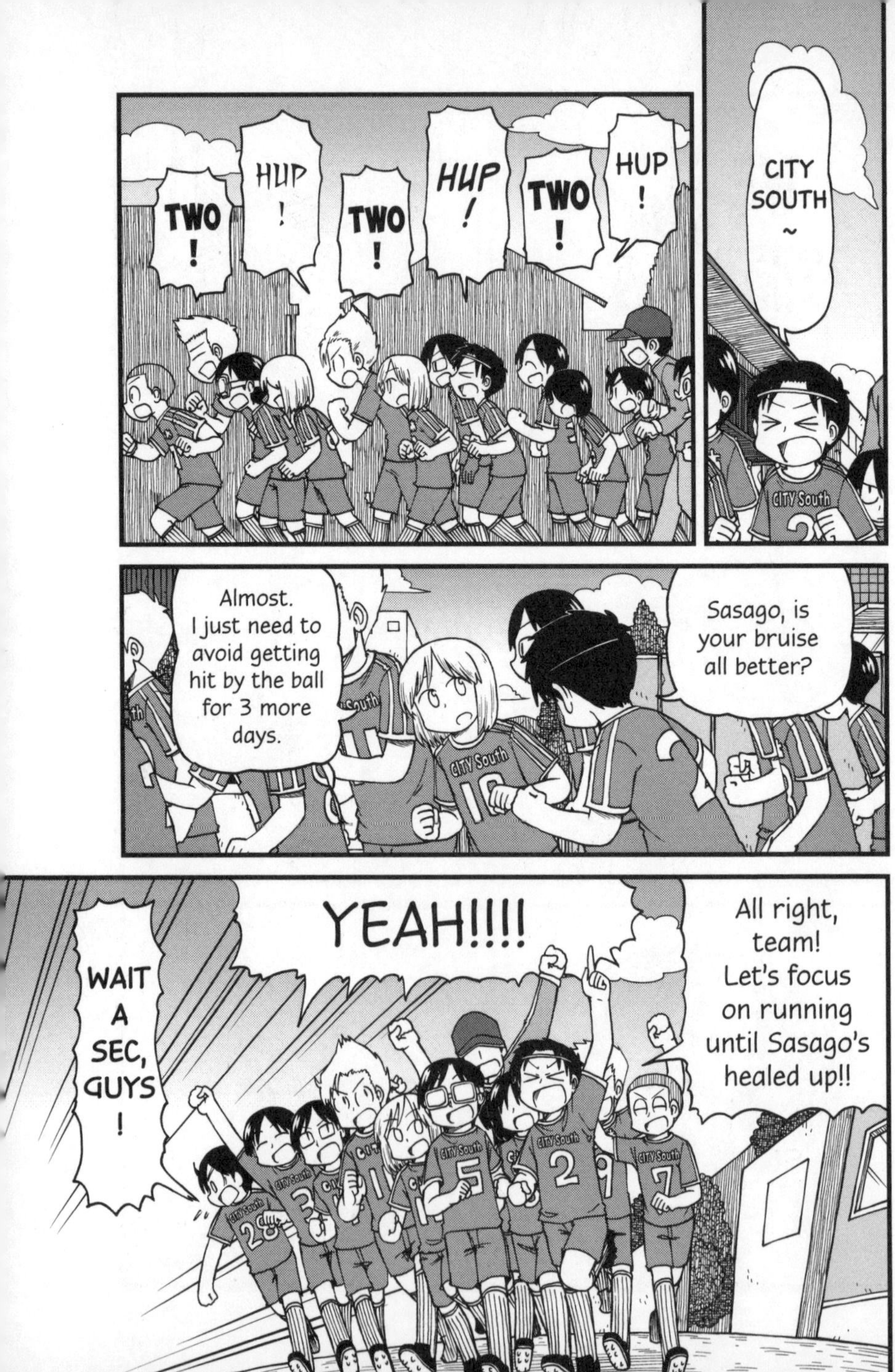
CITY SOUTH ~
HUP !
TWO !
HUP !
TWO !
HUP !
TWO !
Sasago, is your bruise all better?
Almost. I just need to avoid getting hit by the ball for 3 more days.
All right, team! Let's focus on running until Sasago's healed up!!
YEAH!!!!
WAIT A SEC, GUYS !

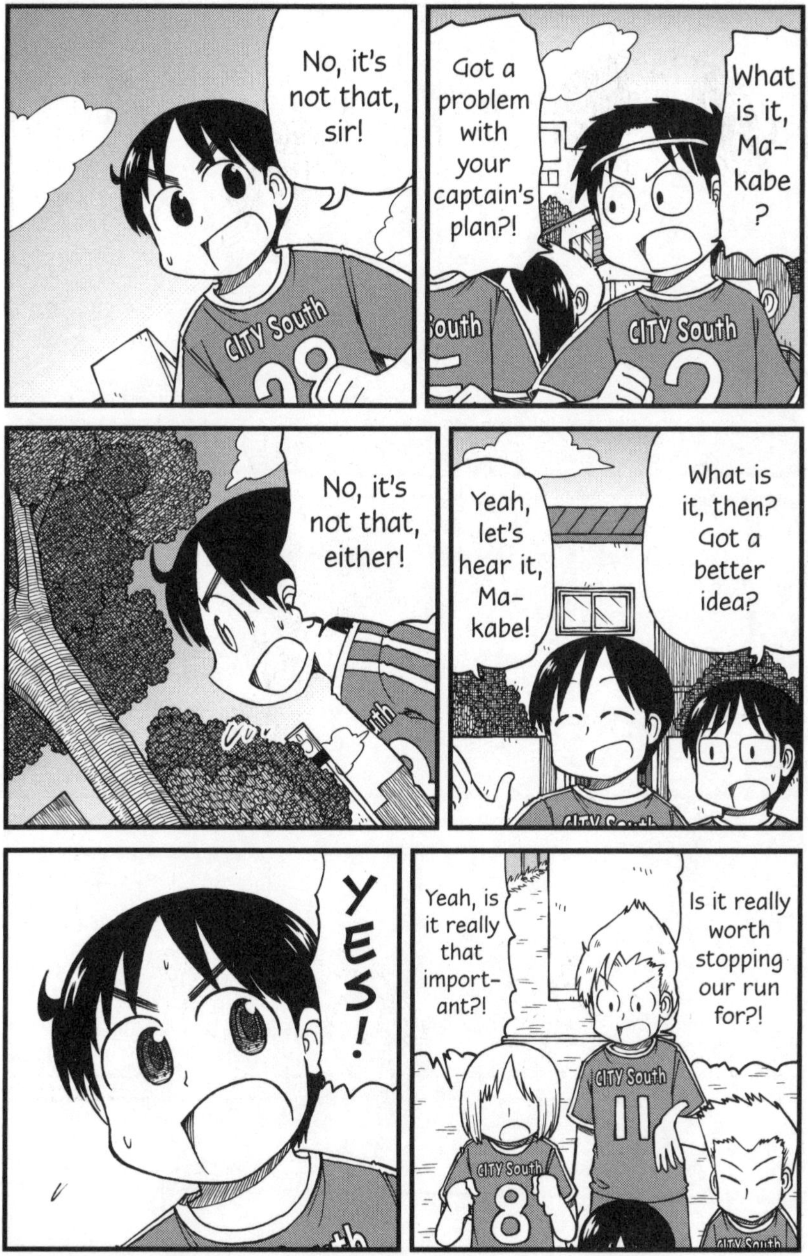
What is it, Ma-kabe?
Got a problem with your captain's plan?!
No, it's not that, sir!
What is it, then? Got a better idea?
Yeah, let's hear it, Ma-kabe!
No, it's not that, either!
Is it really worth stopping our run for?!
Yeah, is it really that import-ant?!
YES!

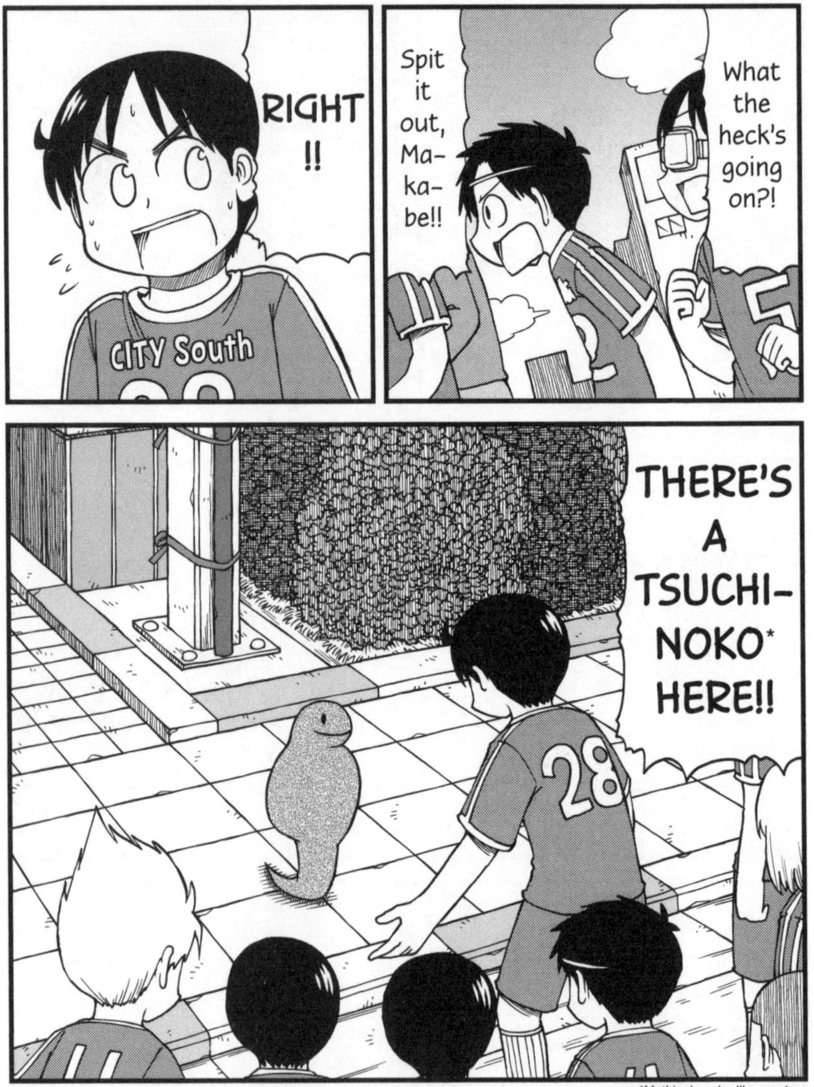
What the heck's going on?!
Spit it out, Ma-ka-be!!
RIGHT!!
CITY South
THERE'S A TSUCHI-NOKO* HERE!!
28

*Mythical snake-like creature

Chapter 51 Legendary Creature

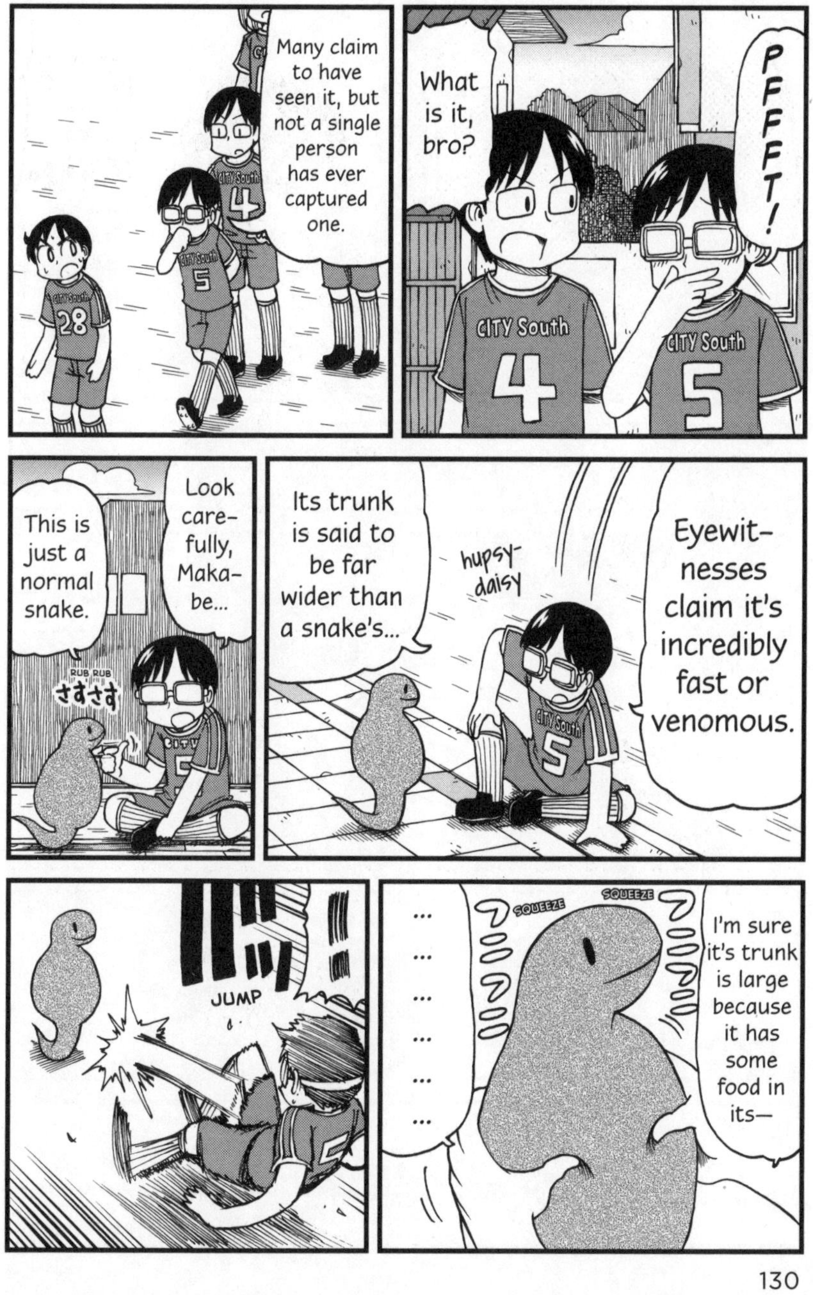
PFFFT!
What is it, bro?
Many claim to have seen it, but not a single person has ever captured one.
Eyewit-nesses claim it's incredibly fast or venomous.
hupsy-daisy
Its trunk is said to be far wider than a snake's...
Look care-fully, Maka-be...
This is just a normal snake.
RUB RUB
さすさす
I'm sure it's trunk is large because it has some food in its—
SQUEEZE
SQUEEZE
...
...
...
...
...
...
JUMP

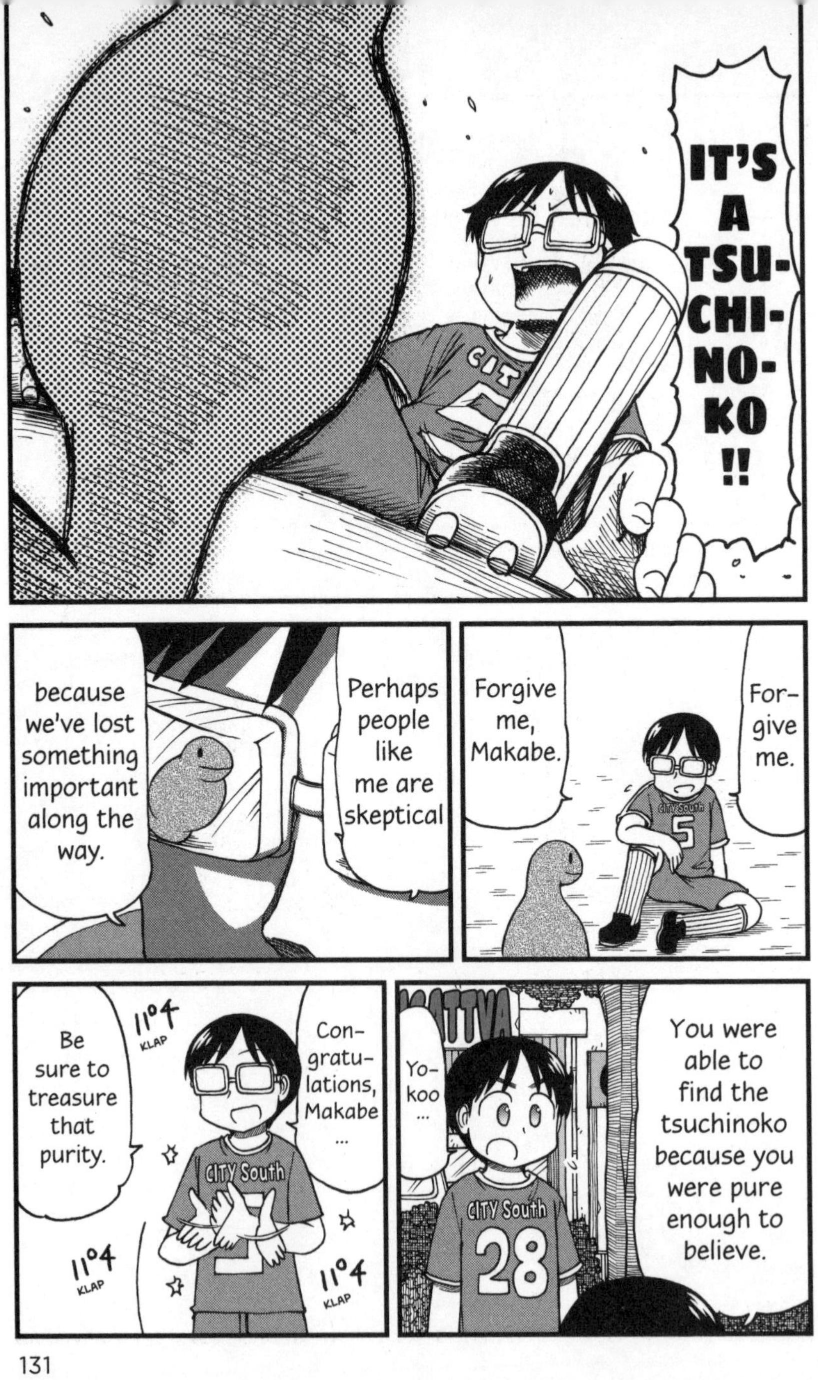
IT'S A TSU-CHI-NO-KO!!
For-give me.
Forgive me, Makabe.
Perhaps people like me are skeptical
because we've lost something important along the way.
You were able to find the tsuchinoko because you were pure enough to believe.
Yo-koo...
Con-gratu-lations, Makabe...
KLAP
KLAP
KLAP
Be sure to treasure that purity.

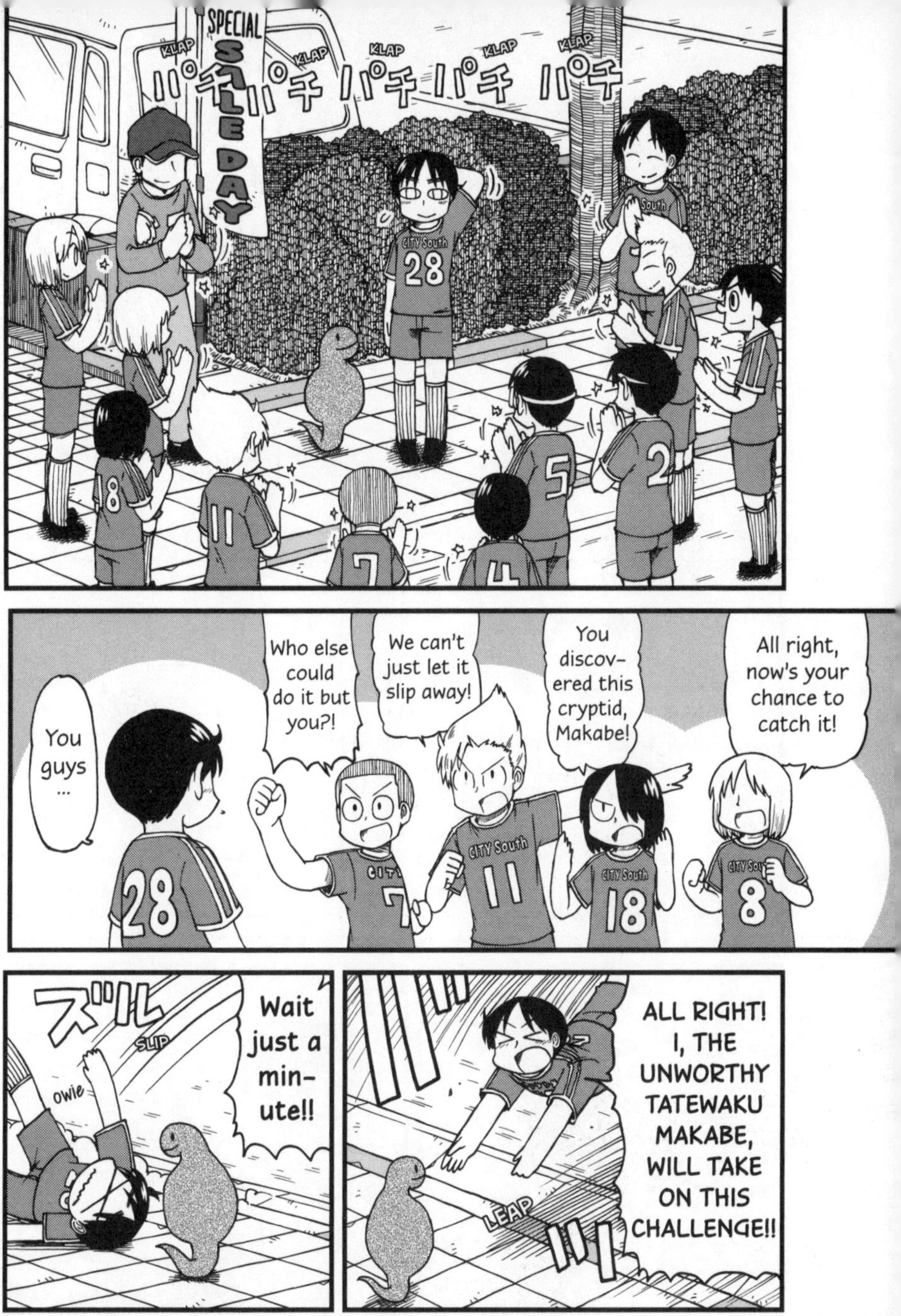
SPECIAL
SALE DAY
パチ パチ パチ パチ パチ
KLAP KLAP KLAP KLAP KLAP
All right, now's your chance to catch it!
You discovered this cryptid, Makabe!
We can't just let it slip away!
Who else could do it but you?!
You guys ...
ALL RIGHT! I, THE UNWORTHY TATEWAKU MAKABE, WILL TAKE ON THIS CHALLENGE!!
LEAP
Wait just a min-ute!!
ズル
SLIP
owie

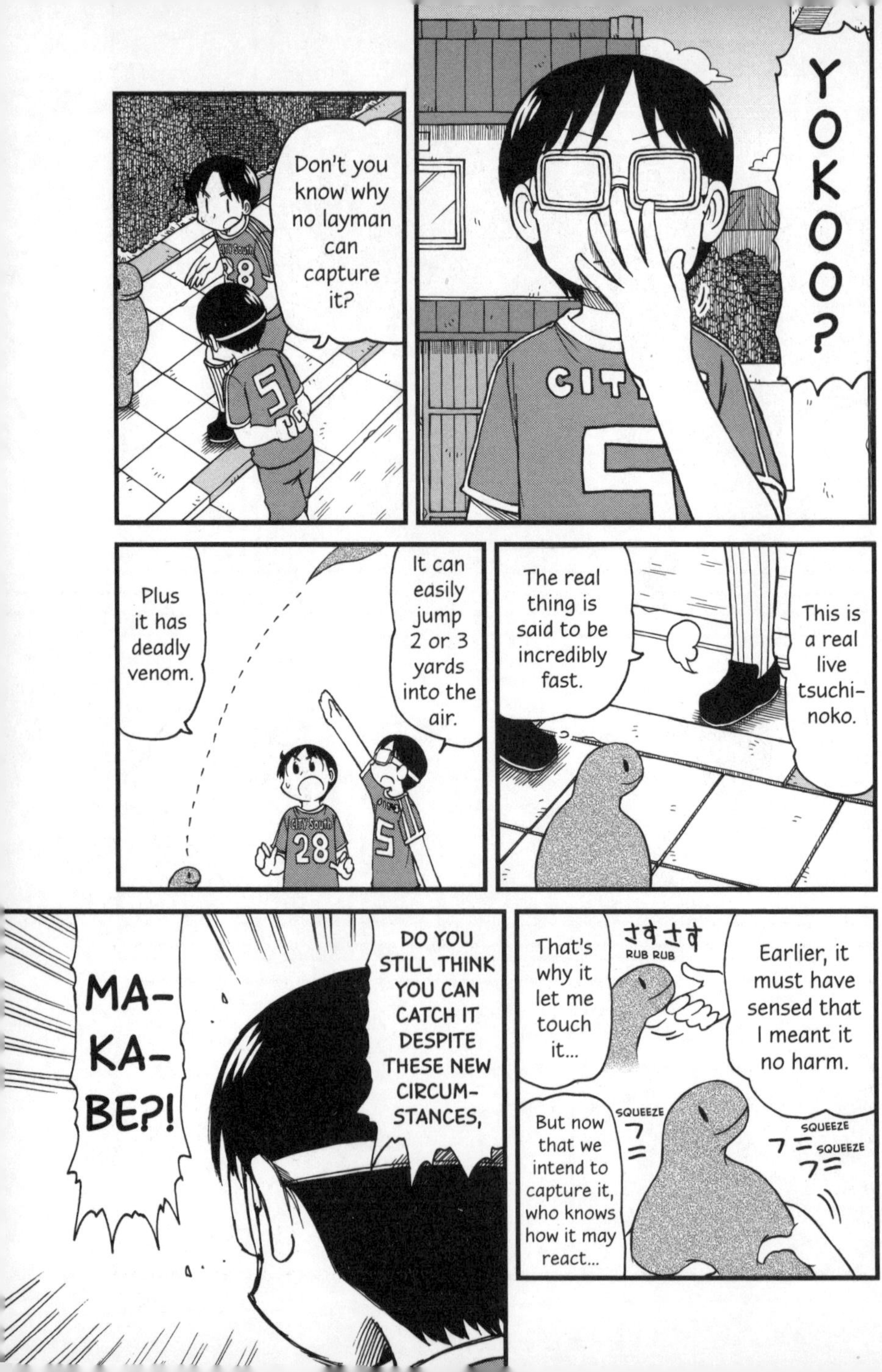
YOKOO?
Don't you know why no layman can capture it?
This is a real live tsuchinoko.
The real thing is said to be incredibly fast.
It can easily jump 2 or 3 yards into the air.
Plus it has deadly venom.
Earlier, it must have sensed that I meant it no harm.
さすさす RUB RUB
That's why it let me touch it...
フニ SQUEEZE
フニ SQUEEZE
フニ SQUEEZE
But now that we intend to capture it, who knows how it may react...
DO YOU STILL THINK YOU CAN CATCH IT DESPITE THESE NEW CIRCUMSTANCES,
MA-KA-BE?!

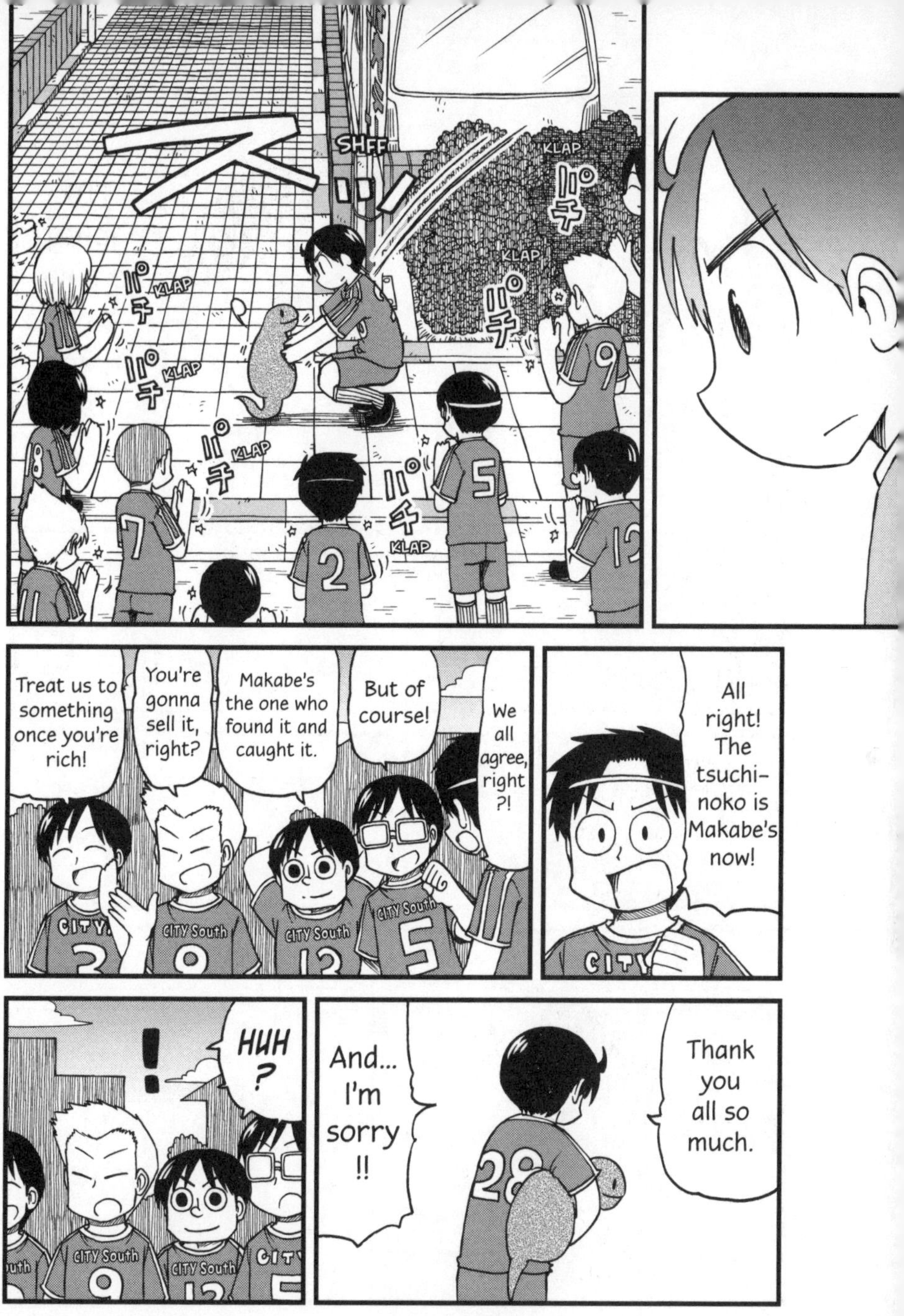
SHFF
KLAP
パチ
KLAP
パチ
KLAP
パチ
KLAP
パチ
KLAP
パチ
KLAP
パチ
KLAP
All right! The tsuchi-noko is Makabe's now!
We all agree, right?!
But of course!
Makabe's the one who found it and caught it.
You're gonna sell it, right?
Treat us to something once you're rich!
Thank you all so much.
And... I'm sorry !!
HUH ?
!

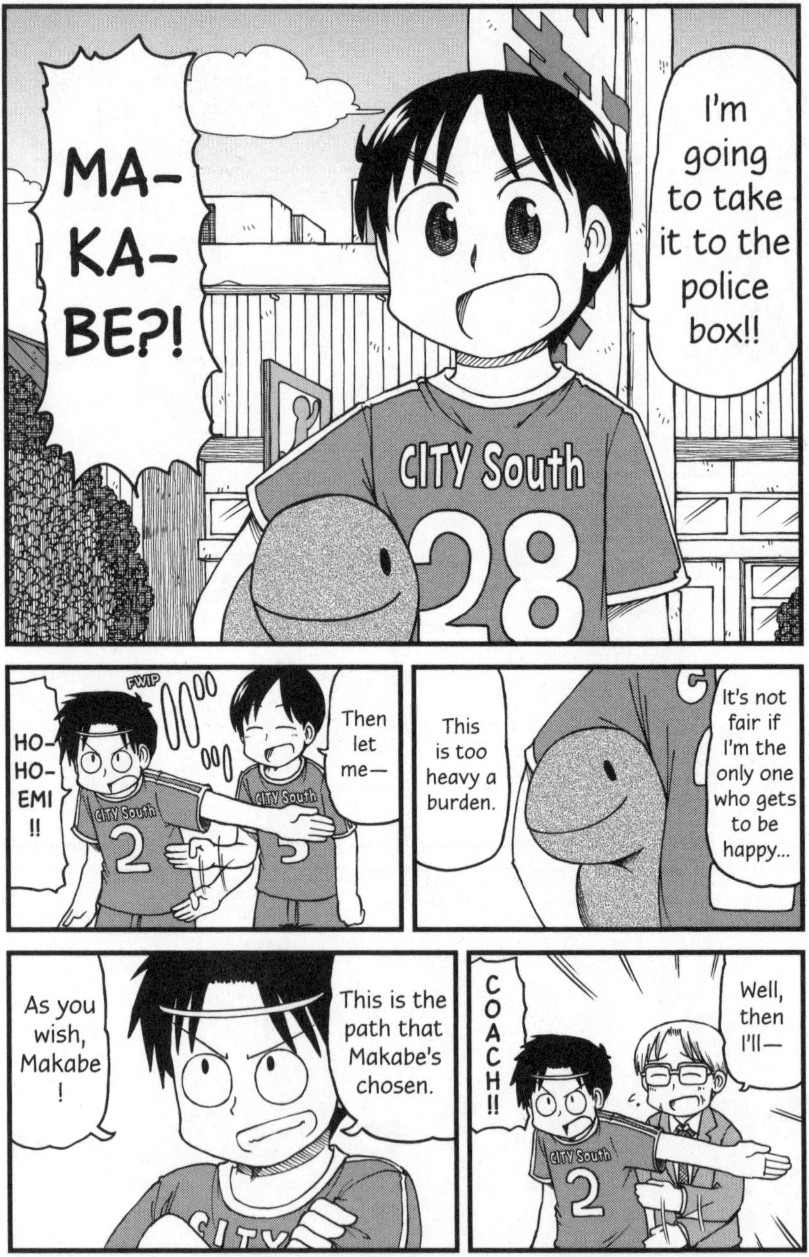
I'm going to take it to the police box!!
MA-KA-BE?!
CITY South
28
It's not fair if I'm the only one who gets to be happy...
This is too heavy a burden.
Then let me—
FWIP
HO-HO-EMI!!
Well, then I'll—
COACH!!
This is the path that Makabe's chosen.
As you wish, Makabe!

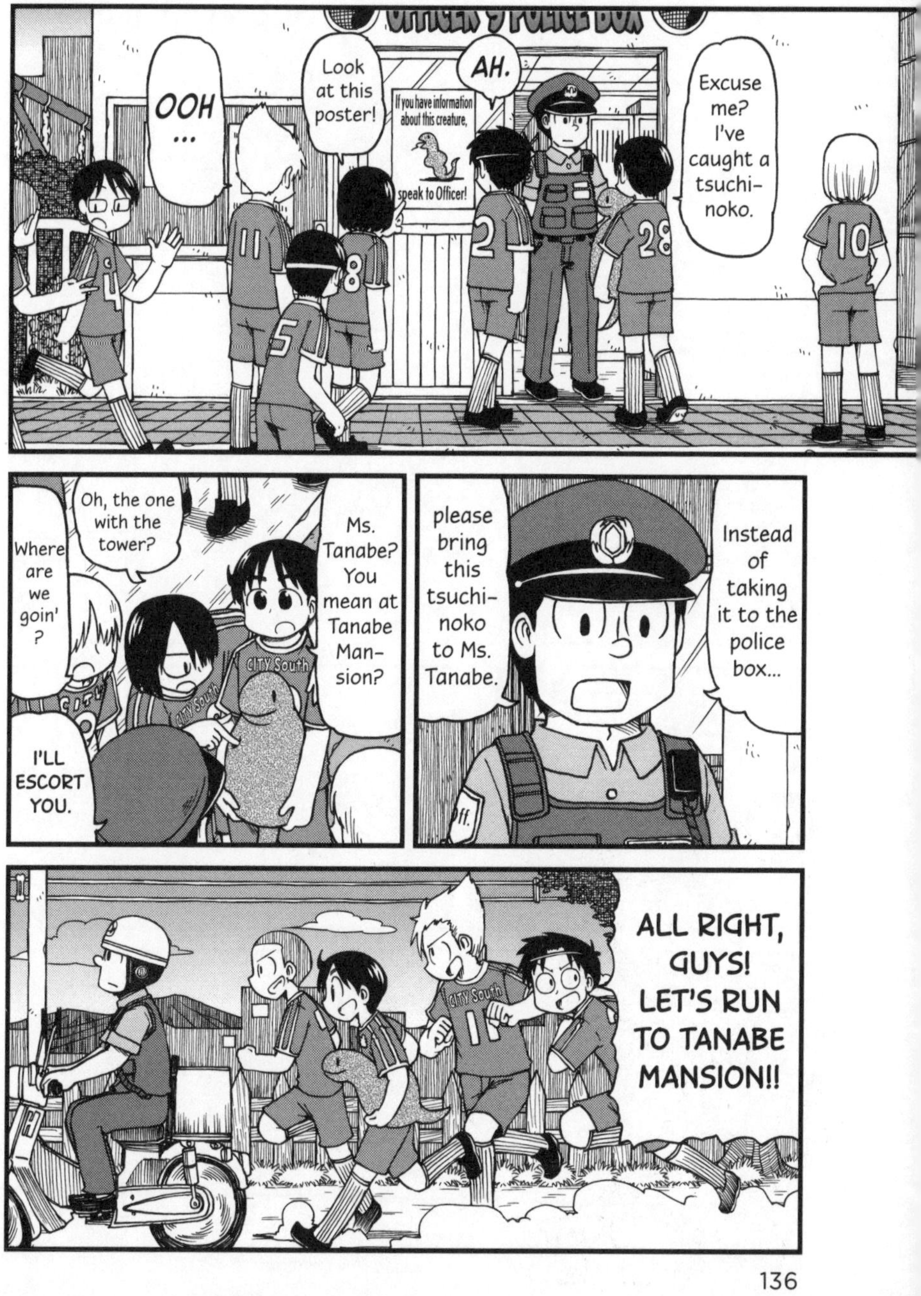
OFFICER'S POLICE BOX
Excuse me? I've caught a tsuchinoko.
AH.
If you have information about this creature, speak to Officer!
Look at this poster!
OOH ...
Instead of taking it to the police box...
please bring this tsuchinoko to Ms. Tanabe.
Ms. Tanabe? You mean at Tanabe Mansion?
Oh, the one with the tower?
Where are we goin'?
I'LL ESCORT YOU.
CITY South
ALL RIGHT, GUYS! LET'S RUN TO TANABE MANSION!!

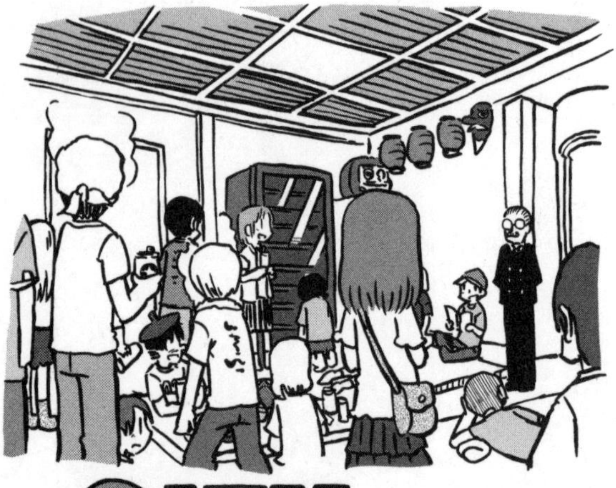

CITY

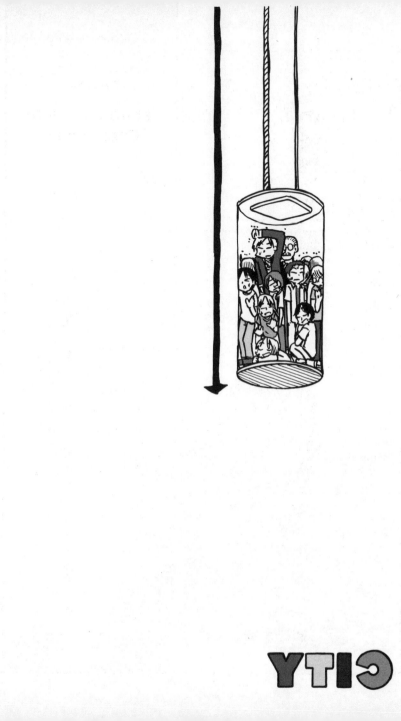

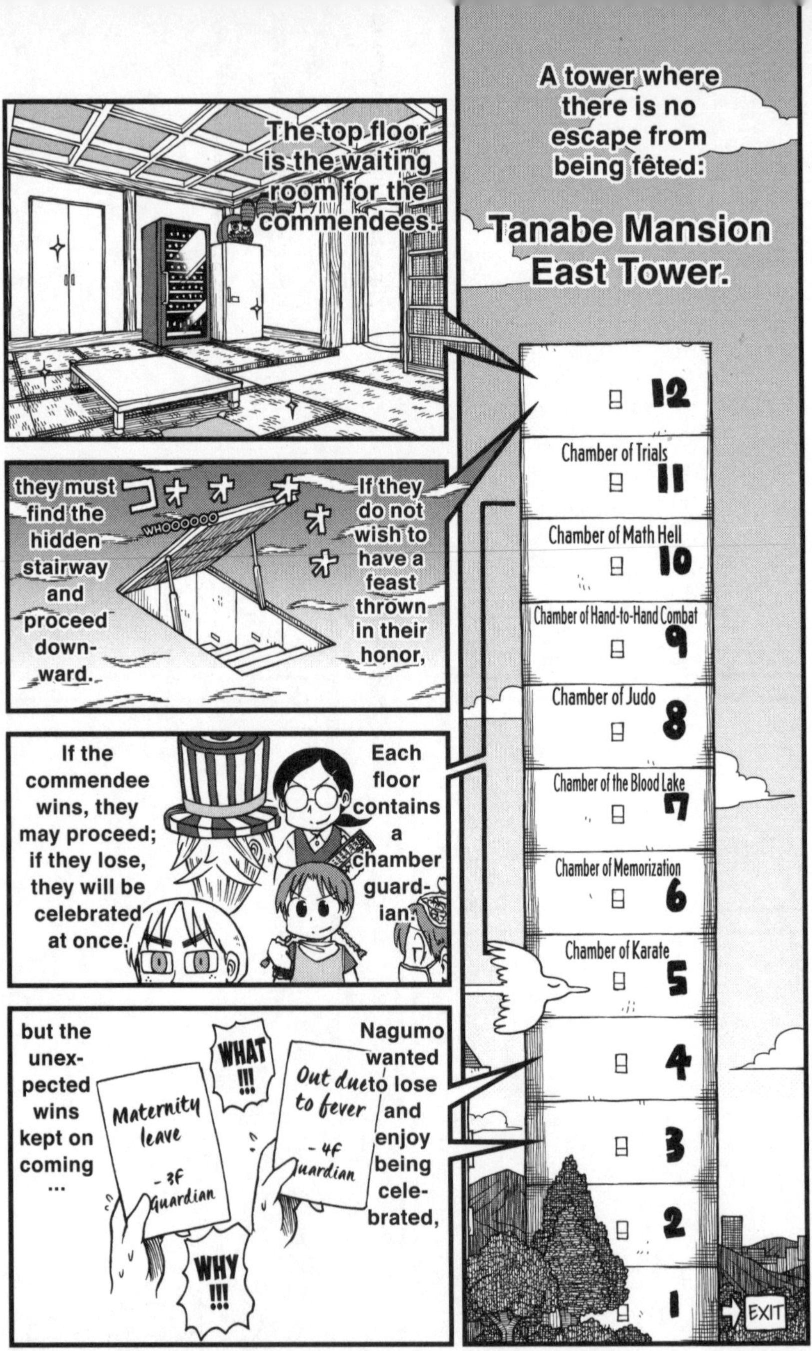
A tower where there is no escape from being fêted:
Tanabe Mansion East Tower.
12
Chamber of Trials
11
Chamber of Math Hell
10
Chamber of Hand-to-Hand Combat
9
Chamber of Judo
8
Chamber of the Blood Lake
7
Chamber of Memorization
6
Chamber of Karate
5
4
3
2
1
EXIT
The top floor is the waiting room for the commendees.
If they do not wish to have a feast thrown in their honor,
コオオオオオ
WHOOOOOO
they must find the hidden stairway and proceed downward.
Each floor contains a chamber guardian.
If the commendee wins, they may proceed; if they lose, they will be celebrated at once.
Nagumo wanted to lose and enjoy being celebrated,
Out due to fever
- 4F Guardian
WHAT!!!
Maternity leave
- 3F Guardian
WHY!!!
but the unexpected wins kept on coming ...

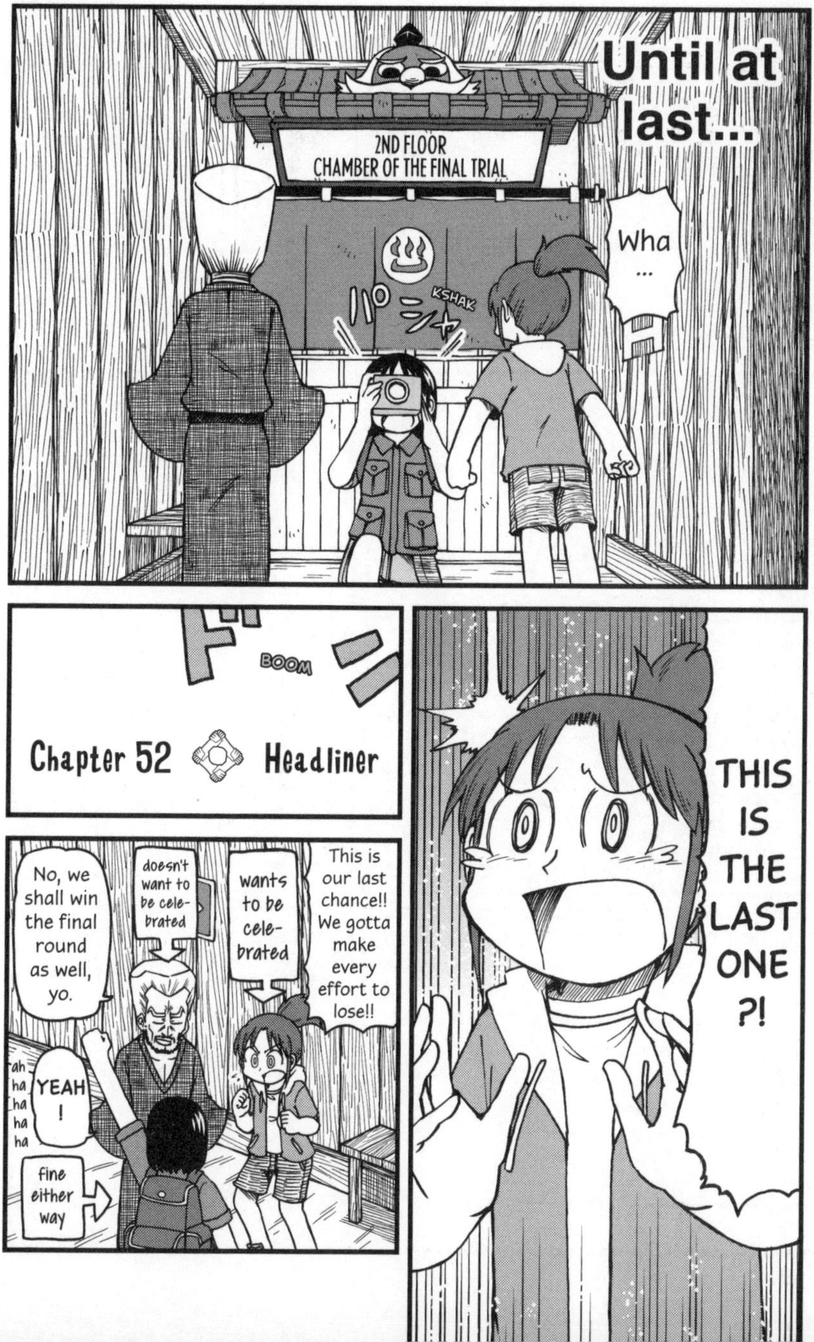
2ND FLOOR
CHAMBER OF THE FINAL TRIAL
Until at last...
Wha...
KSHAK
THIS IS THE LAST ONE?!
BOOM
Chapter 52 Headliner
This is our last chance!! We gotta make every effort to lose!!
wants to be celebrated
doesn't want to be celebrated
No, we shall win the final round as well, yo.
YEAH!
ah ha ha ha ha
fine either way

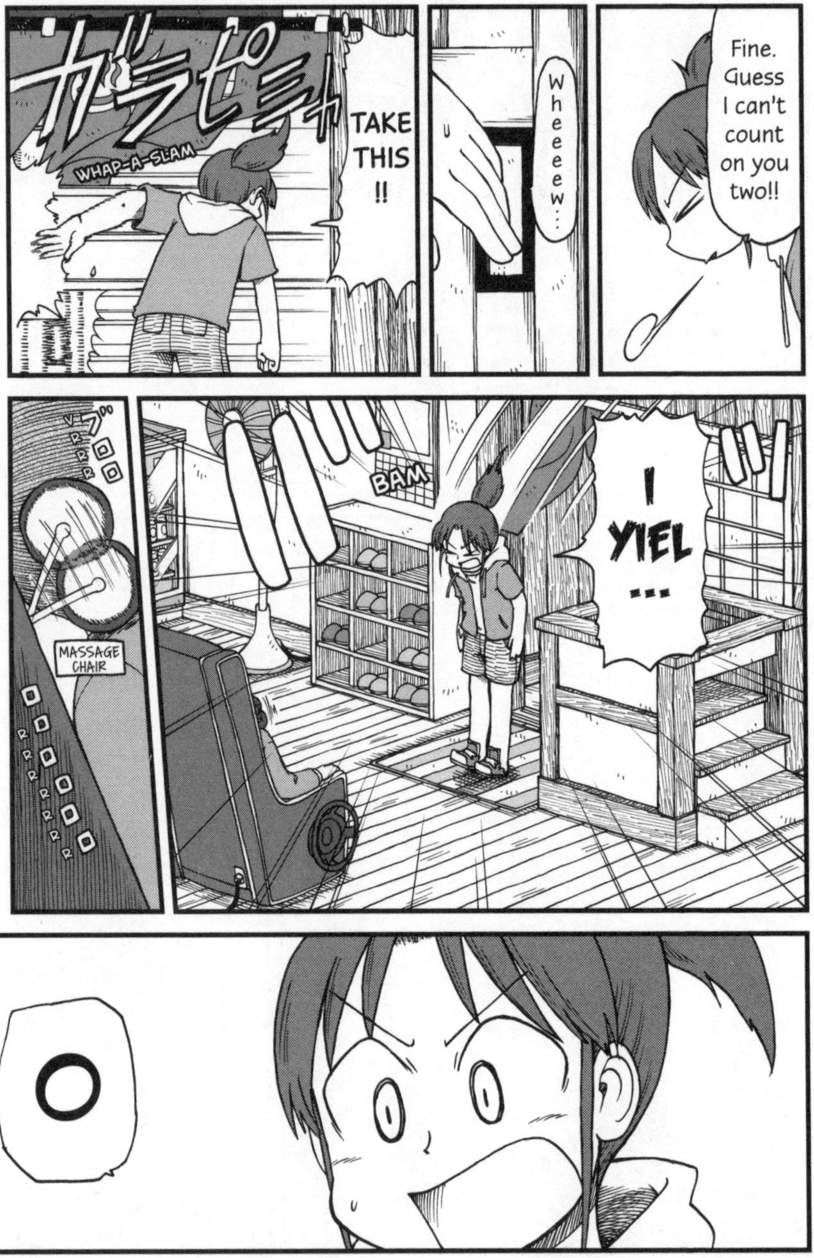
Fine. Guess I can't count on you two!!
Wheeeew...
TAKE THIS!!
WHAP-A-SLAM
I YIEL ...
BAM
MASSAGE CHAIR
O

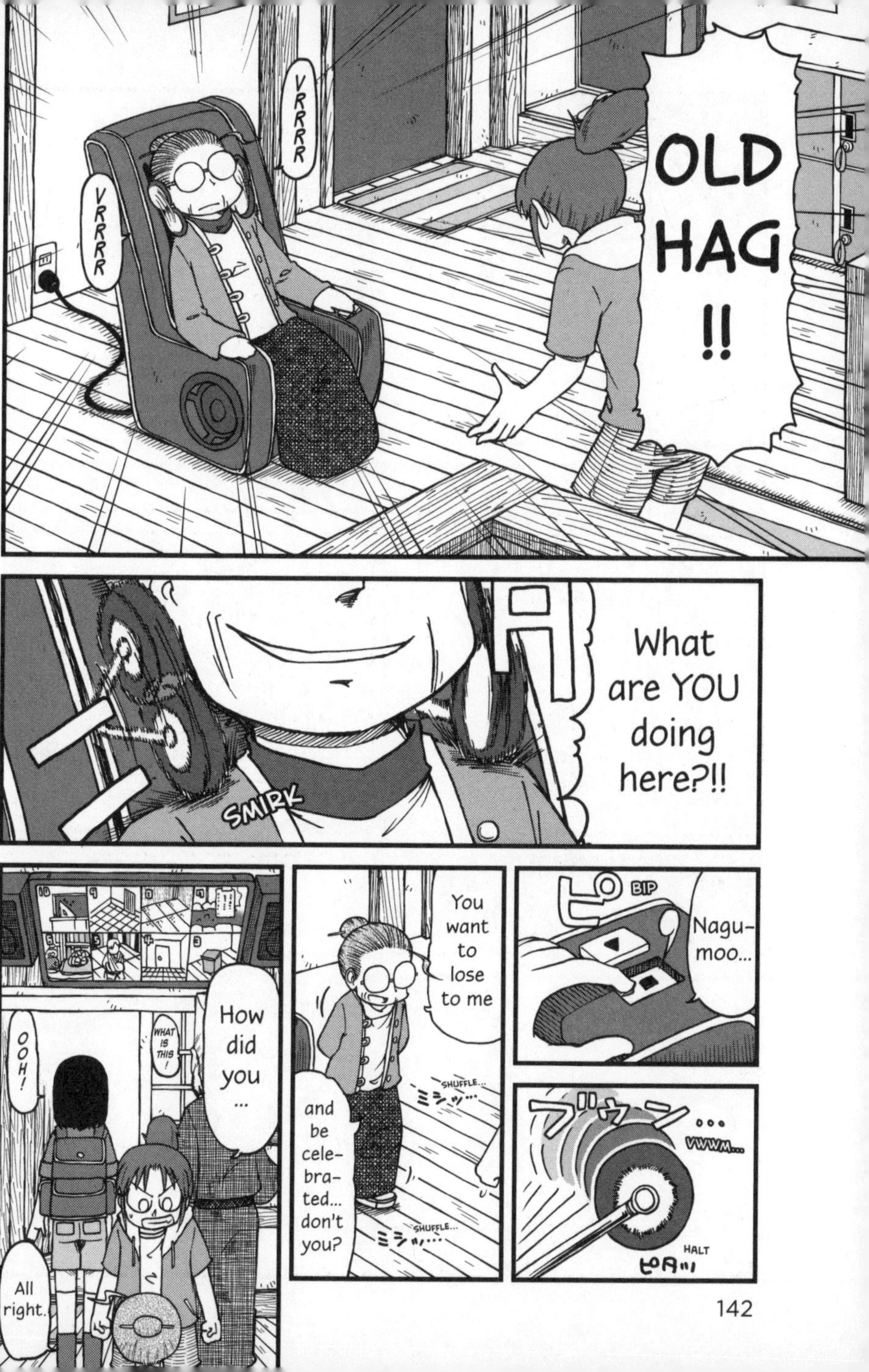
VRRRR
VRRRR
OLD HAG !!
What are YOU doing here?!!
SMIRK
ピ BIP
Nagu-moo...
ブウーン… VWWM...
ピタッ HALT
You want to lose to me
SHUFFLE...
and be cele-bra-ted... don't you?
SHUFFLE...
How did you ...
WHAT IS THIS!
OOH!
All right.

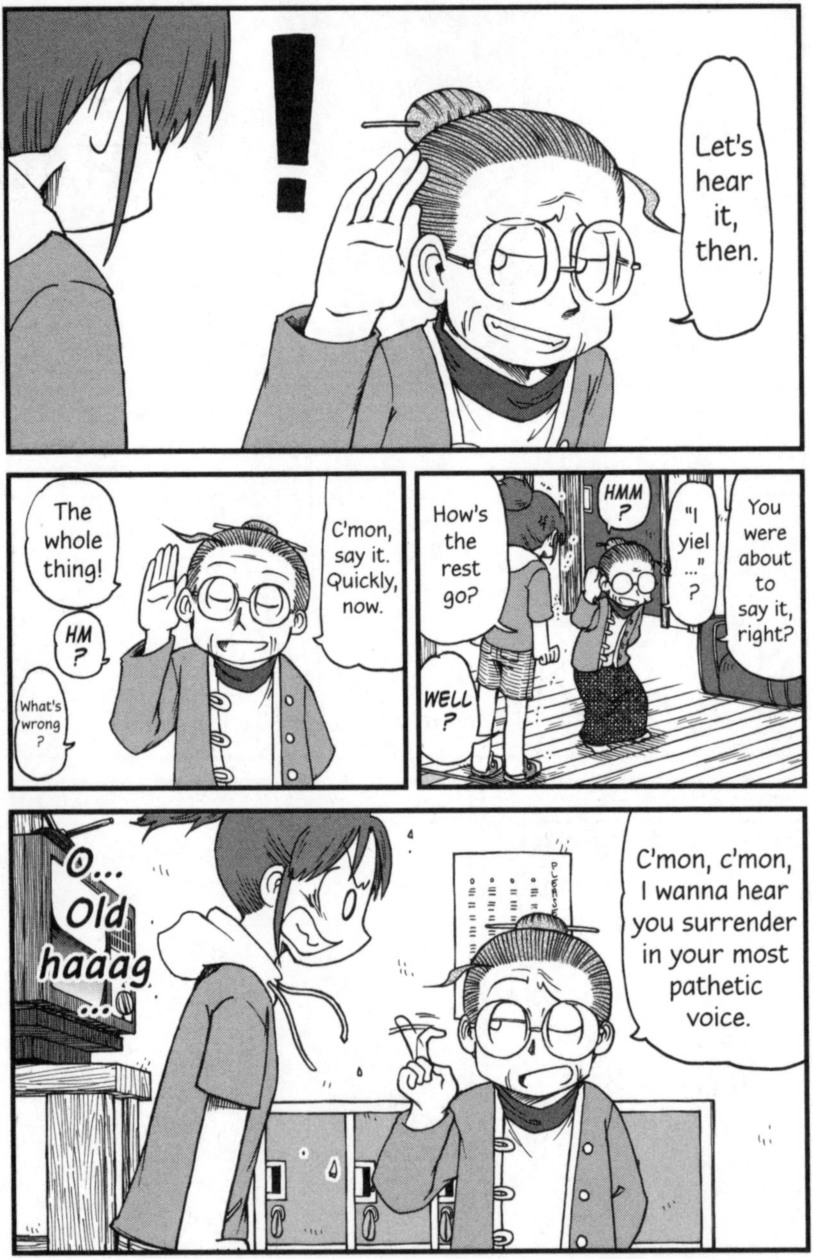
!
Let's hear it, then.
You were about to say it, right?
"I yiel ..."?
HMM?
How's the rest go?
WELL?
C'mon, say it. Quickly, now.
The whole thing!
HM?
What's wrong?
C'mon, c'mon, I wanna hear you surrender in your most pathetic voice.
O... Old haaag...

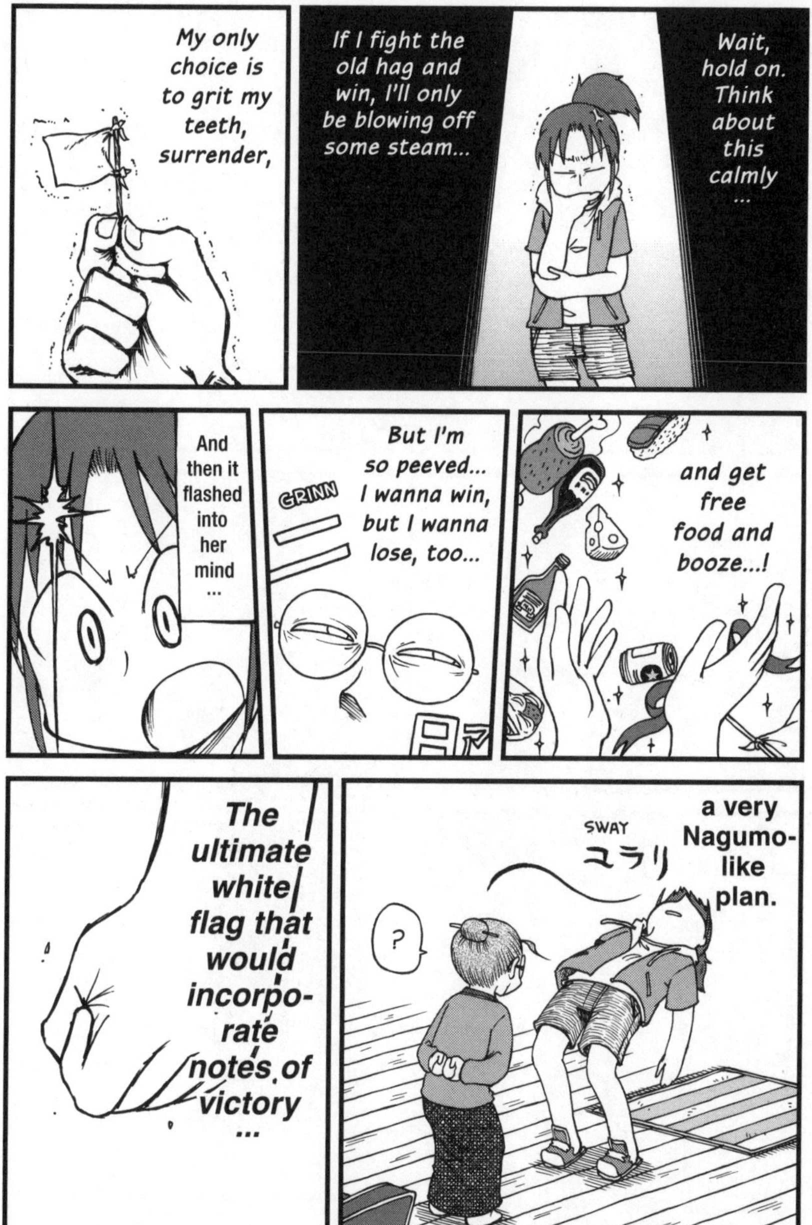

Wait, hold on. Think about this calmly ...
If I fight the old hag and win, I'll only be blowing off some steam...
My only choice is to grit my teeth, surrender,
and get free food and booze...!
But I'm so peeved... I wanna win, but I wanna lose, too...
GRINN
And then it flashed into her mind ...
a very Nagumo-like plan.
SWAY
ユラリ
?
The ultimate white flag that would incorporate notes of victory ...

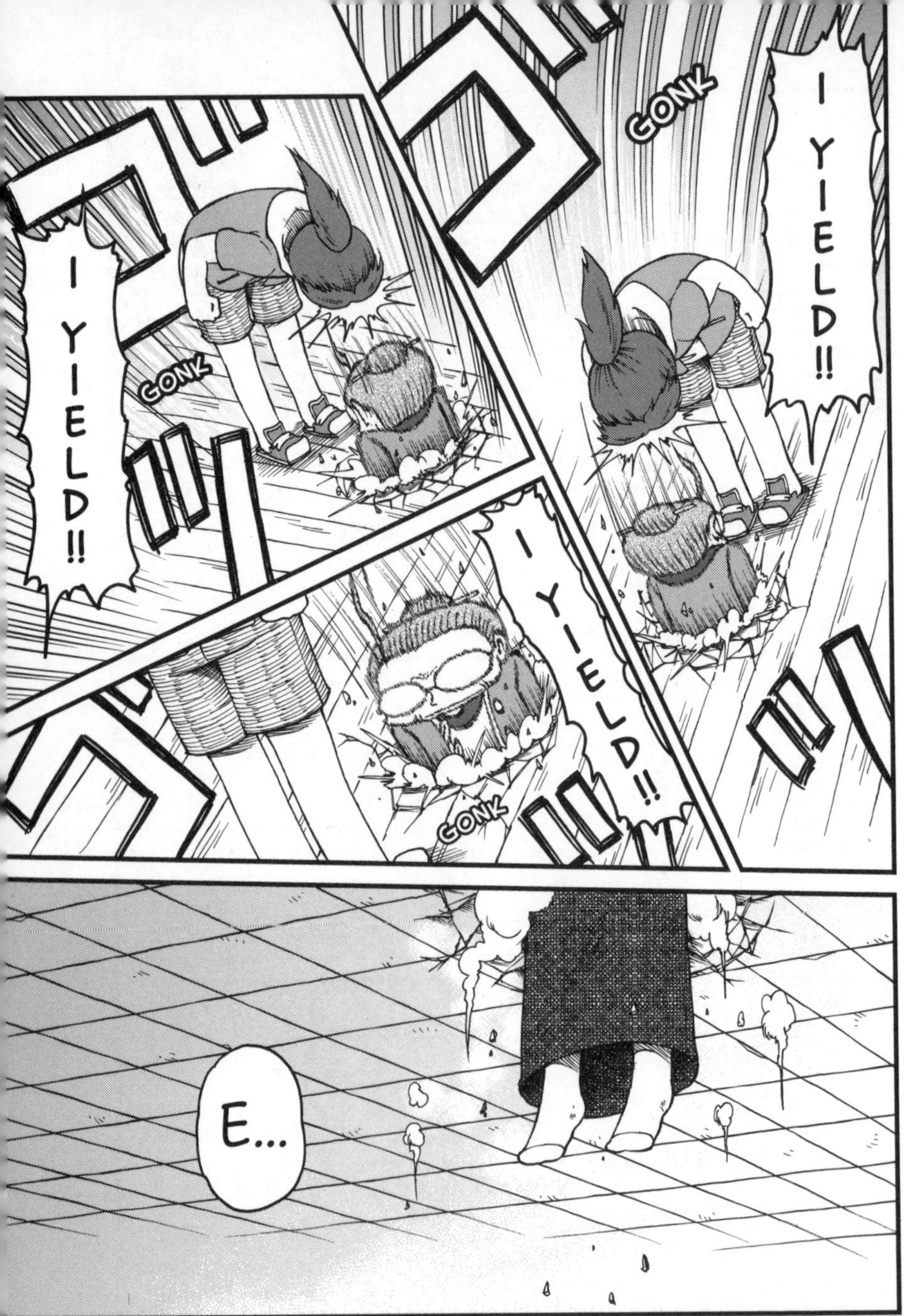
GONK
I YIELD!!
GONK
I YIELD!!
I YIELD!!
GONK
E...

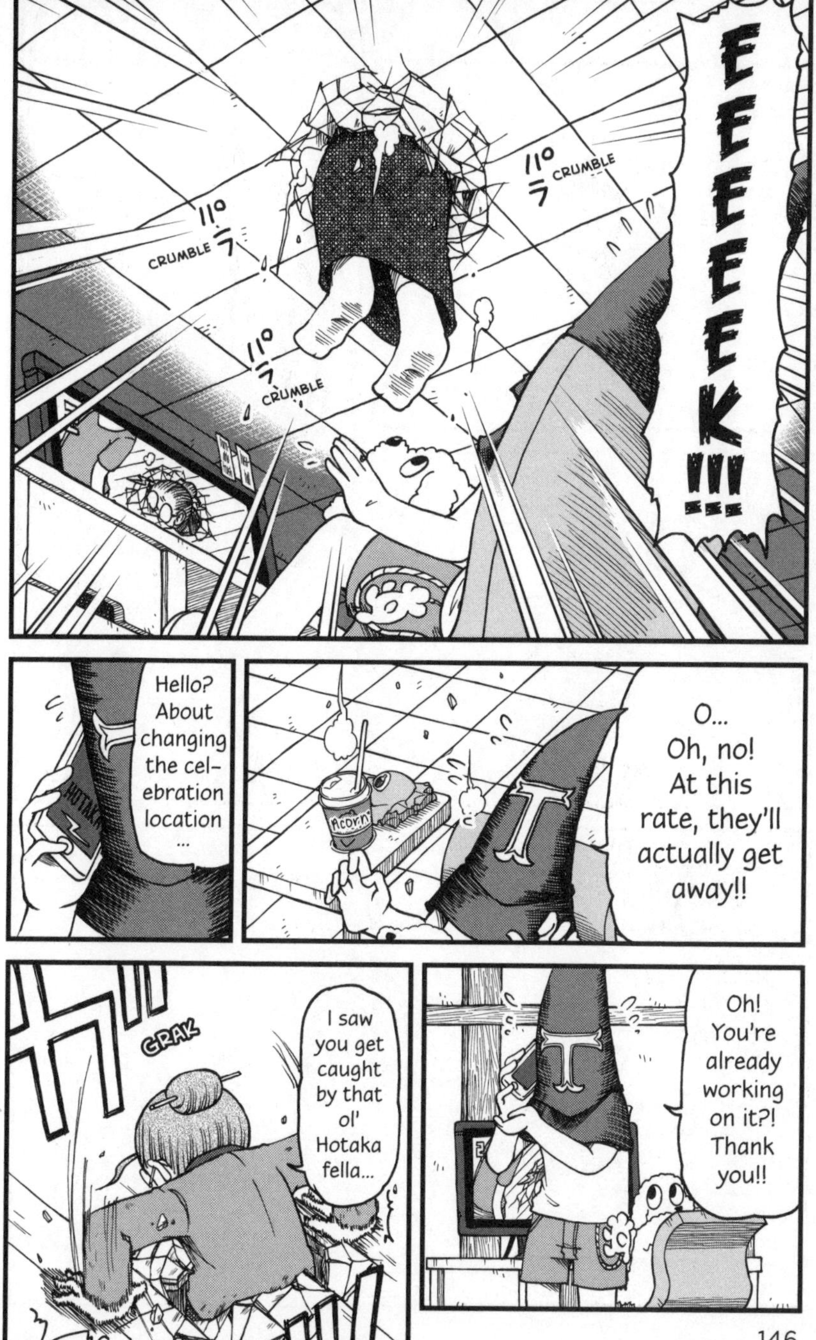
EEEEEK!!!
CRUMBLE
CRUMBLE
CRUMBLE
O... Oh, no! At this rate, they'll actually get away!!
Acorn
Hello? About changing the cel-ebration location ...
HOTAKA
Oh! You're already working on it?! Thank you!!
I saw you get caught by that ol' Hotaka fella...
GRAK

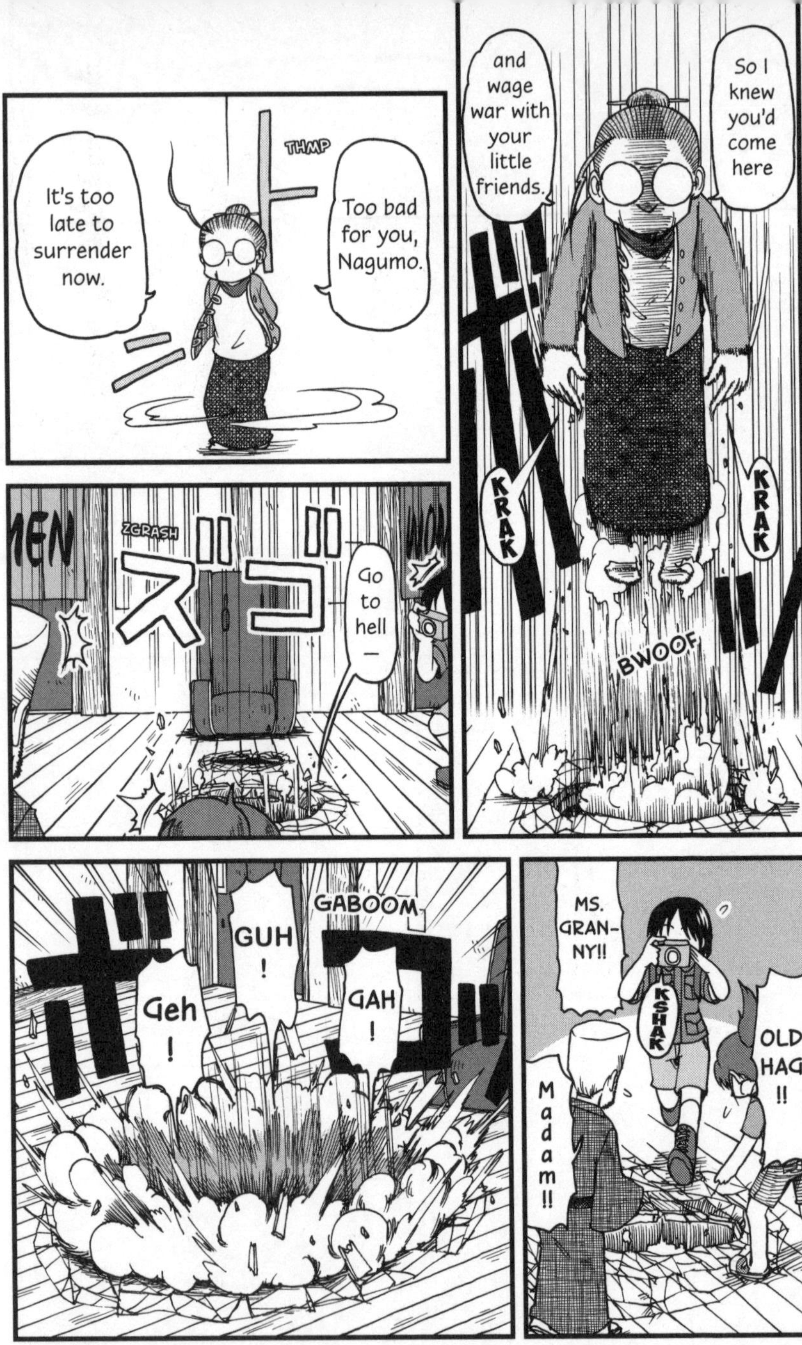
So I knew you'd come here
and wage war with your little friends.
KRAK
KRAK
BWOOF
THMP
Too bad for you, Nagumo.
It's too late to surrender now.
ZGRASH
Go to hell —
MS. GRAN-NY!!
KSHAK
OLD HAG!!
Madam!!
GABOOM
GAH!
GUH!
Geh!

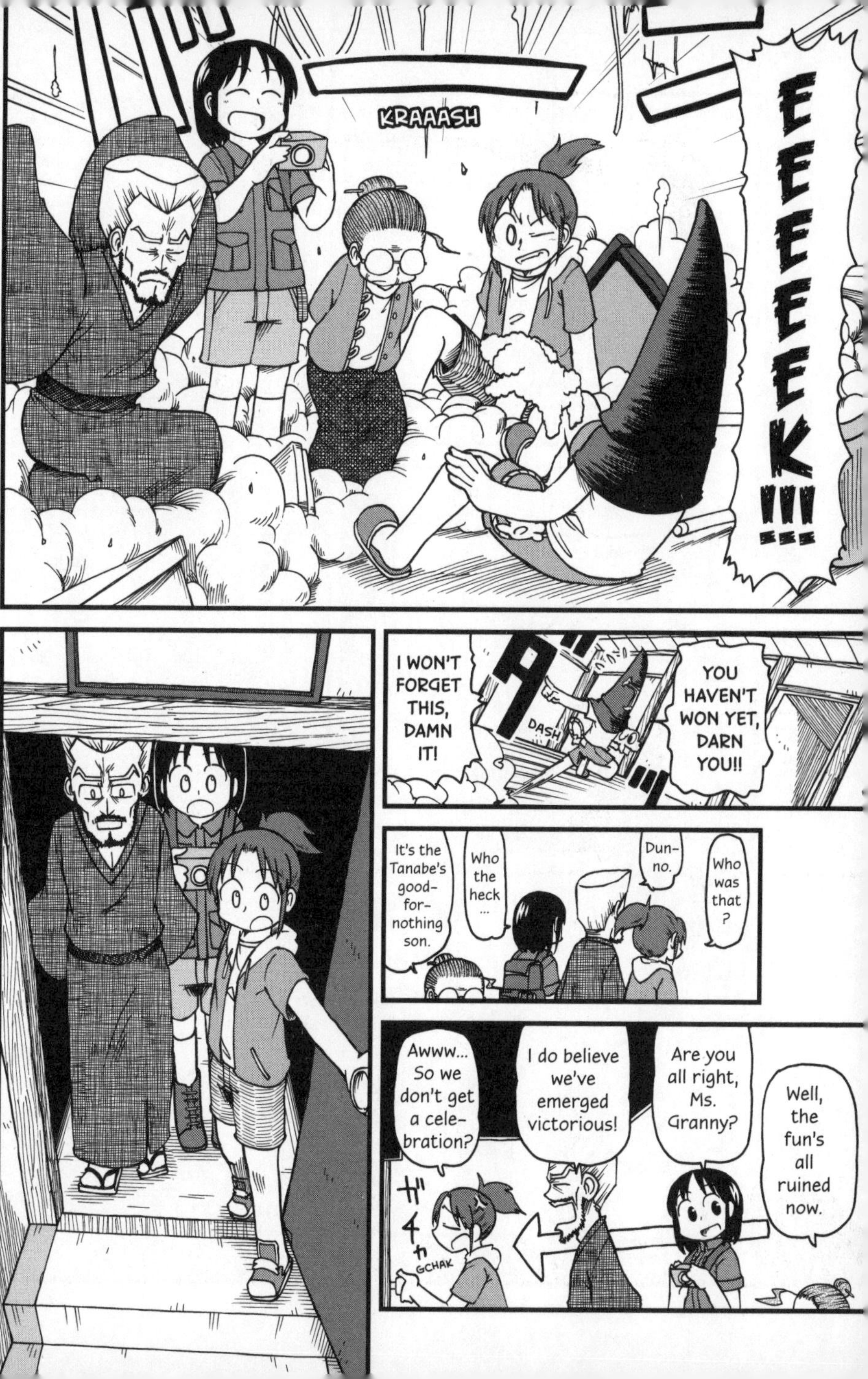
EEEEEK!!!
KRAAASH
YOU HAVEN'T WON YET, DARN YOU!!
DASH
I WON'T FORGET THIS, DAMN IT!
Who was that?
Dun-no.
Who the heck...
It's the Tanabe's good-for-nothing son.
Well, the fun's all ruined now.
Are you all right, Ms. Granny?
I do believe we've emerged victorious!
Awww... So we don't get a celebration?
GCHAK

Chapter 53 ◇ Celebration

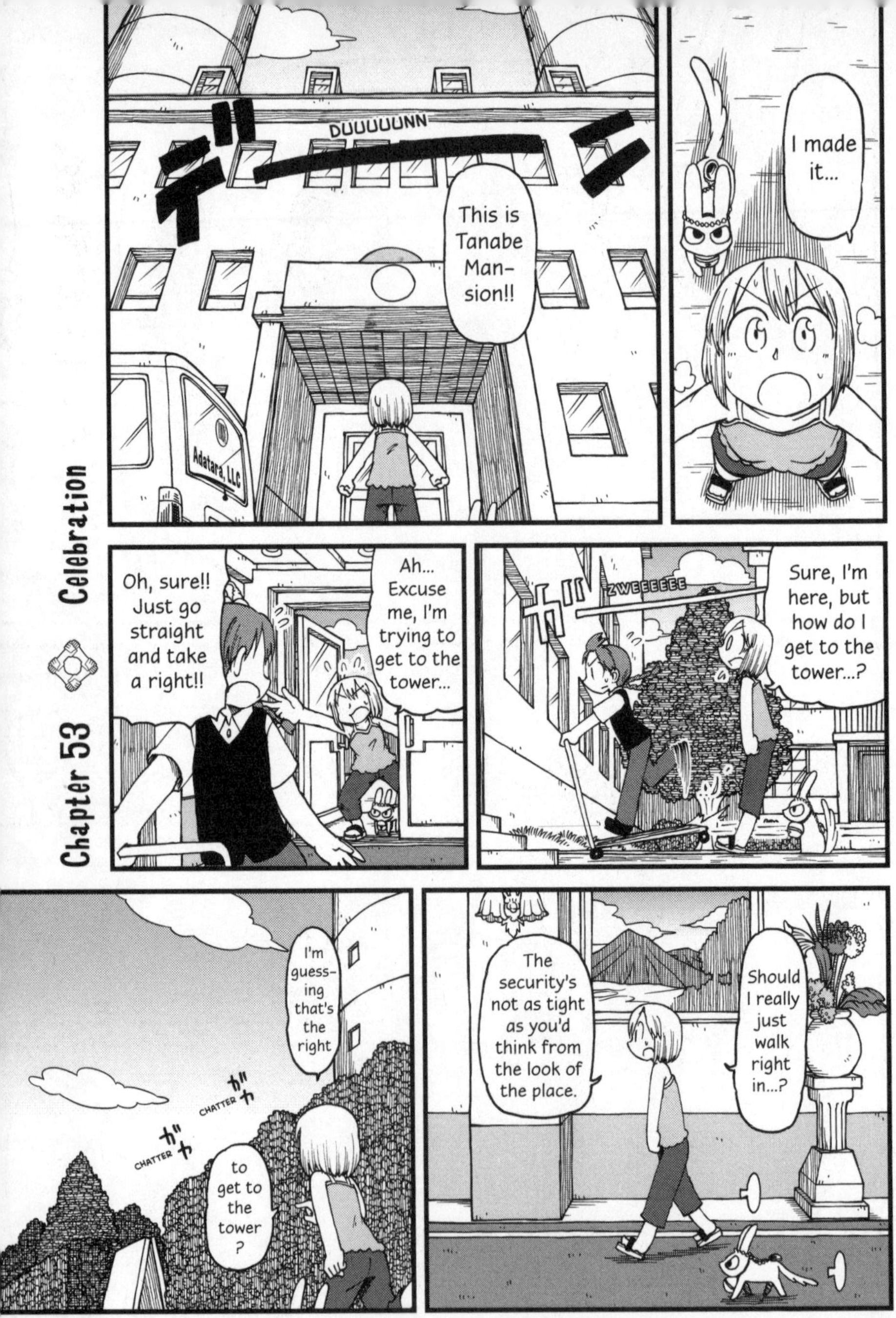

I made it...
DUUUUUNN
This is Tanabe Mansion!!
ZWEEEEEE
Sure, I'm here, but how do I get to the tower...?
Ah... Excuse me, I'm trying to get to the tower...
Oh, sure!! Just go straight and take a right!!
Should I really just walk right in...?
The security's not as tight as you'd think from the look of the place.
I'm guessing that's the right
CHATTER
CHATTER
to get to the tower?

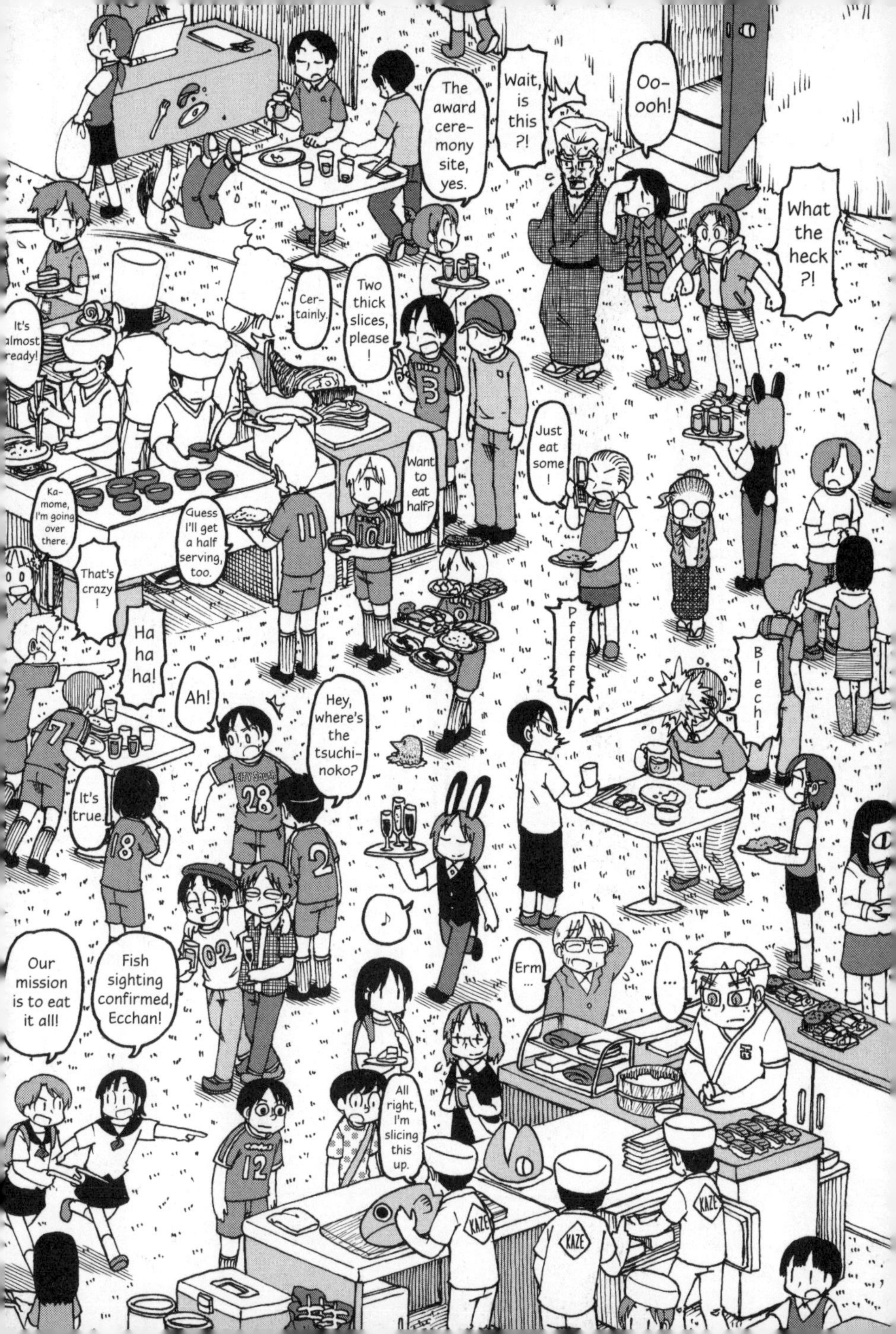
What the heck?!
Oo-ooh!
Wait, is this?!
The award ceremony site, yes.
Two thick slices, please!
Certainly.
It's almost ready!
Just eat some!
Want to eat half?
Guess I'll get a half serving, too.
Kamome, I'm going over there.
That's crazy!
Blech!
Pfffff
Hey, where's the tsuchinoko?
Ah!
Ha ha ha!
It's true.
♪
...
Erm...
All right, I'm slicing this up.
Fish sighting confirmed, Ecchan!
Our mission is to eat it all!
KAZE
KAZE
KAZE

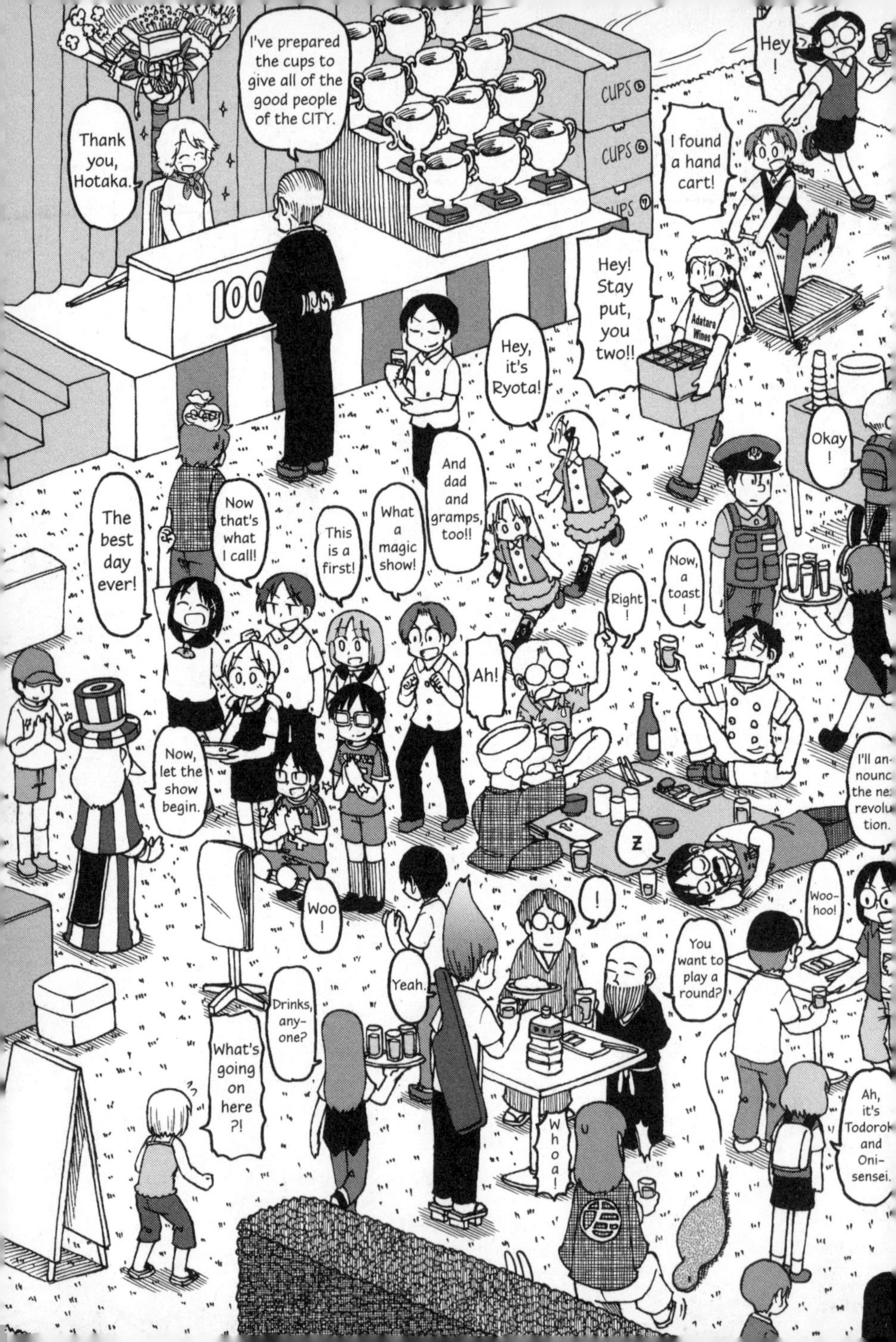
Hey!
I've prepared the cups to give all of the good people of the CITY.
Thank you, Hotaka.
CUPS
CUPS
CUPS
I found a hand cart!
100
Hey! Stay put, you two!!
Adatara Wines
Hey, it's Ryota!
Okay!
And dad and gramps, too!!
What a magic show!
This is a first!
Now that's what I call!
The best day ever!
Now, a toast!
Right!
Ah!
I'll an- nounc the ne revolu tion.
Now, let the show begin.
Z
Woo-hoo!
!
Woo!
You want to play a round?
Yeah.
Drinks, any- one?
What's going on here?!
Ah, it's Todorok and Oni- sensei.
Whoa!

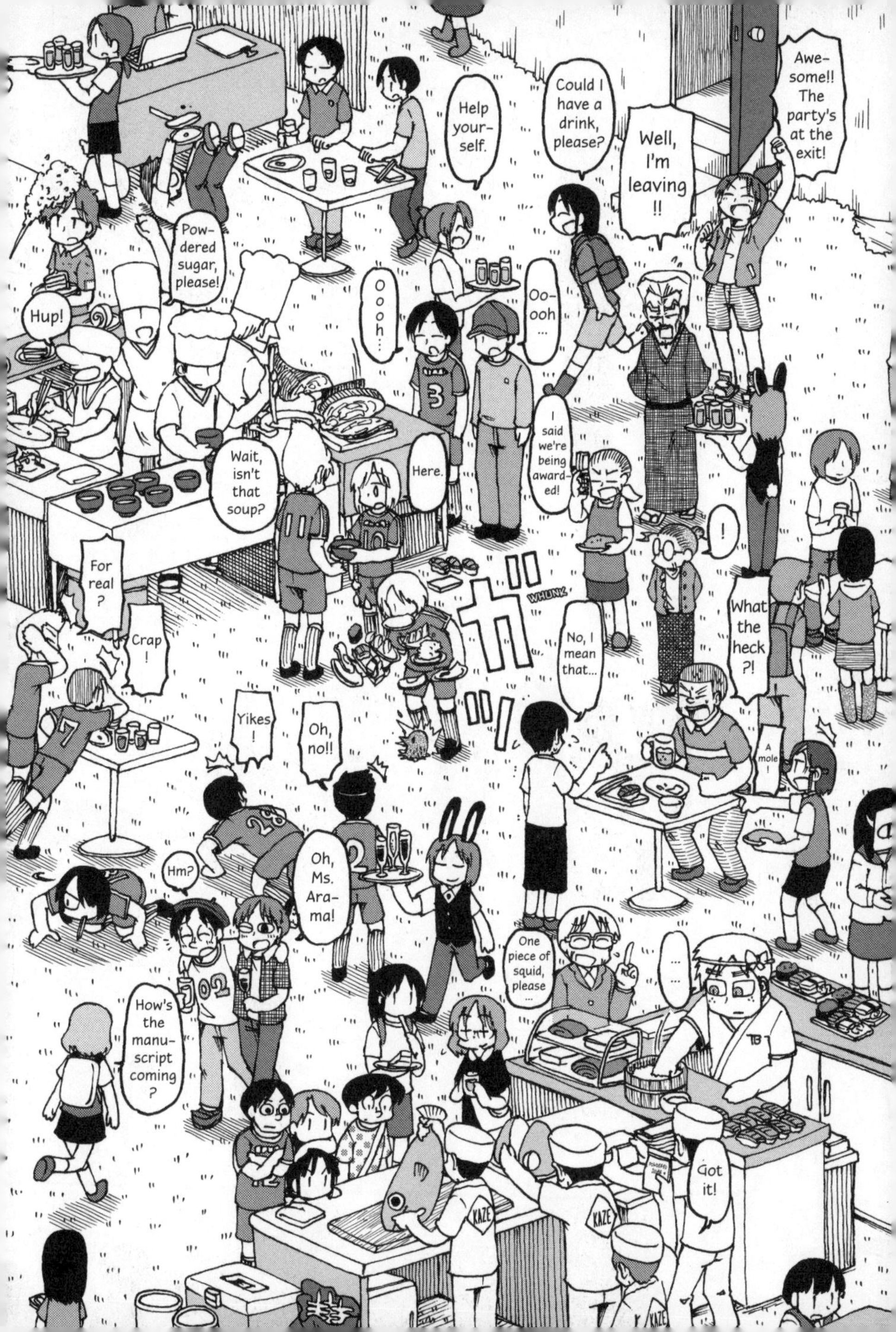
Awe-some!! The party's at the exit!
Well, I'm leaving !!
Could I have a drink, please?
Help your-self.
Pow-dered sugar, please!
Hup!
Oo-ooh ...
Oooh...
I said we're being award-ed!
Here.
Wait, isn't that soup?
!
What the heck ?!
No, I mean that...
WHUNK
For real ?
Crap !
A mole !
Oh, no!!
Yikes !
Oh, Ms. Ara-ma!
Hm?
... ...
One piece of squid, please ...
How's the manu-script coming ?
Got it!
KAZE
KAZE
KAZE

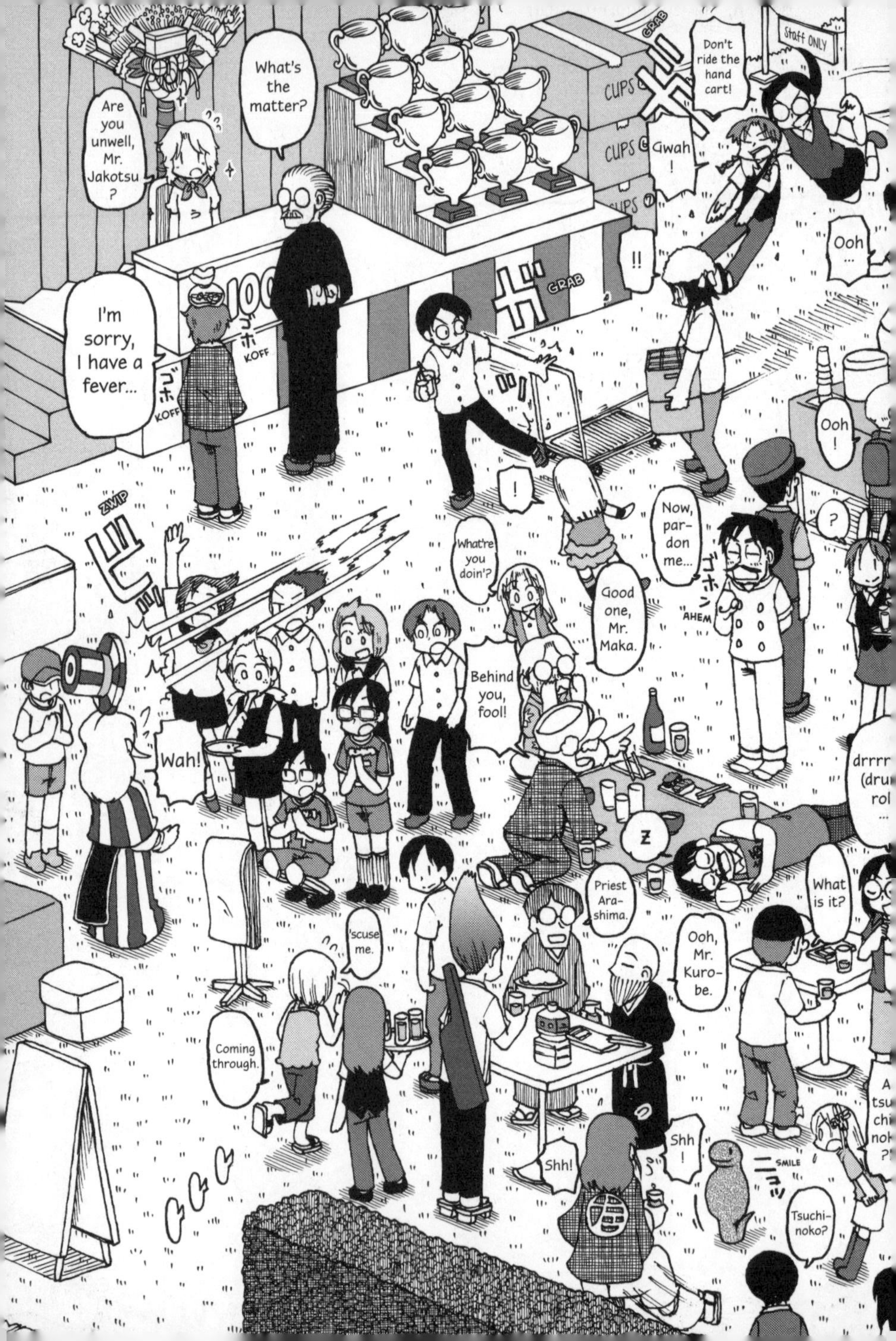
Staff ONLY
Don't ride the hand cart!
GRAB
CUPS
CUPS
CUPS
Gwah!
What's the matter?
Are you unwell, Mr. Jakotsu?
Ooh...
!!
GRAB
100
KOFF
I'm sorry, I have a fever...
KOFF
Ooh!
!
?
Now, pardon me...
AHEM
Good one, Mr. Maka.
What're you doin'?
ZWIP
Behind you, fool!
Wah!
drrrr (dru rol ...
Z
What is it?
Priest Arashima.
Ooh, Mr. Kurobe.
'scuse me.
Coming through.
A tsu chi nok ?
Shh!
Shh!
SMILE
Tsuchinoko?

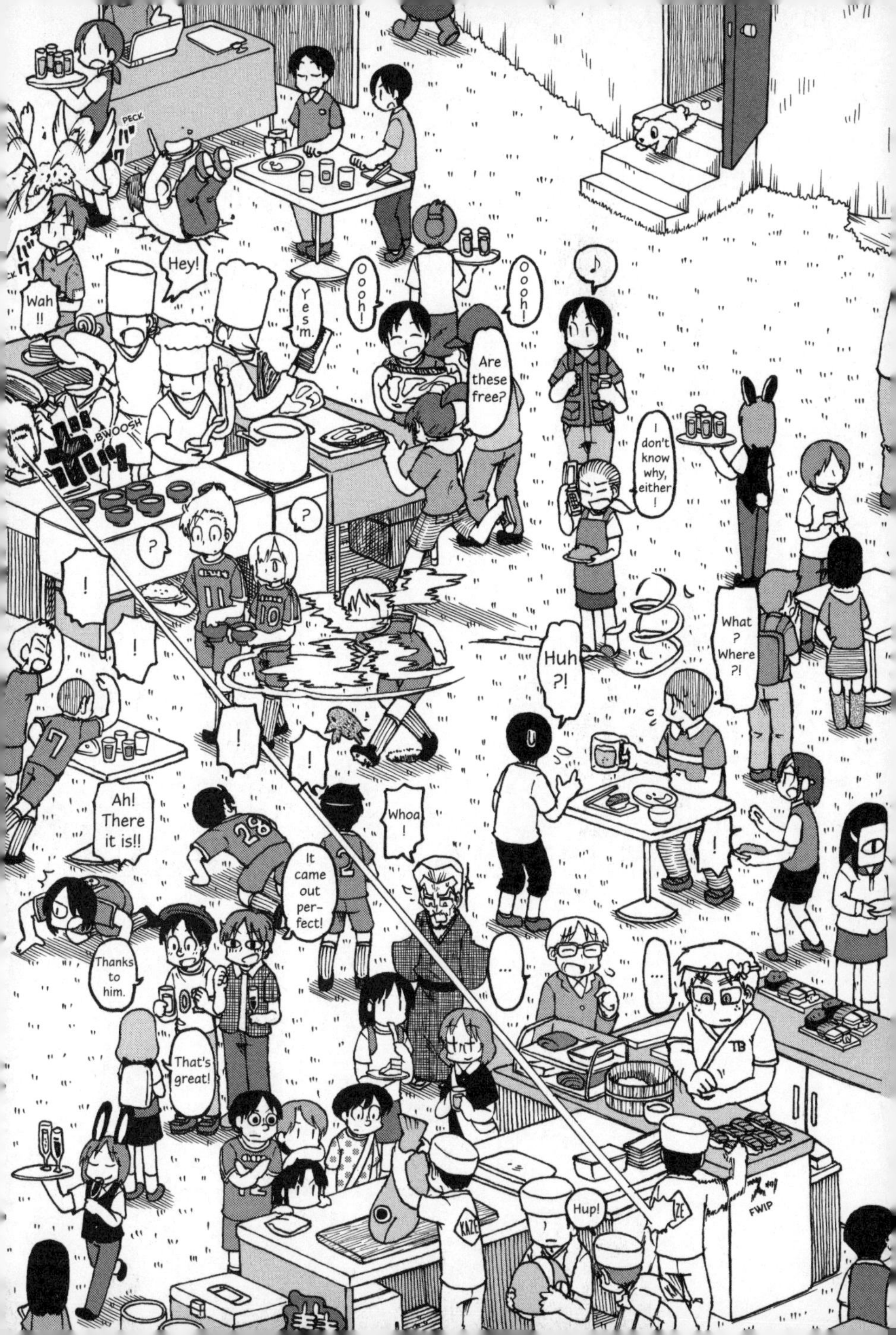

♪
Oooh!
Oooh!
Yes'm.
Hey!
PECK
Wah!!
PECK
Are these free?
I don't know why, either!
BWOOSH
?
?
!
What? Where?!
Huh?!
!
!
!
!
Whoa!
Ah! There it is!!
It came out perfect!
...
...
Thanks to him.
That's great!
Hup!
FWIP

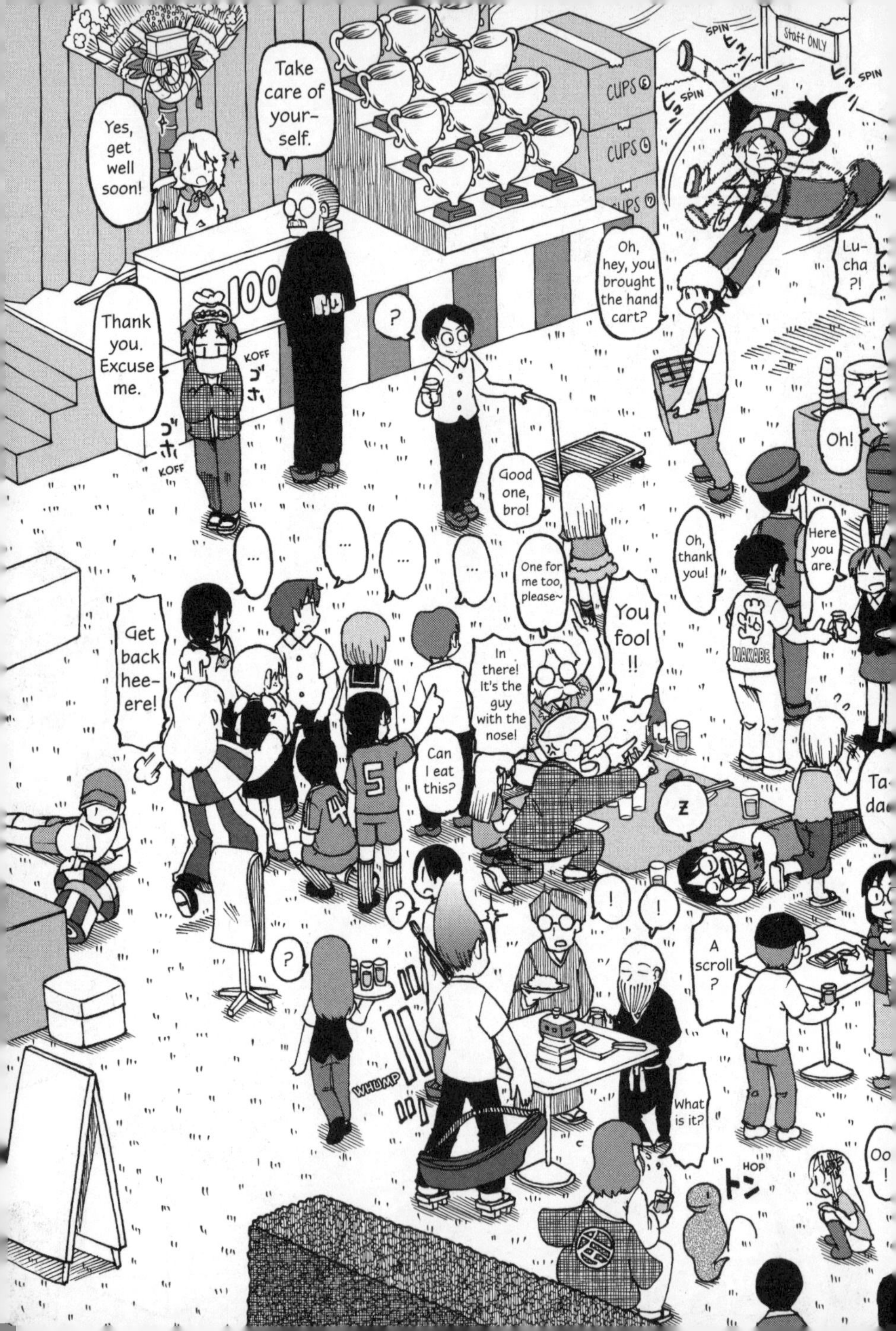

Staff ONLY
SPIN
SPIN
SPIN
Lu-cha?!
Oh, hey, you brought the hand cart?
CUPS 5
CUPS 6
CUPS 7
Take care of your-self.
Yes, get well soon!
100
?
Thank you. Excuse me.
KOFF
KOFF
Oh!
Here you are.
Oh, thank you!
Good one, bro!
One for me too, please~
...
...
...
...
You fool!!
MAKABE
In there! It's the guy with the nose!
Get back hee-ere!
Ta-da
Z
Can I eat this?
5
4
A scroll?
!
!
?
?
WHUMP
What is it?
HOP
トン
Oo!

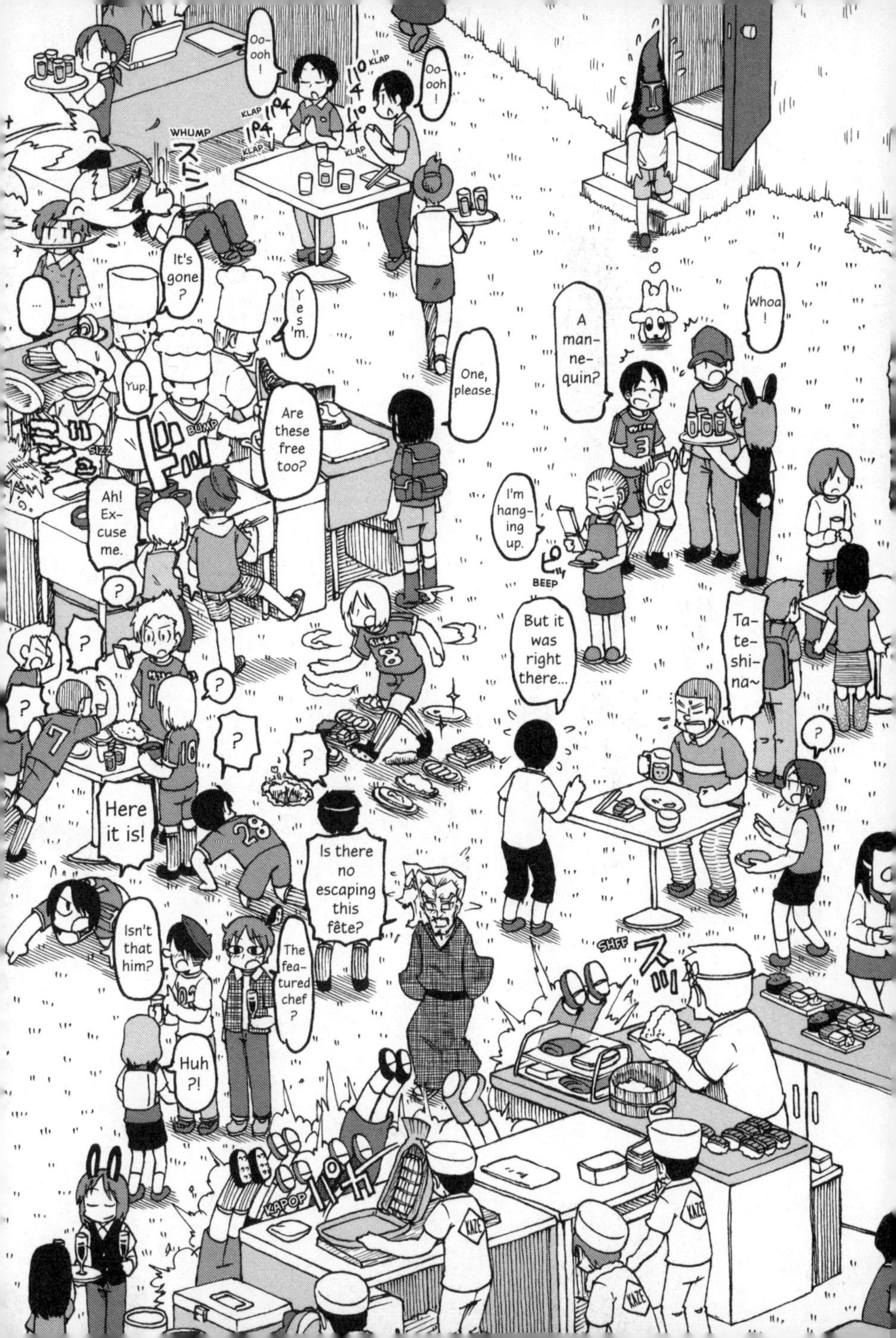

Oo-ooh!
KLAP
KLAP
Oo-ooh!
KLAP
KLAP
WHUMP
ストン
Whoa!
A mannequin?
One, please.
Yes'm.
It's gone?
...
Yup.
Are these free too?
BUMP
SIZZ
I'm hanging up.
BEEP
Ah! Excuse me.
Tateshina~
But it was right there...
?
?
?
?
?
?
?
Here it is!
Is there no escaping this fête?
The featured chef?
Isn't that him?
Huh?!
SHFF
KAPOP

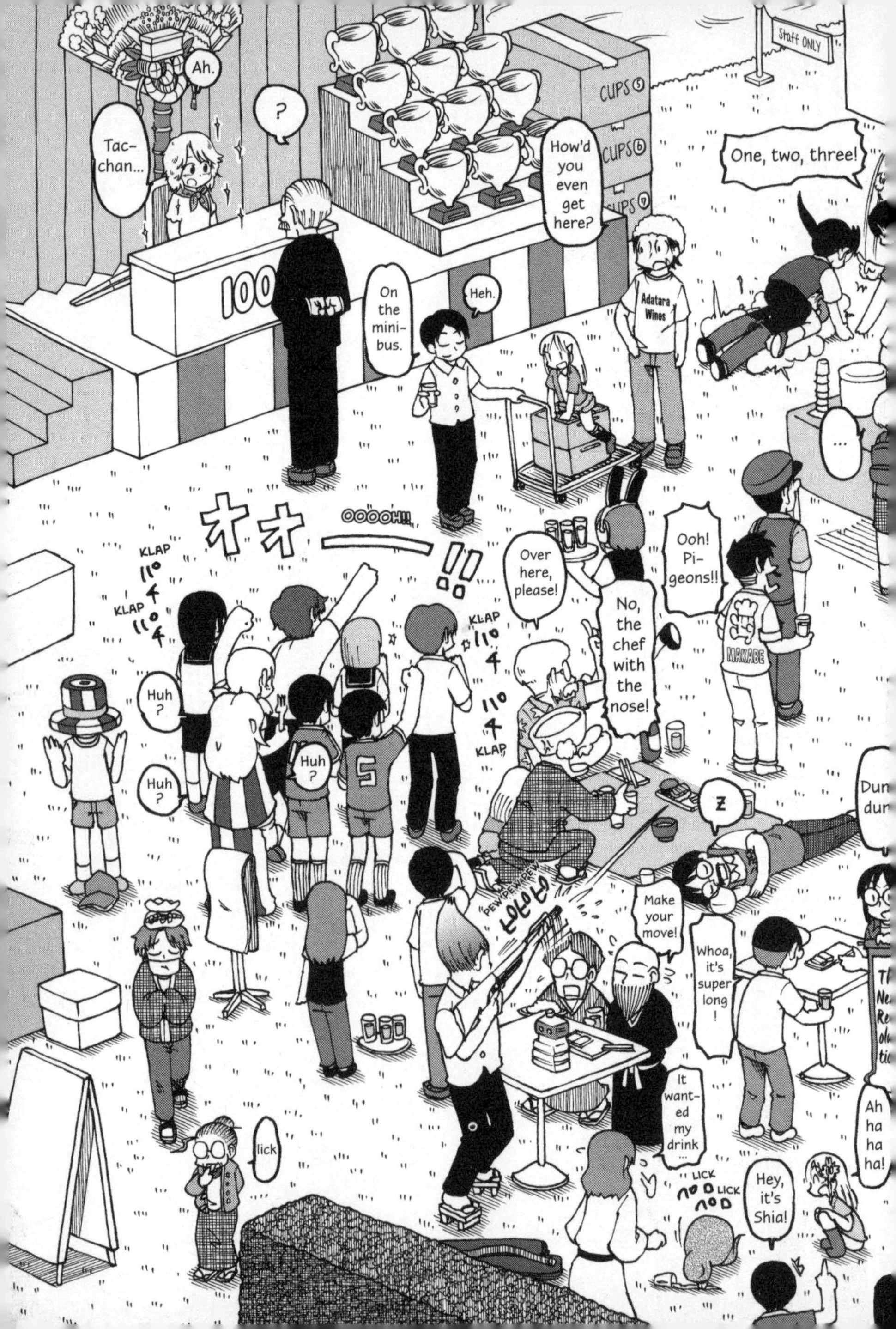
Staff ONLY
CUPS 5
CUPS 6
CUPS 7
One, two, three!
How'd you even get here?
Ah.
?
Tac-chan...
Adatara Wines
100
Heh.
On the mini-bus.
...
Ooh! Pigeons!!
MAKABE
Over here, please!
No, the chef with the nose!
OOOOH!!
オオー!!
KLAP パチ
KLAP パチ
KLAP パチ
パチ KLAP
Huh?
Huh?
Huh?
5
Dun dur
Z
Make your move!
PEW PEW PEW
ピピピ
Whoa, it's super long!
Ah ha ha ha!
It wanted my drink...
Hey, it's Shia!
LICK ペロ
LICK ペロ
lick

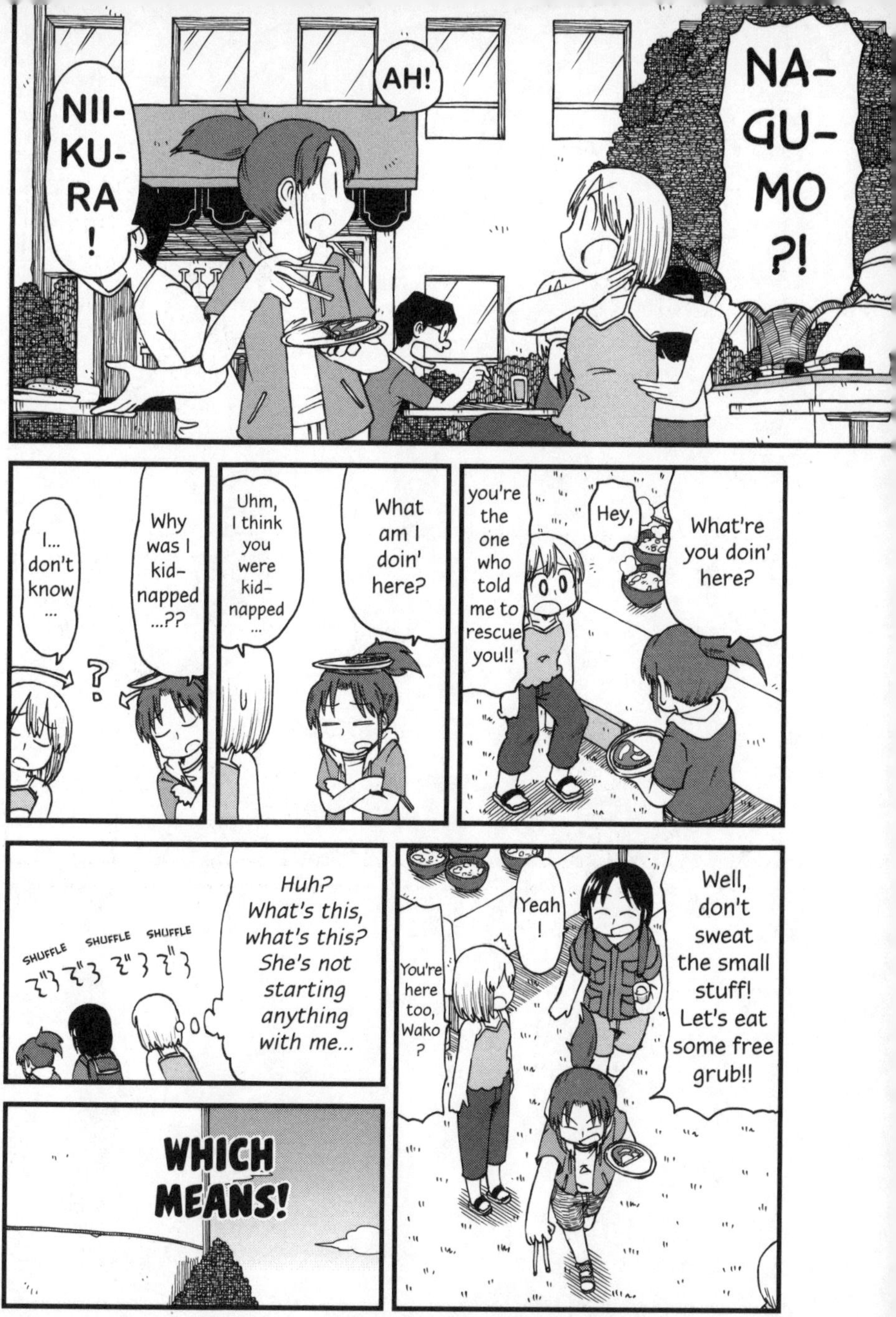
NA-GU-MO?!
AH!
NII-KU-RA!
What're you doin' here?
Hey,
you're the one who told me to rescue you!!
What am I doin' here?
Uhm, I think you were kid-napped...
Why was I kid-napped...??
I... don't know...
Well, don't sweat the small stuff! Let's eat some free grub!!
Yeah!
You're here too, Wako?
Huh? What's this, what's this? She's not starting anything with me...
SHUFFLE SHUFFLE SHUFFLE
WHICH MEANS!

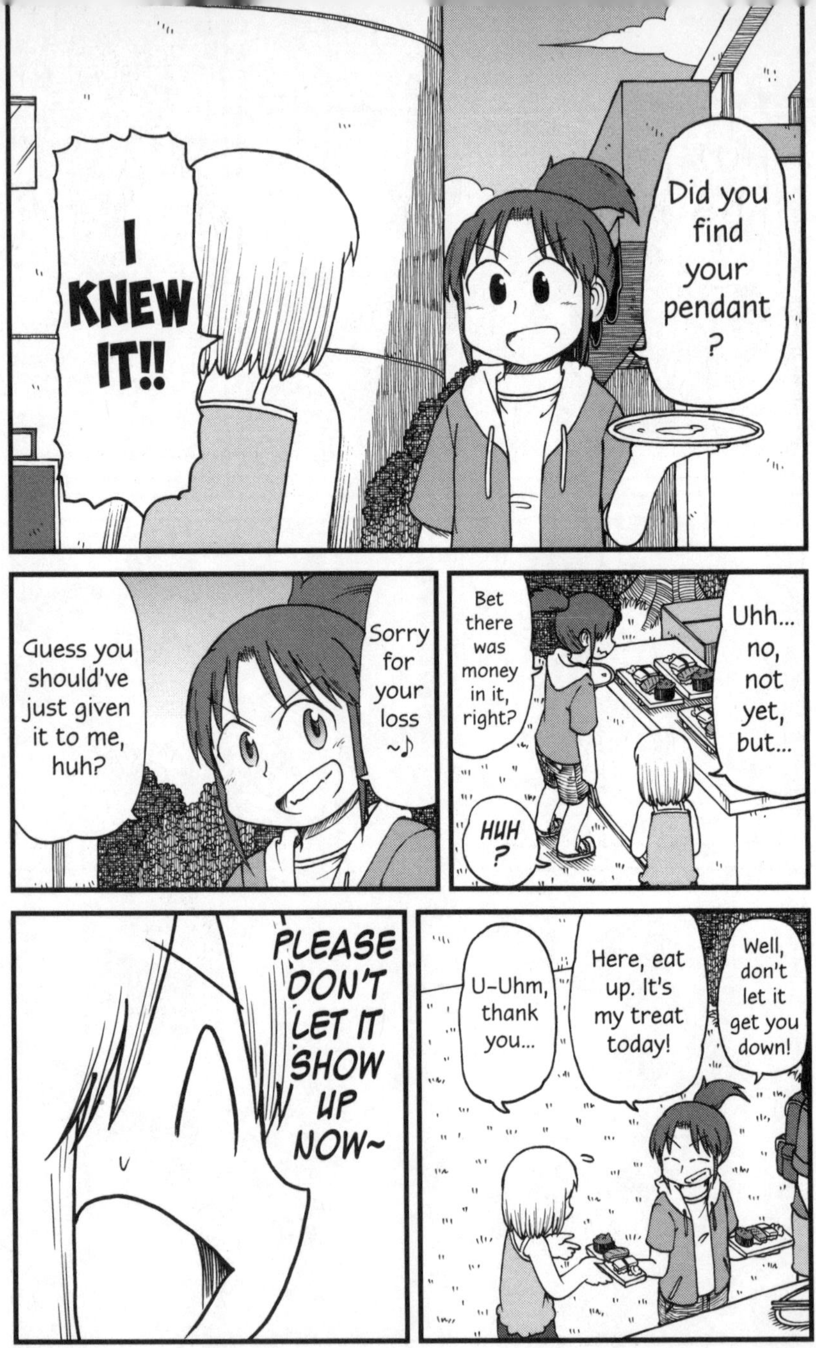
Did you find your pendant?
I KNEW IT!!
Uhh... no, not yet, but...
Bet there was money in it, right?
HUH?
Sorry for your loss ~♪
Guess you should've just given it to me, huh?
Well, don't let it get you down!
Here, eat up. It's my treat today!
U-Uhm, thank you...
PLEASE DON'T LET IT SHOW UP NOW~

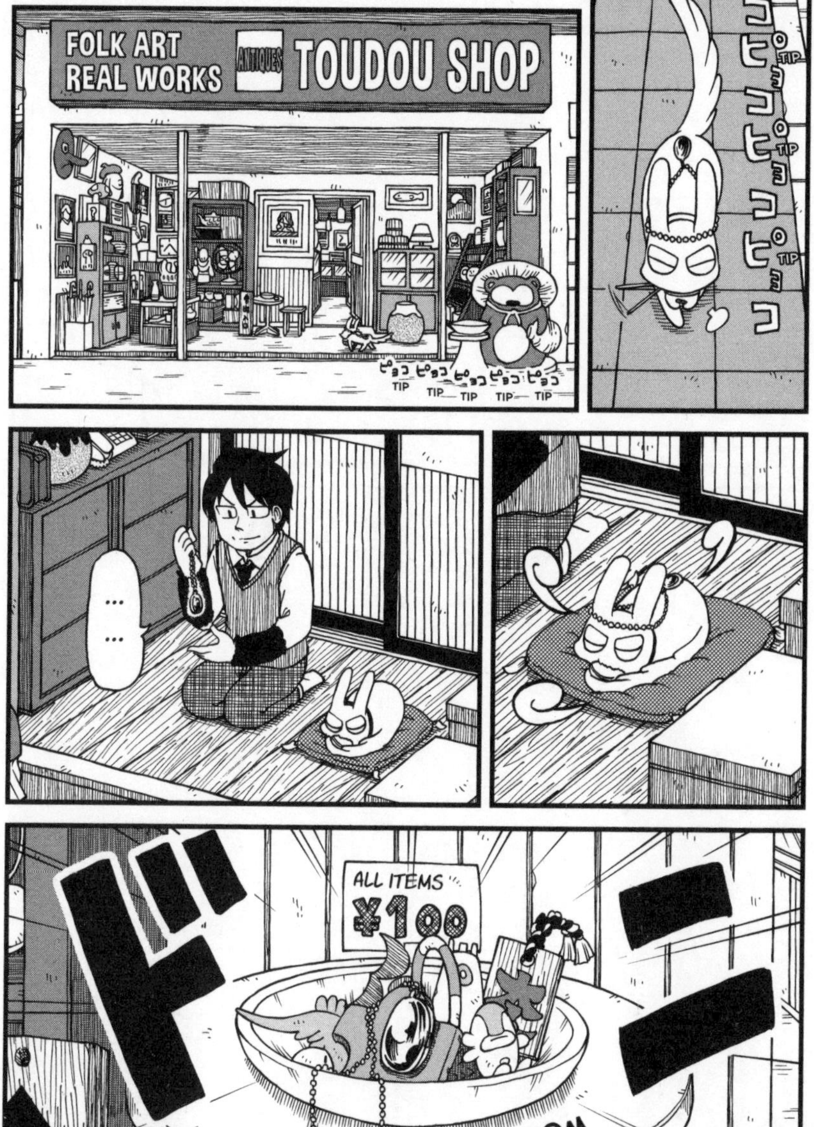
ピョコ TIP
ピョコ TIP
ピョコ TIP
ピョコ TIP
FOLK ART
REAL WORKS
ANTIQUES
TOUDOU SHOP
ピョコ ピョコ ピョコ ピョコ ピョコ
TIP TIP TIP TIP TIP
...
...
ALL ITEMS
¥100
ドーン
BOOM

CONTENTS

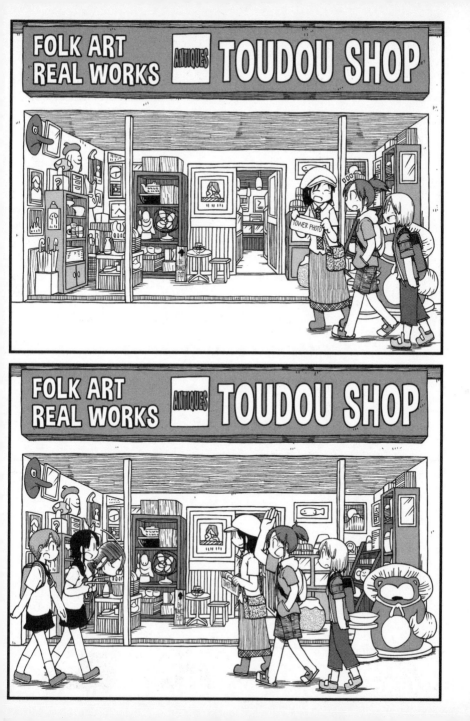

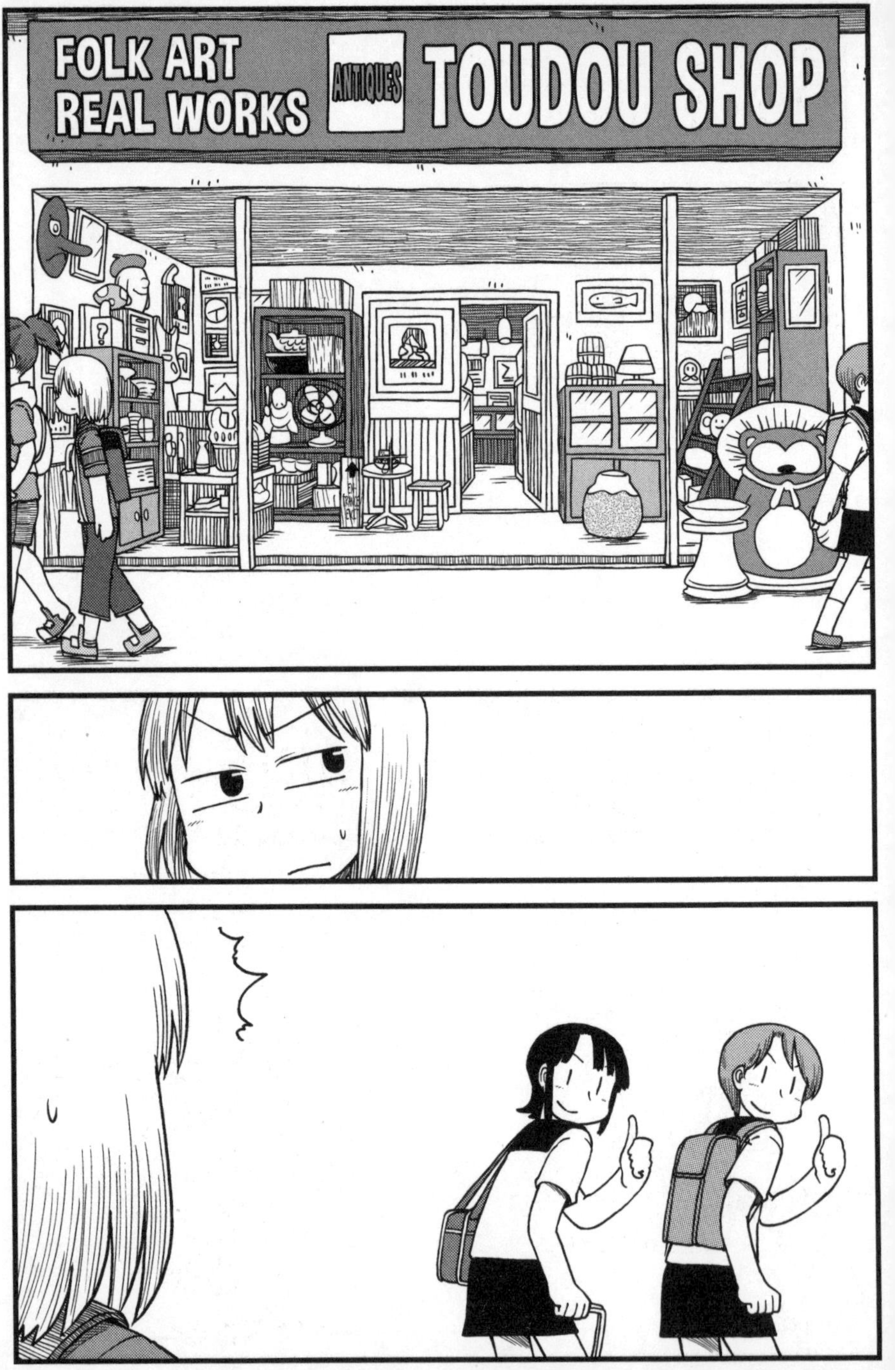
FOLK ART
REAL WORKS
ANTIQUES
TOUDOU SHOP

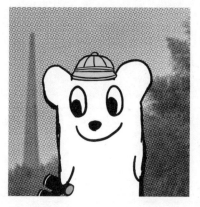

Recent Author Photo

Western Cuisine Makabe
City Branch
Thank You For
Your Patronage

XX/XX/XXXX

Omelet Rice	¥700
-No egg	-¥100

Check #2
Table #2

Subtotal	¥600
Tax	¥ 48

Total	¥648
Cash	¥23,648
Change	¥23,000
Total Points	1 Point

This Month's Request
The weather has gotten hot.
Please take care to avoid
catching a cold.

Receipt #4377

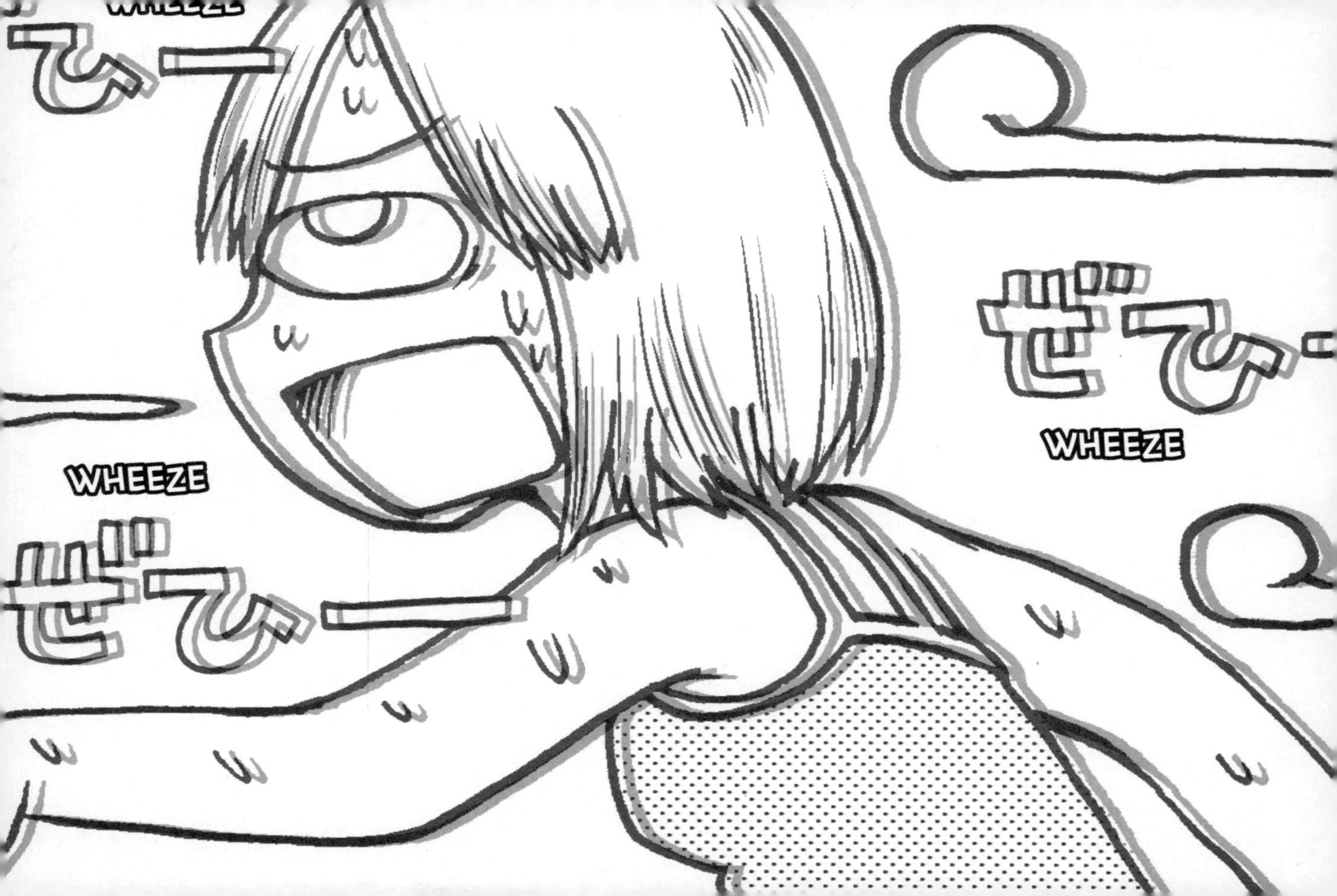
ぜひー
WHEEZE
ぜひー
WHEEZE
ひー

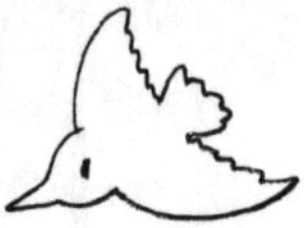

CITY

4

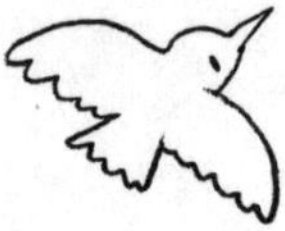

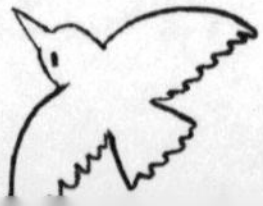

define "ordinary"

in this just-surreal-enough take on the "school genre" of manga, a group of friends (which includes a robot built by a child professor) grapples with all sorts of unexpected situations in their daily lives as high schoolers.

the gags, jokes, puns and random haiku keep this series off-kilter even as the characters grow and change. check out this new take on a storied genre and meet the new ordinary.

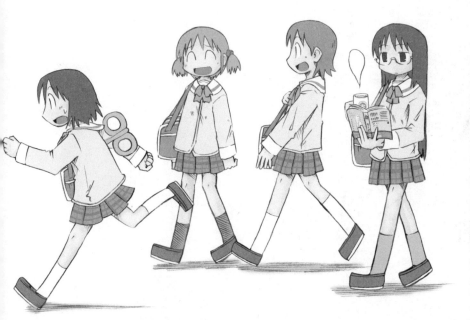

all volumes
available now!

nichijou

my ordinary life

keiichi arawi

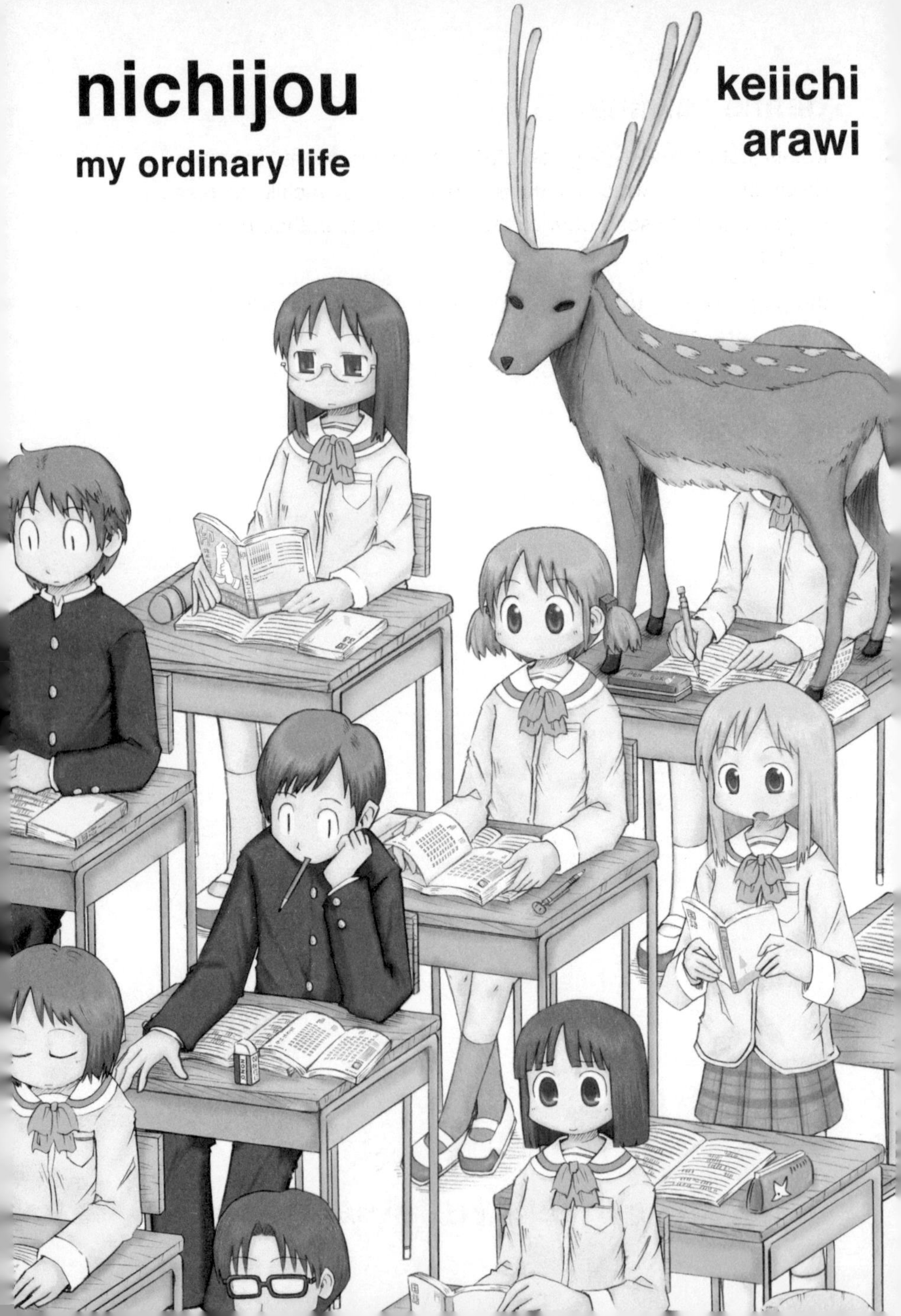

The follow up to the hit manga series *nichijou*, ***Helvetica Standard*** is a full-color anthology of Keiichi Arawi's comic art and design work. Funny and heartwarming, ***Helvetica Standard*** is a humorous look at modern day Japanese design in comic form.

Helvetica Standard is a deep dive into the artistic and creative world of Keiichi Arawi. Part comic, part diary, part art and design book, ***Helvetica Standard*** is a deconstruction of the world of *nichijou*.

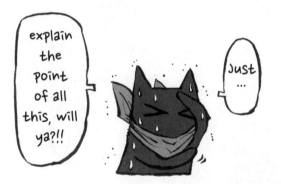

Both Parts Available Now!

Keiichi
Arawi

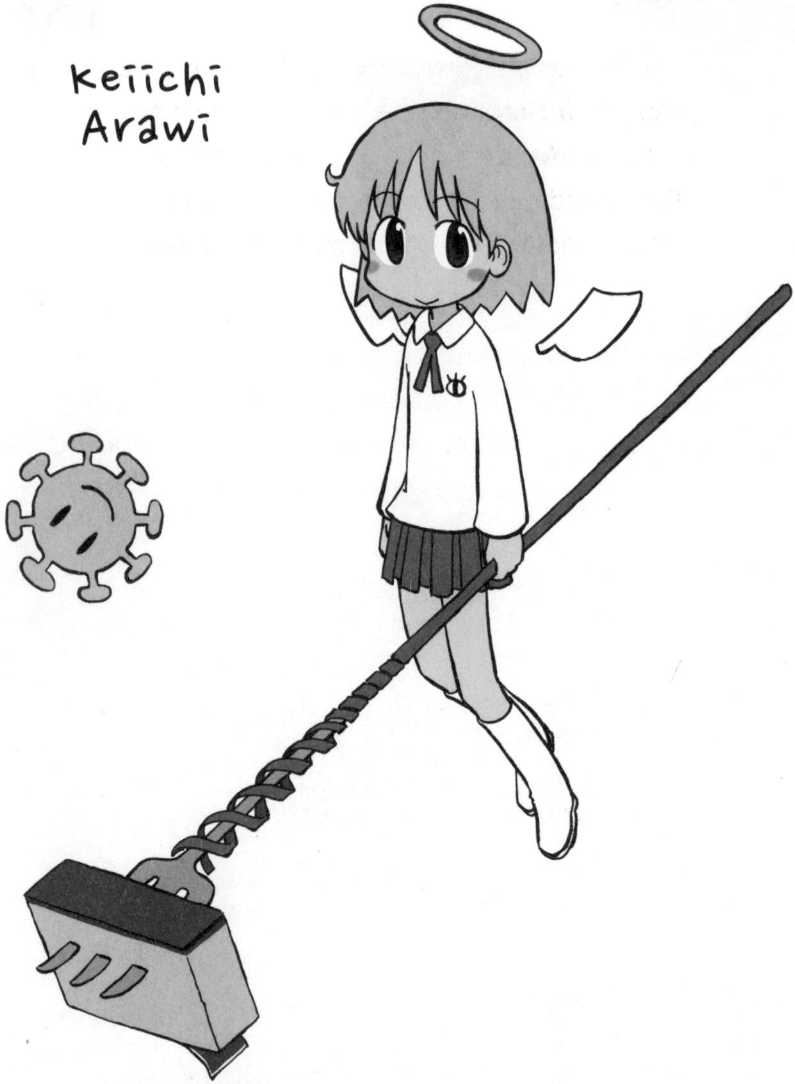

Helvetica Standard

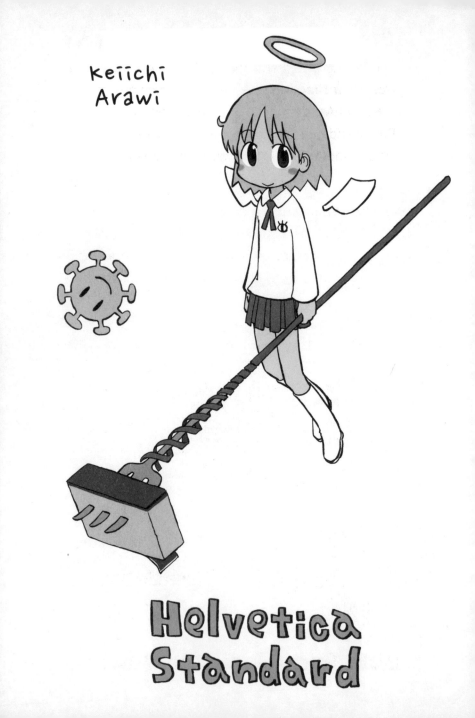

CITY 4

A Vertical Comics Edition

Translation: Jenny McKeon
Production: Grace Lu
Hiroko Mizuno

© Keiichi ARAWI 2018
First published in Japan in 2018 by Kodansha, Ltd., Tokyo
Publication rights for this English edition arranged through Kodansha, Ltd., Tokyo
English language version produced by Vertical, Inc.

Translation provided by Vertical Comics, 2018
Published by Vertical Comics, an imprint of Vertical, Inc., New York

Originally published in Japanese as *CITY 4* by Kodansha, Ltd.
CITY first serialized in *Morning,* Kodansha, Ltd., 2016-

This is a work of fiction.

ISBN: 978-1-947194-26-7

Manufactured in Canada

First Edition

Vertical, Inc.
451 Park Avenue South
7th Floor
New York, NY 10016
www.vertical-comics.com

Vertical books are distributed through Penguin-Random House Publisher Services.